P9-DFE-161

A12901 713476

WITHDRAWN

6107

I.C.C. LIBRARY

Europe

at the

Crossroads

WITHDRAWN

Europe

at the

Crossroads

Will the EU Ever Be Able to
Compete with the United States
as an Economic Power?

I.C.C. LIBRARY

GUILLERMO DE LA DEHESA

McGraw-Hill

New York   Chicago   San Francisco   Lisbon   London
Madrid   Mexico City   Milan   New Delhi
San Juan   Seoul   Singapore
Sydney   Toronto

HC
240
.D38
2006

Copyright © 2006 by The McGraw-Hill Companies, Inc. All rights reserved. Printed in the United States of America. Except as permitted under the United States Copyright Act of 1976, no part of this publication may be reproduced or distributed in any form or by any means, or stored in a data base or retrieval system, without the prior written permission of the publisher.

1 2 3 4 5 6 7 8 9 0   DOC/DOC   0 9 8 7 6 5

ISBN 0–07–145959–6

This publication is designed to provide accurate and authoritative information in regard to the subject matter covered. It is sold with the understanding that the publisher is not engaged in rendering legal, accounting, or other professional service. If legal advice or other expert assistance is required, the services of a competent professional person should be sought.

—From a declaration of principles jointly adopted by a committee of the American Bar Association and a committee of publishers.

McGraw-Hill books are available at special quantity discounts to use as premiums and sales promotions, or for use in corporate training programs. For more information, please write to the Director of Special Sales, Professional Publishing, McGraw-Hill, Two Penn Plaza, New York, NY 10121–2298. Or contact your local bookstore.

This book is printed on recycled, acid-free paper containing a minimum of 50% recycled, de-inked fiber.

CONTENTS

AUTHOR'S NOTE

Some months ago, French and Dutch voters rejected the European Union's new Constitutional Treaty, and the United Kingdom was forced to delay its Treaty referendum. These decisions were a blow to the European Union's constitutional process as well as to the reforms needed to make the European Union competitive in the global marketplace. When I began this book, I sought to explain how the European Union reached this point and where it needed to go to reach its goal of becoming an economic power on a par with the United States. In the face of these decisions, understanding the underlying economic forces and realities becomes even more crucial, because these rejections will delay the reforms necessary to meet the challenges of enlargement, globalization, and the European Union's rapidly aging population.

November 2005

FOREWORD

H ow well is Europe doing?

Badly, say some economists. The European economy has stalled and since the start of the new millennium has shown much lower growth than the US economy. Unemployment has remained high. And the standard of living, measured by gross domestic product (GDP) per capita at purchasing power parities (PPP) prices, is still 30 percent below that of the United States, the same gap that existed in 1970.

This diagnosis is incorrect, according to other economists. There is little question that Europe is going through a cyclical slump, due in part to too tight a monetary policy, and due in part to a general feeling of gloom and doom among consumers. But the underlying reality is in fact much brighter. European firms are doing well. Their profits are high. Productivity, measured by output per hour of work, is close to that of the United States. The difference in GDP per capita comes for the most part from the fact that the Europeans work less than their US counterparts. They work fewer hours a week, take longer vacations, retire earlier. And this is a smart choice: As productivity increases, increasing both consumption and leisure seems quite appropriate.

The first group of economists would again disagree with this. Europe is not in a cyclical slump. The low growth rate of the 2000s is just the continuation of a steady decline in growth in Europe since the 1970s. It is the result of slow strangulation from rigidities of all kinds, from generous welfare benefits in the labor market, to restrictions on how firms can operate, to limits to competition in the goods market, to high tax rates. People take long vacations because of confiscatory taxation, not because they love the seaside.

This is ideology, not economics, retort the defenders of Europe. The slowdown in growth since 1970 reflects catching up, nothing deeper. "Eliminating labor rigidities" is a code phrase for reducing social protection. But social protection is good, and many countries in Europe are living proof that social protection is consistent with efficiency and growth. Look at the Scandinavian countries, look at the Netherlands. Sure, reforms are needed in Europe, as they are in all countries in the world. But they involve tweaking, not wholesale elimination of existing institutions.

Leave the past behind, comes the reply. Even if we were to concede that Europe has not done so badly, the future is bleak. European countries are aging, and aging much faster than is the United States. Birth rates are lower, immigration more limited. This is a challenge that the welfare state in general, and the retirement systems in particular, cannot meet. Major changes will have to come, both in the delivery of health care and in the generosity of retirement benefits.

There are always problems on the horizon, say the Europhiles. The United States has to finance its defense budget. Europe has to deal with its aging problem. Both will find a solution in some way or another, but not without enduring political and budget crises. The proportion of GDP spent on health care will increase, reflecting higher income, technological improvements, and longer life expectancy. But changes in the composition of spending happen all the time. We spend more on vacations than we used to, and we do not see it as a major issue.

And the debate goes on, becoming more and more heated. At the center are fundamental questions: Can one have a generous welfare state and still let the entrepreneurial spirit thrive? Is there a viable European model, an alternative to the US model?

Don't expect this book to provide the definitive answer to these questions. No respectable book should, because we don't know it. We do, however, have a great deal of information that we can use to make predictions. And this book tells you what we know so far. It is intended to provide you with the facts and nothing but the facts. It guides you through the mountain of statistics compiled by national statistical institutes, international statistical agencies, and individual researchers. It warns you about the difficulties of comparing statistics across countries. It tells you what we know about labor productivity, about total factor productivity, about employment, about capital. It summarizes what we know and do not know about the effects of particular labor market institutions and of reforms on goods markets. It gives you the basic facts about coming demographic trends and their implications for retirement systems and for health care. It tells you about the different policy trade-offs, such as how much retirement age would have to increase and/or how much benefits would have to decrease in order to balance the retirement systems.

In short, the book provides the basis for an informed discussion, and thus a more productive debate. This debate is one I have engaged in with Guillermo for the past decade. I am more optimistic than he about Europe, perhaps because I live far away, perhaps because I am an eternal optimist. I believe that rich countries should be able to provide both a high level of social protection and economic efficiency. I see many problems with the way social protection is designed in Europe today. But I also see a process of reform, in both the goods and in the labor market. It is a messy process, because reforms create winners and losers, because reforms often have short-term costs and long-term benefits, and because the costs are often salient and the benefits often diffuse. Nevertheless, I expect the process of reform to continue and Europe to do well. Am I right? Is Guillermo's more sober assessment correct? We shall see. Meanwhile, we should make sure that we, and all other participants in the debate, have our facts right. This book will help to achieve that end.

OLIVIER BLANCHARD
Cambridge, MA, September 2005

PREFACE

After almost 50 years, Europe's economic and political consolidation is now well underway. The European Union (EU) has united important political and economic policies, and its political borders have increased from the six original members of the Common Market to today's 25 member states. In the next two years, membership will increase to 27 and in the not too distant future to 33—increasing until it covers most of historical Europe. This alliance allows the EU to increasingly operate as a single market for goods, services, labor, and capital. The EU's greatest achievement, thus far, is the creation of this large alliance without war or forced annexation, making it the first large union of sovereign states in history to be built by a democratic process.

From the start, the EU had a clear priority and political objective: to permanently consolidate peace in Europe after two of the bloodiest wars in history. But the passage of time and the fall of communism brought a second priority: becoming an economic power capable of counterbalancing the United States' growing weight in the world economy.

Not everybody agrees with this second priority. For many European leaders and politicians, the EU should consolidate a model of liberal democracy that combines economic efficiency and social cohesion, making itself a model of growing prosperity that the world sees as the most balanced and inclusive way of living. These leaders feel that the EU should not worry if the US economy continues to outpace Europe's, as long as the EU maintains a reasonable level of prosperity and a high level of inclusion and cohesion. According to Jacques Delors, a former president of the European Commission and a staunch defender of this view, "Europeans should attempt to create a grand liberal democracy, which combines competition as an element of fostering economic growth, cooperation as an instrument of building political consensus, and solidarity as a factor of achieving a more integrated union and a deeper social cohesion."

While the social objective in many ways defines the EU and differentiates it from the US, it is equally clear that the economic objective is also being pursued. Creating the euro as a reserve currency that can compete with the dollar for world monetary dominance and enlarging the EU both point clearly to the desire to create an economic power that can stand on equal footing with the US in international political and economic issues. A recent German Marshall Fund poll found widespread support for the idea that "the EU should become a superpower like the US."

Though it is difficult to compare the US and the EU when the latter has not yet achieved political unity, there is a growing conviction among EU citizens that the union needs to become a federation or confederation of states similar to the United States. While this seemed to be one of the long-term objectives underlying the recent European Convention debate and its project of creating a European constitution, unfortunately the strong divide between "federalists" and the "intergovernmentalists" who would like the EU to remain as is has finally turned in favor of the latter. Article One of the recently approved (but not ratified) Constitutional Treaty keeps the definition of the EU as a "Union of the citizens and the States of Europe." Nevertheless, the Constitutional Treaty has taken another positive step toward deepening the political union to face the challenges posed by its ambitious enlargement plan.

The EU's expansion toward the east is also based on a political objective—achieving an area of stable peace and security to the east—that makes it easier for the newcomers to consolidate their rapid transition to full democracy and capitalism. Although this enlargement will give the EU more economic and political weight in the world and a larger single market in which to reap further economies of scale, it will also make economic decision making more complex, increase the average income differences among EU citizens and countries, and reduce the share less developed members and regions receive from the EU budget.

This book surveys most of the recent official literature and data on how the European Union is fulfilling its economic and social targets to gauge: (1) how well the EU is catching up with the US in terms of economic performance and prosperity levels, and (2) how well the EU will be able to sustain its distinctive social model. While the book's contents may appear to be rather technical for a layperson, its goal is to provide a useful overview for a wide spectrum of readers and to explain in simple and understandable terms the main economic issues facing the EU today and in the future.

To show the European Union's probabilities of achieving its economic and social goals, this book reviews the available analyses and official data concerning the EU's persistent economic underperformance over the past decades. The book then analyzes the causes of the slower growth and examines the reforms that need to be implemented in order to improve the EU's future growth rate and standards of living while still preserving its social model.

NOTE ON STATISTICAL SOURCES AND COMPARATIVE MEASUREMENT ISSUES

In order to measure the EU's economic performance with respect to the United States over the last 30 years, this book uses statistics provided by the European Commission in official documents published by the Directorate General for Economic and Financial Affairs and EUROSTAT. Organization for Economic Cooperation and Development (OECD) statistics are also used for the United States' data and when European Union statistical sources are not available or need further explication.

One persistent critique made when comparing the EU's average economic performance to that of the US is that although in most comparable ratios the EU performs worse, there are always some member countries that have better ratios. However, this critique is not valid because the US also has some states or regions that fare much better than the national average. The idea is to compare the average performance of the two economies, not individual member states or countries. Nevertheless, when possible we single out some member countries that are much above or much below these averages. As a matter of fact, there is only one EU country that can rival any of the US states in GDP per capita—Luxembourg—but it has fewer than half a million inhabitants. The other 14 member countries have a lower GDP than the US, while there are only four US states that have a lower GDP per capita than the EU average.[1]

From the outset, we must stress that the international comparisons of growth patterns are constrained by a number of measurement issues. First, after the shift to the new System of National Accounts (SNA) agreed to in 1993, member countries have adopted the new measurement techniques at different speeds and with different levels of comprehensiveness.

Second, the method to construct price indexes for information and communication technology (ITC) equipment varies between countries, which affects the estimates of output growth in both ITC production industries as well as in industries that use ITC equipment extensively. Some countries try to account for the rapid quality changes in ITC by applying so-called hedonic pricing, that is, unbundling the market price of a computer into its most important technical characteristics and pricing each characteristic separately. When this adjustment is not made, the price index is computed from the price per computer unit, and the quantity index is based on the number of units produced or sold without considering each product's quality and performance. This hedonic method is also applied by some countries, notably the US, to other products such as cars or durable goods, while in the EU the traditional method of pricing per unit is the norm. Therefore, the estimated productivity of ITC and other manufacturing industries is underestimated unless hedonic methods are used to account for possible changes in their output.

Third, measurement problems are compounded by the notorious difficulty of measuring output in some service sectors, including those where the quality aspects of output are important, for example, financial intermediation.

Fourth, another inherent complication of international growth performance in the short and medium term is that cross-country differences in output growth rates and levels may reflect different cyclical positions as well as underlying differences in performance. Despite some evidence of reduced cyclical divergence in most recent years,[2] the 1990s saw large differences in the US and EU business cycles. To control for these problems, this book frequently uses trend series analyses, using the Hodrick-Prescott Filter (1997), which tend to eliminate these cyclical differences.

Fifth, GDP measures have an important shortcoming as indicators of prosperity because they capture only the part of production that takes place in the market sector and can be statistically recorded. Output in the informal, black, or illegal markets and the unrecorded output of households themselves are not recorded, which gives a certain advantage to the US over the EU, where unrecorded sectors show higher levels.[3]

Finally, there are differences between how the US and EU account for capital depreciation. The US uses a higher rate of depreciation the first year and then a declining rate every year after—the loss of value of equipment goods is higher in the first year than in the second, less in the second than in the third, and so on—while the EU uses the same rate of depreciation every year.

These measurement problems may be the reason why there are differences among the major statistical bases to estimate the level of GDP per capita and their determinants. For the IMF, the Euro Area does not have a productivity problem since, according to its estimates, hourly productivity is higher in the Euro Area than in the US, and all the differences in per capita GDP are due solely to the lower number of hours worked in the EU. For EUROSTAT, based on its structural indicators, however, a completely different picture emerges, suggesting that 45 percent of the gap in living standards between the Euro Area and the US are due to lower labor productivity per hour, with the remaining 55 percent due to lower number of hours worked. Finally, the OECD estimates suggest a position that lies roughly between the two previous estimates, namely that the Euro Area has a productivity problem, but it is not as severe as suggested by EURO-STAT, and that one-third of the GDP per capita difference with the US is due to lower productivity and two-thirds are due to the lower number of hours worked.

NOTES

1   Bergstrom and Gidehag, 2004

2   Dalsgaard et al., 2002

3   Schneider, 2002

Europe
at the
Crossroads

CHAPTER 1

THE EUROPEAN
UNION ECONOMY:
YESTERDAY
AND TODAY

As the title of this book suggests, Europe is at an economic cross-roads. In Lisbon in 2000, European Union (EU) leaders set ambitious goals to make the EU an economic power on a par with the United States, but progress has been slow. Politics have stalled reform efforts, and the challenges of growth, enlargement, globalization, and aging remain. EU citizens have long been recipients of a very generous social welfare system, but what will happen when financing that system becomes too expensive? Before embarking on a path for the future, it is important to understand how this point was reached, which means looking at the numbers.

Between 1975 and 2002, the US economy grew, on average, at a faster rate than the EU's in terms of average real gross domestic product (GDP). As Table 1.1 shows, in the mid-1970s US and EU growth differed by 1.1 percent, and although the EU's growth began catching up with that of the US in the late 1980s, at the turn of the new century, the gap was back to nearly its original level. In other words, over the last 28 years, the US has had an average annual real growth of 3.2 percent versus only 2.3 percent for the EU. An area of focus for EU leadership should be the growing GDP gap with the US.

While GDP paints an interesting picture, the most accurate way to compare the relative economic strength of countries is by measuring their exchange rates, that is, by converting their GDP to a single currency, not in market price terms, but in terms of purchas-

TABLE 1.1   Growth of Real GDP in EU Member States and in the United States, 1975–2002

(average annual growth in percent,
ranked according to 1995–2002 performance)

	1975–1985	1985–1990	1990–1995	1995–2002
Ireland	3.5	4.6	4.7	7.8
Luxembourg	2.4	6.4	5.4	5.5
Finland	2.9	3.3	–0.7	4.4
Netherlands	1.9	3.1	2.1	3.5
Spain	1.6	4.5	1.5	3.5
Greece	2.1	1.2	1.2	3.5
Portugal	3.0	5.5	1.8	3.5
Sweden	1.5	2.3	0.6	2.7
U. K.	1.9	3.3	1.6	2.5
Belgium	2.1	3.1	1.5	2.5
Denmark	2.1	1.3	2.0	2.5
Austria	2.4	3.2	2.0	2.4
France	2.4	3.3	1.1	2.4
Italy	3.0	2.9	1.3	1.8
Germany	2.2	3.4	2.0	1.6
EU-15	2.3	3.2	1.5	2.3
USA	3.4	3.2	2.4	3.3

Source: European Competitiveness Reports, 2001 and 2003

ing power parities (PPP). PPP allows us to see the exact purchasing power of each unit of income or GDP. By these standards, the US has multiplied its GDP in PPP terms 7.6 times, while the EU has only multiplied its GDP 6.6 times between 1975 and 2002.

According to European Commission statistics,[1] in 1991 the total EU GDP, in PPP terms, was exactly 103 billion euros larger than that of the US. By 2003, however, US GDP was estimated to be 622 billion euros larger, which means that in only 12 years, the US had outpaced the EU by 725 billion euros, or 7.7 percent of the total EU GDP—an amount equal to approximately 85 percent of the GDP of Spain.

In 2004, 10 Central and Eastern European countries became EU members, and two more will join over the next few years, adding more GDP to the Union as a whole. In PPP terms, these countries will collectively add around 100 billion euros to the global EU GDP; while this addition will make the EU's GDP larger, it does not capture the entire story.

While from 1991 to 2002, the US growth rate was 1.2 percent higher than the EU's, this growth seems to be explained by the US's higher population growth, which reached an average annual rate of 1 percent compared to the EU's 0.25 percent. A more meaningful comparison should take this growth into account by concentrating mainly on GDP per capita, which is the measure commonly used to compare the standard of living among countries.

Figure 1.1 compares the evolution of GDP per capita between 1970 and 2002 in PPP terms and shows that the levels have widened slightly.[2] For example, if we think of the US as equal to 100, then the EU's GDP per capita was 69 in 1970, 71 in 1982, 70.5 in 1991, and then dropped back down to 69 in 2002. In other words, the EU's

FIGURE 1.1   Level of GDP per Person in 1995 Market Prices

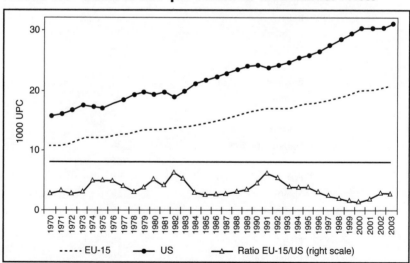

(Left scale is in 1995 units of buying power; estimated for 2001; predictions for 2002–2003; right scale is the ratio of EU to US)

Source: European Competitiveness Reports, 2001 and 2003

GDP returned to the starting point. The gap has continued to increase even though the population of the US has increased by 35.3 million people and the EU's by only 14.1 million.

Table 1.2 shows that the GDP per capita levels of most of the larger European Union countries in 2001 were close to the average across the European Union; only Spain's was much below average. Smaller countries like Denmark, Ireland, the Netherlands, Belgium, and Austria all had GDPs levels that were above the average. EU expansion to the east, however, will lower the average GDP per capita levels even further—if the 10 countries which have most recently joined had been full members in 2001, the total EU average GDP per capita in PPP terms would fall to 21,900 euros; that is 65 percent of the US average.

TABLE 1.2   GDP per Capita in EU Member States, US, and Japan in 2001 in PPS (US = 100)

Luxembourg	137
Ireland	83
Denmark	83
Netherlands	79
Austria	75
Belgium	73
Germany	72
Italy	70
Finland	70
United Kingdom	70
Sweden	69
France	68
Spain	57
Portugal	50
Greece	49
EU-15	69
United States	100
Japan	72

Source: European Commission services

In order to explore corrective measures, we need to look at how the EU got to this point by examining specific parts of the economy, such as employment, work hours, market regulations, productivity, and capital, to see what role each plays. This discussion is quite technical because the problems and solutions are quite complex.

CALCULATING ECONOMIC GROWTH

We need to begin by looking at how we measure economic growth. According to standard growth theory, a nation's long-term economic growth is determined by how quickly and efficiently it accumulates and uses capital and labor. Until very recently, we analyzed economic production by essentially linking output to input. But recent research has refined and extended the analysis to consider factors such as creativity, innovation, scientific research, technology development, entrepreneurship, and dynamism.[3] Today, the main controversy in contemporary growth theory focuses on the relative importance of factor accumulation, that is, increases in labor, capital, land, and entrepreneurship and their efficient use versus technical progress, especially the role of physical and human capital investment in driving economic growth.

In standard neoclassical growth theory,[4] output is produced by capital and labor. Economic growth is compatible with technical progress, which acts as if it were increasing the available amount of labor. In the long term, output per capita and productivity grow at a rate based on technical progress, which is exogenous to the model. Whereas increases in investment tend to show decreasing returns to scale and raise the growth rate only during the transition to higher levels of economic growth, that is, only when growth is balanced with capital in the so-called steady state.

Because investment is determined endogenously—based on variables within the model—economic policy cannot, on a sustained basis, raise productivity growth by increasing available capital (capital deepening, thus the investment/product coefficient tends to be constant in the long term). This is the reason why early growth accounting exercises identified a large *Solow residual* (not explained by the accumulation of labor and capital), or what is the same as a high total factor productivity growth (TFP), which attributes the main role in growth to technological progress.[5] Under these circumstances, when adjusted for demographic differences, richer countries tend to grow at a slower rate than poorer countries. However, in recent decades this relationship has weakened among OECD countries and can be reconciled with the data only by looking at the relationship between the growth rate and the initial conditions (after controlling for other political, institutional, and geographical variables).[6]

This standard neoclassical theory was challenged by new so-called endogenous growth models,[7] which explain long-term growth by relaxing assumptions about diminishing returns to capital and including technological progress as endogenous. For example, some authors add human capital to physical capital to derive a concept of *broad capital* characterized by constant or even increasing returns to scale.[8] Others introduce externalities to the capital accumulation whereby private returns to scale may be diminishing but social returns can be constant or increasing because of either *learning by doing*[9] or research and development (R&D).[10] With constant or increasing returns to broad capital, the long-term growth rate becomes endogenous because it depends on investment decisions which, in turn, could be influenced by policy and institutions.

In these theories, a firm's production is defined by company-specific variables (capital, labor, and R&D inputs) and a shift term called *index of technology*, which is a function of the stock of knowledge available to all firms—that is, knowledge-generating activities such as R&D become a public good. This shift term reflects learning by doing or the influence of human capital. These theories consider innovation and especially the accumulation and diffusion of technical knowledge as the driving force of long-term growth, and they try to shed some light on how they affect technical progress and factor accumulation. In addition, knowledge accumulation (through investment) becomes the key mechanism for achieving technical progress because knowledge and technical advances need capital in order to raise productivity. Therefore, without more investment in human and physical capital, knowledge, and R&D, technical progress would not necessarily contribute to higher growth rates. As a result, "broad capital" accumulation becomes a fundamental element for achieving higher growth.

Although not yet fully conclusive, new evidence by the OECD and the European Commission finds that the amount of capital invested and the age of the capital are main determinants of TFP growth.[11]

A GROWTH ACCOUNTING EXERCISE

In order to explain why EU and US economic performance differs, we need to separate the different inputs that support growth through a methodology called *growth accounting*. Growth accounting breaks GDP growth into accumulation and utilization of labor and capital as well as their combined productivity. The rest, that is, the output growth that cannot be explained by these production factors, is considered techncal progress and treated as a residual measured by TFP.[12] Using this growth accounting framework, we can separate the EU and US growth components.

Employment Growth

The simplest, though least recommended, labor measure is a head count of jobs or employees. However, this measure fails to reflect changes in average work time, people who hold multiple jobs, self-employment, and the quality of labor. This simple measure can be refined by (1) extending it to total employment, including both wage and salary earners and the self-employed, and (2) estimating total hours "actually" worked, instead of "contractual" hours, to capture shifts toward shorter hours, longer paid vacations, and more part-time work.[13]

Table 1.3 shows EU and US employment growth between 1975 and 2002 as well as their 2002 employment rate levels, that is, the number of people employed as a percentage of the total labor force.[14] Based on this data, the US has had a higher annual average rate of labor accumulation and utilization. In the last 28 years, the EU's average employment growth rate was 0.55 percent, compared to the US rate of 1.62 percent—nearly three times higher. This difference in labor accumulation and utilization is probably the main factor behind the growth gap between the two economies.

TABLE 1.3   Employment Growth in EU Member States and in the Unites States, 1975-2002

		(average annual growth in percent, ranked according to performance, 1995-2002)			
	1975–1985	1985–1990	1990–1995	1995–2002	Employment rate in 2002
Ireland	0.0	1.1	1.9	4.6	68
Spain	−1.6	3.3	−0.5	2.7	59
Luxembourg	0.0	1.4	0.5	2.6	66
Netherlands	0.5	2.3	1.1	2.4	77
Finland	0.5	0.3	−3.8	1.8	66
France	0.2	1.0	−0.2	1.5	63
U.K.	−0.2	1.8	−0.9	1.1	71
Belgium	−0.4	1.0	−0.2	0.9	60
Italy	0.8	0.8	−0.7	1.1	59
Denmark	0.5	0.1	−0.5	0.8	76
Sweden	0.5	1.0	−2.2	0.8	75
Greece	1.2	0.7	0.6	0.6	56
Germany	0.2	1.4	−0.3	0.5	69
Austria	0.1	0.7	0.2	0.5	74
Portugal	−0.3	1.1	−0.5	0.4	78
EU-15	0.1	1.4	−0.5	1.2	66
US	2.2	2.0	0.9	1.4	75

Source: European Competitiveness Reports, 2001 and 2003

In addition, in 2002 the US employment rate was much higher than the EU's. In the US, 75 percent of the working-age population (people aged 15 to 64) had a job, while in the EU only 66 percent were employed—9 percentage points less. Only the Netherlands, Sweden, and Denmark had rates comparable to the US, while Italy, Spain, and Greece all had rates below 60 percent.

Table 1.4 shows how employment rates are distributed by age and gender. The average gap between the EU and US is much larger for women and older workers, 13.5 percentage points and 9.5 percentage points, respectively. This lower rate is due in large part to the differences in the participation rate, that is, the number of people actively looking for a job, which was 77.5 percent in the US versus 70 percent in the EU. Only Denmark and Sweden had higher rates than the US. Female participation rates have an even wider gap at 10 percentage points. For older workers, the difference favors the US by 11.5 percent.[15] In other words, if the EU had the same employment rate as the US, it would have had around 16 million more jobs!

Part of this large gap in the participation rates results from the US's larger internal population growth and immigration rates; also immigrants tend to have more children. While the EU population

TABLE 1.4   Employment and Participation Rates (2002)

	US	EU
Participation or Activity Rate	77.5%	70.0%
Male Participation Rate	83.5%	77.0%
Female Participation Rate	70.0%	60.0%
Older Workers (aged 55–64)	59.0%	40.0%
Employment Rate	**75.0%**	**66.0%**
Male Employment Rate	80.0%	72.5%
Female Employment Rate	68.0%	54.5%
Older Workers Employment Rate	57.5%	48.0%

Participation Rate = percentage of working age population (aged 15 to 64) actively seeking employment.
Employment Rate = percentage of working age population (aged 15 to 64) employed.
Source: EUROSTAT

grew at only 0.4 percent per year between 1991 and 2000, the US population increased 1.2 percent, or three times more. At the same time, the US employment rate grew 5 percent while the EU's grew only 1 percent. However, demographic trends cannot be considered as fully exogenous to growth, given that the probability of finding employment tends to be highly correlated with the birth rate.[16]

It is striking to see that the EU employment rate in 2002 was still lower than in 1975 when it reached 67 percent, despite the fact that it has been growing steadily since 1994 when it was at 62 percent (see Figure 1.2). On the contrary, the US rate, which began in 1975 at a lower level has been growing steadily (except for a drop at the beginning of the 1980s), peaking in 1999 and then dropping slightly over the last four years.[17]

The other main reason for the US's higher employment rate has to do with labor costs. From the standpoint of economic efficiency, real wage restraint is desirable only if past wages rose faster than productivity; otherwise excessive wage levels can become a

FIGURE 1.2   Though Rising, the Employment Rate in the EU Is Much Lower than in the US

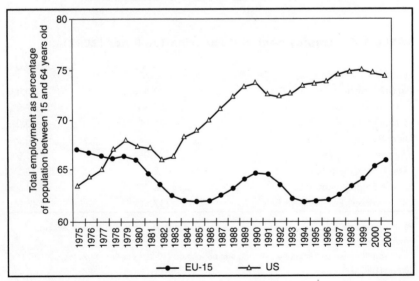

Source: European Competitiveness Report, 2001

barrier to job creation. Figure 1.3 shows how total real labor costs outpaced gains in the EU's productivity in the 1970s, but that productivity growth caught up with labor costs during the 1980s and even moved ahead of labor costs in the 1990s.[18] By contrast, productivity outpaced the growth of total labor costs in the US throughout the past two decades, perhaps contributing to its relatively stronger employment growth as well as to its relative stagnation in compensation.[19] Nevertheless, after 1995 labor costs and wage growth accelerated markedly in the US in stark contrast to the EU.

FIGURE 1.3   The Rise in Real Labor Cost, Work Productivity, and Employment, 1970–2001

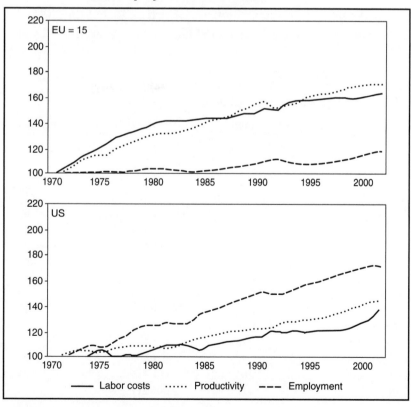

Source: OECD Employment Outlook, 2003

Another important measure of labor accumulation is the number of hours worked annually per average person employed; this figure also tells us the level of part-time employment as well as total working time per year for those employed full time. Part-time employment is 13.9 percent of total employment in the EU and 13 percent in the US. However, the rates in the EU vary widely from 33 percent in the Netherlands and 23 percent in the UK to 7.9 percent in Spain and 4.8 percent in Greece.[20] Although EU women have a lower employment rate than do US women, they play a larger role in part-time employment with 76.7 percent versus 67.5 percent.

There are two basic ways of comparing the average annual hours worked in every country: through the contractual working time or, the more realistic measure, hours actually worked per year. The latter measure shows that in the US the average employed person works around 211 hours more per year than that of the EU. Table 1.5 shows the average effective working time per year in 1990 and in

TABLE 1.5   Average Annual Hours Actually Worked per Person Employed

	1990	2002	Difference
Belgium	1,677	1,599	−118
Denmark	1,491	1,499	8
Finland	1,763	1,686	−77
France	1,657	1,545	−112
Germany	1,541	1,444	−97
Greece	1,919	1,934	15
Ireland	1,920	1,668	−252
Italy	1,675	1,619	−56
Netherlands	1,437	1,340	−97
Portugal	1,881	1,719	−162
Spain	1,824	1,807	−17
Sweden	1,544	1,581	32
United Kingdom	1,767	1,707	−60
European Union	1,676	1,604	−72
United States	1,837	1,815	−22
US/EU	+161	+211	

Source: OECD Employment Outlook, 2003

2002.[21] In the US, the average employed person worked 1,837 hours per year in 1990 and 1,815 hours in 2002—a reduction of 22 hours. In the EU, they worked 1,676 hours per year in 1990 and only 1,604 hours per year in 2002—a reduction of 72 hours.[22]

This working time gap is the result both of shorter work weeks (approximately 35.6 hours in the EU versus 40.3 hours in the US) and/or longer paid holidays in the EU. For instance, US workers have an average holiday entitlement of 16 days per year, but most employees take only 14. By contrast, in the EU at least one month of paid vacation is viewed as an inalienable right. Italian workers get 39.5 paid days off each year, French workers 35, German workers 39, and Spanish workers 30. Even the British, although much closer to the so-called US business culture, get an average of 25 days. This statistic shows a very clear and entrenched social preference among EU citizens for more leisure and less working time.[23]

Social factors   Social choices such as fewer working hours must be respected not only because they are the will of majority, but because it seems natural for people to demand more leisure as their real income levels increase. However, an increasing use of labor potential, both in terms of employment and hours worked, does not always imply a welfare improvement for all workers. Working fewer hours can be economically inefficient unless higher productivity and/or higher employment fill the productivity gap caused by fewer working hours. This was the case in the EU for many years, while the US needed to have higher employment growth and more working hours to compensate for its lower productivity growth; however, this is no longer the case. The EU has simply used some its productivity improvement to increase leisure rather than income, while the US has done the opposite.[24] This explanation can still be right for France or even Germany, which have higher productivity levels than those of the US, but not for the EU as a whole. The main issue here is that in the last eight years both the employment rate and productivity gap have slowly grown in favor of the US, which should be a major cause of concern for EU policymakers.

In addition, the EU's increasing social rejection of immigrants, as they become a larger percentage of total EU population, could be potentially damaging in the long term, especially when immigrants reach the threshold of a certain percentage of the total population. If the EU's persistently declining fertility rate and increasing life expectancy are not compensated for by higher immigration rates, the average age of the population may increase faster, and the EU would be faced with an economy that is less innovative, entrepreneurial, or productive (the young are those who consume, innovate, and take risks) creating insurmountable fiscal problems for generations to come.

Market regulation   A number of institutional factors affect labor utilization, including the level of competition. When factor and product markets are more regulated and less flexible, competition, investment, and employment creation decrease. Table 1.6 shows a product market regulation index developed by Nicoletti, Scarpetta and Baylaud (2002). If we average the EU countries, the index is 160 compared to the US index of 100. The index varies widely among member countries with Italy and France at 230 and 210, respectively, while others have a very low index, such as the UK with 50.

In terms of factor market regulation, a number of indexes show the inflexibility of the EU labor markets. For example, as the importance of innovation and the need for restructuring becomes greater, the importance of labor mobility also increases and comes at a premium. Flexibility allows firms to match employment more closely with output levels, which also helps match the skills and abilities of the labor force with specific tasks by enabling firms to redeploy (internal flexibility) or to change their skill composition (external flexibility) more easily. An index developed by Obstfeld and Peri (2002) shows that interregional mobility between 1990 and 1995 was more than the double in the US than in Italy, three times higher than in Germany, and more than three times larger than in the UK. An index of intercompany mobility developed by Auer and Cazes (2001) measures flexibility by the number of years someone works for the

TABLE 1.6   Indices of Product Market Regulation, 1998

	Inward-oriented	Outward-oriented	All
Austria	118	54	140
Belgium	270	63	190
Denmark	190	54	170
Finland	230	63	190
France	270	103	210
Germany	190	54	140
Greece	270	132	220
Ireland	80	43	80
Italy	330	49	230
Netherlands	180	54	140
Portugal	210	107	170
Spain	220	68	160
Sweden	170	84	140
UK	50	43	50
Australia	120	43	90
Canada	100	215	150
Japan	180	102	150
New Zealand	140	95	130
Norway	220	215	220
Switzerland	220	132	180
US	110	87	100

Source: Nicoletti, Scarpetta, and Boylaud, 2002

same company. This index shows average job tenure in the EU is 10.5 years versus 6.8 years in the US.[25]

Another way of measuring labor mobility is through the immigration rate, measured by the percentage of foreign labor within the total. According to the OECD Employment Outlook (2001), the US reached 12 percent in 1998 versus only 5 percent in the EU. There member country rates varied widely with Germany at 9 percent, France at 5.6 percent, and Italy and Spain at only 2 percent and 1.5 percent, respectively. While these EU percentages have grown—Italy and Spain each to more than 5 percent, Germany to more than 10 percent, and France to more than 7 percent—the US immigration rate has also grown to 16 percent. Another indirect index for measuring labor market mobility is the percentage of public sector employment in both economies—15 percent in the US versus 19.3 percent in the EU.[26]

Labor market regulation can also be measured by the employment protection indices.[27] Such indices measure the restrictions companies face in dismissing regular and temporary employees. Table 1.7 shows that the US protection index is 3.5 times lower than the EU's.[28]

Nickell and Nunziata (2000) developed another indirect measure of labor market regulation through the indices of trade union density and trade union coverage. These indices show that the proportion of wage earners who are union members is 40 percent in the

TABLE 1.7   Employment Protection Indices

	Late 1980s (narrow)	Late 1990s (narrow)	Late 1990s (broad)	Change, late 1980s–1990s (narrow)
Austria	2.2	2.2	2.3	0
Belgium	3.1	2.1	2.5	–1.0
Denmark	2.1	1.2	1.5	–0.9
Finland	2.3	2.0	2.1	–0.3
France	2.7	3.0	2.8	0.3
Germany	3.2	2.5	2.6	–0.7
Greece	3.6	3.6	3.5	0
Ireland	0.9	0.9	1.1	0
Italy	4.1	3.3	3.4	–0.8
Netherlands	2.7	2.1	2.1	–0.6
Portugal	4.1	3.7	3.7	–0.4
Spain	3.7	3.1	3.1	–0.6
Sweden	3.5	2.1	2.6	–1.3
UK	0.5	0.5	0.9	0
Australia	0.9	0.9	1.2	0
Canada	0.6	0.6	1.1	0
Japan	n/a	2.4	2.3	n/a
New Zealand	n/a	2.6	0.9	n/a
Switzerland	1.0	1.0	1.5	0
US	0.2	0.2	0.7	0

Note: The "narrow" measures represent protection for regular and temporary contracts: the "broad" measure takes account of collective dismissal legislation.

Source: OECD Employment Outlook, 1999, cited in "What Have Two Decades of British Economic Reform Delivered?" D. Card, R. Freeman, NBER Working Paper 8801, February 2002.

EU versus only 15 percent in the US, and that the proportion of wage earners covered by collective agreements is 80 percent in the EU versus only 20 percent in the US.[29]

Another factor that negatively affects the use of labor is taxes on low-wage labor, including contributions to social security. Higher tax rates result in lower incentives for workers to work and for employers to hire. According to the OECD,[30] the tax rate on low-wage earners in 2000 was 37 percent in the EU but only 28 percent in the US.[31] A similar trend appears in total taxes on total labor. In 2002, the EU's average implicit tax rate on total labor was 40 percent versus only 24 percent in the US. In 2001, the EU tax wedge (the difference between gross pay and take home pay) for a single worker with no children at the average production wage was 43.1 percent versus 30 percent in the US and 33 percent in the ensemble of the OECD countries. The entire difference was accounted for by social security contributions. This interaction between social protection and economic performance in the EU has turned into a negative spiral in the last decade. Because of the lower growth of European employment rates, lower productivity growth, and the growing number of dependants, higher social contribution charges were required to maintain a consistent level of social benefits.

The International Monetary Fund's (2003) very interesting empirical analysis of the relationship between unemployment and the Euro Area's[32] labor market institutions sums up this issue well.[33] The study, using the IMF's global economy model (GEM), shows that if the European labor markets became as competitive as those in the US, then European GDP would increase by about 5.5 percent over the long term. Consumption and investment would be boosted by similar amounts, and unemployment would be reduced by more than 3.5 percent.[34] In addition, if the euro area product markets were as competitive as those in the US, the impact would be nearly double with GDP increasing by 10 percent in the long run (corresponding to one-half of the estimated productivity gap between the two regions), and unemployment could fall by about 6.5 percent, bringing European unemployment to levels unseen since the early 1970s.

Productivity

Productivity is measured using two different ratios. The first is the average GDP produced by every employed person, which results from dividing the total annual GDP by the average number of people employed during the same year. The second is the average GDP per hour worked, which we get by dividing the annual GDP by the average number of hours worked during the same year. Both ratios can be measured by their average annual rate of growth or by their average level in a specific year.

Table 1.8 shows how during the last 28 years the annual average rate of productivity growth per person employed has evolved.[35]

TABLE 1.8   Labor Productivity in the EU and US, 1975–2002

(average annual growth of GDP per employed person in percent, ranked according to performance in 1995–2002)

	1975–1985	1985–1990	1990–1995	1995–2002	Labor productivity in 2002 (US = 100)
Ireland	3.5	3.5	2.7	4.1	87
Luxembourg	2.3	5.0	4.9	2.8	145
Portugal	3.3	4.4	2.3	2.6	48
Finland	2.4	3.0	3.2	2.7	76
Greece	1.0	0.5	0.7	2.8	59
Austria	2.3	2.5	1.9	1.8	70
Sweden	1.0	1.2	2.8	1.8	67
Belgium	2.5	2.1	1.7	1.5	92
U.K.	2.2	1.5	2.5	1.6	72
Denmark	1.6	1.2	2.5	1.6	76
France	2.3	2.2	1.2	1.2	78
Germany	2.0	2.0	2.3	1.1	71
Netherlands	1.4	0.8	1.0	0.9	72
Italy	2.2	2.0	2.0	0.7	82
Spain	3.2	1.2	2.0	0.8	65
EU-15	2.2	1.8	2.0	1.0	73
US	1.2	1.2	1.5	2.2	100

Source: European Competitiveness Reports, 2001 and 2003

Over the whole period, the EU's average annual rate of productivity growth has been slightly higher: 1.79 percent versus 1.51 percent. However, between 1995 and 2002, the US rate has been much higher: 2.2 percent versus 1.0 percent—more than double. While it may seem that the EU has been able to trade part of this higher productivity for leisure rather than income,[36] in the last seven years the trend has reversed.

Nevertheless, in spite of the EU's persistently higher productivity growth, in 2002, the US level was much higher. If we think of US productivity as 100, then the EU level is only 73—27 percentage points lower. Luxembourg was the only EU country with a higher level than the US, but given its small size, it is not representative. The countries with the next highest levels are Belgium at 92, Spain at 91, and Ireland and Italy, at 87 and 82, respectively. Of the larger countries, France is at 78, the UK 72, and Germany 71. Part of these EU differentials may result from the relative levels of unemployment: those countries with higher unemployment rates seem to have higher output per employee than those with lower levels.

Beginning in 1975, EU productivity grew steadily from 66 percent of the US average to its peak of 78 percent in 1993. In 2001 and 2002, productivity dropped to 73 percent. Therefore, in the last eight years the gap has been widening. According to the European Competitiveness Report (2003), in 2002 productivity increased by 2.81 percent in the US but only by 0.32 percent in the EU.

Measuring productivity by GDP per person employed should be complemented by the productivity per hour worked. Since the EU has a much lower employment rate, its productivity per person employed tends to be higher. Such a measure negates the large differences in part-time employment that causes countries with higher levels of part-time labor to have lower productivity. Between 1990 and 2002, the annual average GDP growth rate per hour worked was 1.8 percent in the EU versus 1.5 percent. However, between 1996 and 2002, the trend reversed and has been higher in the US with 1.86 percent versus 1.27 percent.[37] Figure 1.4 shows this change in productivity per hour for both economies between 1985 and 2002.

FIGURE 1.4   **Levels of Productivity (GDP per Hour)**
in the EU and in the US (1995 = 100)

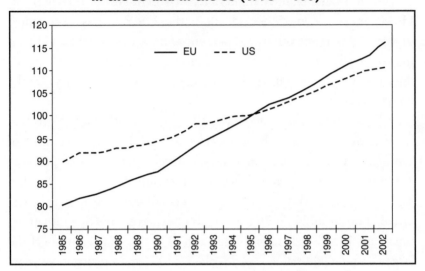

Source: WIFO calculations using Gröningen Growth and Development Centre data

While both economies began with a gap of 10 percentage points, today the gap is only 6 percentage points, and is higher in the US.

In addition, as shown in Table 1.9,[38] in 1999 the level of output per hour worked in the US was 15 percentage points higher than in the EU, much higher than previously calculated. The member countries differ greatly: Luxembourg, Belgium, and Netherlands have higher levels than the US, while Italy and France are very close to the US average, and Greece and Portugal are more than 40 percentage points lower. In 2003, according to EUROSTAT database, the gap level between the US and the EU has been reduced to 12.7 percentage points.

Because the levels of output per hour worked in some large EU countries are very close to US levels, some researchers believe that hourly productivity is the indicator to watch.[39] But others show that the EU's annual GDP growth rate per hour has fallen from around 2.6 percent per year in the first half of the 1990s to 1.4 percent per year since 1995, a drop of 1.2 percent.[40] During this same period, the US increased its hourly productivity growth from 1.2 percent to

TABLE 1.9   Comparative Levels of GDP per Capita and Labor Productivity, 1999

	GDP per Capita	GDP per Person Engaged	GDP per Hour Worked
United States	151	132	115
EU Total	100	100	100
Austria	109	95	90
Belgium	110	125	128
Denmark	119	100	99
Finland	101	101	99
France	101	108	113
Germany	106	99	102
Greece	67	79	74
Ireland	98	99	94
Italy	103	114	113
Luxembourg	185	194	199
Netherlands	115	99	119
Portugal	73	66	63
Spain	81	91	81
Sweden	102	94	95
United Kingdom	101	95	92
EU (excluding UK)	100	101	102

Note: In these calculations the EU total is the sum across all member states, not the average of the 15 countries.
Source: O'Mahony, H.M. Treasury, 2002

2.0 percent, increasing the gap with the EU. The EU's decline does not simply reflect a cyclical phenomenon because the period after 1995 was not worse for business and GDP was always positive.

As shown in Figure 1.5, there is no clear correlation between employment rates and productivity. The US has both high employment and high productivity, while Italy, Spain, and Greece have low levels of both. There is also a low correlation between average annual hours worked and output per employed person. The US has lower productivity per employed person than Japan, although the average employed person in Japan works approximately the same number of hours. In addition, Italy, France, and Germany have greater productivity rates than the UK but employed people work fewer hours. The

FIGURE 1.5   Levels of Employment and Productivity in the EU and in the US

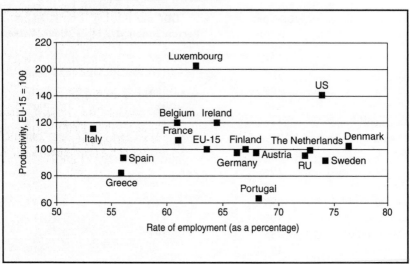

Productivity: GDP per person employed in 2001 (EUROSTAT, structural indicators).

Source: Employment: OECD Employment Outlook (Book B, Employment:Population ratios)

reasons why employment and productivity do not correlate could be the different rates of labor flexibility, education levels, or different capital/labor ratios. In the period from 1995 to 2002, average annual employment growth was similar in the EU and US, around 1.3 percent and 1.4 percent, respectively, but the US's average annual productivity grew much faster—2.2 percent versus 1.2 percent—because the US increased its capital deepening (see below) and total factor productivity.

Contrary to the US trend, in EU countries with similar levels of development there is a negative correlation between productivity and labor inputs.[41] This implies a trade-off by which low productivity countries are compensating by working longer hours and/or achieving higher employment rates. As a result, EU countries have been incapable of improving employment without reducing productivity and vice versa. This trade-off suggests an overall limit on the EU's potential growth rate at a time when it is still trying to catch up with the US and when quickly evolving ICT changes should boost potential.

However, we should not mistake this theoretical trade-off for a genuine trade-off between employment and productivity in a long-term dynamic sense. One of the most stylized facts in economics is that over the long term technological progress is neutral with respect to employment. In US history, the process of capital accumulation and technological innovation has not meant the "end of work," despite notions of "factories without workers."

Actual productivity growth can of course deviate from the balanced productivity growth rate over the short to medium term because the capital for labor substitution and the employment neutrality hypothesis do not hold over the short to medium term.[42] Structural reforms in the labor markets may entail temporarily reducing productivity growth below its full potential, but this should not be regarded as a trade-off in any sense. Higher employment implies an unambiguous increase in GDP per capita with no negative implications for the long-run productivity growth. Thus, there is no inherent problem in acting simultaneously on both fronts, raising the balanced rate of productivity using available instruments to stimulate TFP growth, while also encouraging the labor-intensive growth needed to move toward full employment.

If we sum up all the different measures of labor inputs and productivity applied to the European Union and the United States, we see the following:

- In 2002, for every 100 working-age people, the US had 9 more employed than did the EU.
- Each US person employed worked around 211 hours more per year.
- The GDP per employed person in the US was about 27 percentage points higher.
- The US output per hour worked was 15 percentage points higher.

Table 1.10 uses three alternative sources—OECD, EUROSTAT (structural indicators), and GGDC (Groningen Growth and Development Centre)—to summarize the respective standard of living

TABLE 1.10   EU/US Comparisons: Alternative Estimates for 2002 (US = 100)

	OECD data	GGDC	Structural indicators
GDP per capita	72.4	71.7	71.2
GDP per person employed	79.0	77.1	82.6
GDP per hour worked	90.0	91.5	86.8
Components:			
GDP	95.2	94.4	93.7
Population	131.5	131.7	131.5
Persons employed	120.6	122.4	113.4
Annual average hours worked	87.7	84.2	95.2
Total hours worked	105.7	103.2	107.9

Sources: OECD, Gröningen Growth and Development Centre, and EUROSTAT

situations for the US and EU.[43] If we consider the US as 100, then the EU's level of GDP per capita oscillates between 71.2 and 72.4. Its level of GDP per person employed ranges between 77.1 and 82.6, and its level of GDP per hour worked ranges from 86.8 to 91.5.[44]

Capital Deepening

Productivity is also determined by capital deepening, that is, the growth in capital per employed person or hour worked. Capital deepening is a long-term process determined primarily by investment, which measures how much the degree of capital intensity per employee or the substitution of capital for labor has contributed to overall productivity growth. As Table 1.11 shows, from 1975 to 2002 the average annual contribution to productivity was 0.68 percent in the EU versus only 0.32 in the US—almost half. The EU has been leading the US through most of the period, except in the last eight years—0.7 percent versus 0.4 percent—thanks to an investment boom as the quality of ICT products rose and their prices declined steeply, which decisively boosted ICT investment.[45]

Nevertheless, although the EU has had higher annual rates of capital deepening growth for many years, it has not yet been able to match US levels of capital per hour worked. In 1999, the US level

TABLE 1.11   Capital Deepening in EU Member States and in the US, 1975–2002

(average annual contribution to labor productivity growth in percentage points; ranked according to performance from 1995–2002)

	1975–1985	1985–1990	1990–1995	1995–2002
Portugal	1.5	0.8	1.1	1.1
Greece	1.1	0.7	0.6	0.8
Austria	1.0	0.6	1.0	0.7
Germany	0.8	0.2	1.0	0.5
Belgium	1.1	0.5	0.9	0.4
United Kingdom	0.6	0.2	0.8	0.4
Luxembourg	0.6	0.1	0.8	0.4
Denmark	0.5	0.7	0.5	0.4
Italy	0.7	0.6	0.9	0.3
Spain	1.7	0.2	1.3	0.3
France	1.0	0.7	0.9	0.3
Sweden	0.5	0.4	1.0	0.0
Ireland	1.7	0.5	0.1	−0.1
Netherlands	0.9	0.1	0.4	−0.1
Finland	0.9	1.0	1.4	−0.4
EU-1	0.9	0.4	1.0	0.4
United States	0.2	0.1	0.3	0.7

Note: The figures indicate how much (in percentage points) capital deepening or the substitution of capital for labor contributed to overall labor productivity growth.
Source: European Competitiveness Report, 2001 and 2003

was 107 compared to 100 in the EU.[46] Table 1.12 shows the EU's distribution of capital per hour worked. The member countries differed widely—five countries had much higher levels than the US: Belgium, 145; France, 124; Finland, 120; the Netherlands, 115; and Italy, 111. Austria had the same level, 107, but Spain had 90 and the UK had only 81. We should also point out that without the UK, the EU average would be 104, much closer to that of the US.[47]

Total Factor Productivity

TFP is another very important factor behind productivity because it estimates underlying residual productivity. TFP growth is mea-

TABLE 1.12   Relative Levels of Capital per Hour

	Capital per hour worked
United States	107
EU total	100
Austria	107
Belgium	145
Denmark	98
Finland	120
France	124
Germany	102
Greece	67
Ireland	78
Italy	111
Luxembourg	193
Netherlands	115
Portugal	39
Spain	90
Sweden	95
United Kingdom	81
EU 14 (excluding UK)	104

Source: O'Mahony. H.M. Treasury, 2002

sured by the difference between output growth and the growth of factor inputs, that is, the weighted average growth of labor and capital.

An increase in TFP means that more output can be produced from the same amount of labor and capital inputs. As a residual, TFP growth measures how innovation, R&D, and technological progress affect factor intensity and the proper organization of labor and capital. Furthermore, unlike other methods of calculating productivity, TFP reflects changes in the quality of inputs, such as better capital goods or improving skills and education levels. In recent years, one of the key factors enhancing TFP has been investment in new ICT capital goods, which tend to have a higher margin than many other capital goods. Finally, cyclical factors are also likely to have an impact on TFP growth. In periods of rapid growth, utilization and intensity tend to be higher and vice versa.

In the last 28 years, the EU's TFP annual growth has been slightly higher than that of the US. As shown in Table 1.13, the average annual TPF growth rate for the period has been 1.3 percent in the EU versus 1.05 percent. Only from 1995 to 2002 was US TFP growth higher.[48]

In spite of having a higher annual TFP growth, the EU's present level is lower.[49] Table 1.14 shows that given a 1999 EU level of 100, the US was 12 percentage points higher. There is considerably greater variability across EU countries in capital per hour worked and TFP than in productivity. In the case of capital, the large EU countries (except the UK) had capital levels higher than or close to the US. So for these countries, the TFP gap is greater than for productivity. As a result, the productivity gap with the US for large countries is

TABLE 1.13   Total Factor Productivity Growth in EU Member States and the US, 1975–2002

(average annual growth in percentage points, ranked according to performance from 1995–2002)

	1975–1985	1985–1990	1990–1995	1995–2002
Ireland	1.8	2.9	2.6	4.0
Finland	1.5	2.0	1.8	3.3
Greece	–0.2	–0.1	0.1	1.9
Sweden	0.5	–0.8	1.7	1.9
Portugal	1.8	3.6	1.3	1.8
Luxembourg	1.6	3.1	1.9	1.6
Austria	1.3	1.9	1.5	1.5
Belgium	1.3	1.6	0.8	1.2
United Kingdom	1.6	1.3	1.7	1.2
Denmark	1.2	0.5	2.0	1.2
France	1.4	1.7	0.6	1.1
Netherlands	1.1	1.1	1.0	1.1
Italy	1.3	1.5	1.2	0.7
Germany	1.2	1.7	1.1	0.7
Spain	1.6	1.0	0.6	0.5
EU-15	1.4	1.5	1.1	1.0
United States	1.0	0.9	0.9	1.5

Source: European Competitiveness Reports, 2001 and 2003

TABLE 1.14   Total Factor Productivity Levels in 2002

	TPF
United States	112
EU total	100
Austria	87
Belgium	111
Denmark	99
Finland	93
France	104
Germany	101
Greece	86
Ireland	105
Italy	109
Luxembourg	153
Netherlands	113
Portugal	90
Spain	85
Sweden	97
United Kingdom	99
EU 14 (excluding UK)	100

Source: O'Mahony. H.M. Treasury, 2002

mainly explained by TFP. TFP levels are considerably closer to US levels than was the case for productivity. The net effect is that the variation among EU countries is relatively small, especially if Luxembourg is excluded.

As a conclusion of this growth accounting exercise, we can say that an estimated two-thirds of the EU gap with the US in GDP per capita result from lower levels of labor utilization—one-third from lower employment rates, one-third from lower effective working hours, and the last third from lower productivity. While part of the lower utilization reflects shorter EU working hours and may be considered a matter of choice, the much lower participation and employment rates as well as the much higher rate of unemployment do not reflect social preference and should greatly concern the EU because of its rapidly aging population.[50]

The EU productivity and TFP growth rates have been slowly declining over the last four decades while employment has been growing slowly, increasing unemployment quite rapidly. Therefore, the decline in productivity has been far more important for economic growth than has employment. The recent decline in productivity reflects the combined impact of a diminishing capital/labor ratio and declining TFP growth. The EU's recent past has been characterized by a divergence in output trends and productivity growth, as strong employment has contrasted with a further deceleration of productivity. Conversely, the US has experienced both higher job creation and accelerated productivity.

Using standard growth accounting, the European Commission has separated real GDP growth in labor utilization (employment growth) into productivity and TFP growth. As shown in Table 1.15, during the last four decades, GDP growth has fallen from an average of 4.9 percent in the 1960s to 2.1 percent in the 1990s. Although output growth has increased since the mid-1990s, it remains unclear whether this is a trend reversal. The growth figures for 2002 and 2003 do not reflect such a reversal given that the EU is back to a very low growth rate—approximately one-third of US growth. There has been a certain convergence of labor utilization growth rates, although they are still lower in the EU.

TABLE 1.15　Productivity and Output Growth in the EU

	1960s	1970s	1980s	1990s	1996–2000	
Average annual rate of growth in %						
					EU-15	US
Total factor productivity	3.1	1.5	1.3	1.0	1.0	1.8
Labor productivity	4.6	2.7	1.9	1.7	1.3	2.8
Employment	0.3	0.4	0.5	0.4	1.3	1.6
Real gross domestic product	4.9	3.0	2.4	2.1	2.6	4.4
Unemployment rate (%)	2.2	4.0	9.0	9.9	9.8	4.6

Source: European Competitiveness Report, 2001

Factors enhancing TFP   Innovation has become the key driver of economic growth.[51] The long EU postwar expansion was based on an already mature technology trajectory with well-known organizational implications and a rapid diffusion of best practices. The EU was catching up with the US, both through investment and factor accumulation and through imitation of leading-edge technologies. Standardized mass-market products that could be made with long production runs brought significant economies of scale, resulting in an industrial structure dominated by large firms. Assembly-line production absorbed large quantities of unskilled labor coming off the land and some intra-European migration from the Mediterranean basin. The innovation process was heavily incremental in nature. The welfare state favored the establishment of long-term labor relations. Macroeconomic management was directed to aggregate demand while microeconomic management dealt with the unwanted side effects of concentrating production in very few firms and public ownership of enterprises operating as natural monopolies. Public education systems concentrated on primary and secondary education, combined with extensive apprenticeship systems. Higher education, often separated from research activities, played the role of forming elite units for top managers, high-level civil servants, and professionals.

The breakdown of this system did not come suddenly, and it remains in place today in significant areas. Nevertheless, the easy gains from assimilating existing technologies became exhausted, and demand for the output from leading industries became saturated. Because the technologies were now widely available and the knowledge required largely codified, some of these industries were susceptible to offshore production in middle-income, newly industrialized countries with educated workforces and lower labor costs, while others retreated into higher-quality, higher-margin segments, substituting capital for labor and increasing outsourcing. The patterns of consumption and production shifted in favor of different types of products that required different forms of industrial organization. Higher educational standards and changing consumer preferences also led to greater demand for less standardized and more customized products. Growth was not driven by volume but by composition.

Once European countries had to move toward the technology frontier, innovation rather than factor accumulation and imitation became the engine of growth. This called for new organizational forms, less vertically integrated firms, greater mobility both intra- and intercompany, greater flexibility of labor markets, a greater reliance on market finance, and a higher demand for both R&D and higher education. However, the necessary changes in economic institutions and organizations are not taking place on a large scale, and the delay in adjusting the EU's complex institutional system accounts for most of the gap with the US.[52]

There are three key factors that enhance innovation and, therefore, TFP-knowledge, R&D investment, and ICT investment:

1. *Knowledge is basically the labor force's level of education.* Human capital formation may also permanently impact output growth if higher skill levels and knowledge facilitate the adoption of new technologies and/or innovation, which in turn accelerate technological progress. The closer the economy gets to the technology frontier, the greater the importance of higher education. While the basic requirement for the postwar, industry-driven economy was secondary education, in an innovation-driven economy higher education becomes the standard.

Table 1.16 shows the average number of years of schooling for the adult population between 1960 and 2002.[53] The difference between the EU and US has narrowed from 2.8 years in favor of the US in 1960 to 2.2 years in 2002. Only Germany, with 13 years, had similar schooling figures as the US. However, when looking at the quality of education (using reading, scientific, and numeric literacy as proxies for performance), except for reading the US performs below the OECD average; while some European countries far exceed the average (Finland, Ireland, the Netherlands, Sweden, and the UK), and other large European countries—Germany, Italy, and Spain—perform worse than the US.

TABLE 1.16   Average Number of Years of Schooling, 1960–2002

	1960	1965	1970	1975	1980	1985	1990	1995	2002
Belgium	7.7	8.1	8.5	8.9	9.4	9.7	10.1	10.5	11.1
Denmark	10.8	10.9	11.1	11.3	11.5	11.7	11.7	11.9	12.5
Germany	9.9	10.4	11.0	11.5	12.0	12.6	12.9	13.1	13.0
Greece	5.6	5.9	6.2	6.6	7.1	7.5	7.9	8.7	10.2
Spain	5.0	5.1	5.2	5.5	5.9	6.5	7.1	n.a.	9.2
France	8.1	8.6	9.0	9.6	9.9	10.2	10.5	n.a.	10.6
Ireland	7.4	7.5	7.8	8.2	8.5	8.9	9.4	10.1	10.6
Italy	5.4	5.8	6.2	6.6	7.0	7.5	8.0	8.6	9.7
Luxembourg	n.a.	n.a.	n.a.	n.a.	n.a.	n.a.	n.a.	n.a.	0.0
Netherlands	8.1	8.5	8.9	9.4	9.9	10.4	11.0	11.4	11.9
Austria	9.0	9.2	9.3	9.8	10.3	10.9	11.3	11.7	12.4
Portugal	4.4	4.6	4.9	5.3	5.7	6.1	6.4	n.a.	7.2
Finland	7.7	8.2	8.7	9.3	9.9	10.5	11.0	11.4	11.4
Sweden	8.0	8.3	8.6	9.1	9.6	10.1	10.6	11.1	11.7
UK	8.6	8.8	9.1	9.4	9.8	10.2	10.5	n.a.	12.0
EU 15	7.8	8.2	8.5	8.9	9.3	9.7	10.2	n.a.	11.1
US	10.6	11.0	11.3	11.8	12.2	12.4	12.7	13.0	13.3

Note: Figures for Germany before 1990 exclude former GDR, EU average (excluding Luxembourg) weighted by population aged 25–64.
Source: de la Fuente and Domenech (2001) for 1990–1995, Table 4.4 for 2002; European Commission Services for population data.

Table 1.17 shows that the US has both a much higher proportion of workers with higher education than France, Germany, or the UK, and also a much higher percentage of the workforce with lower qualifications (except for the UK).[54] On the other hand, Germany and France have a much higher percentage of workers with secondary education. In 2000, the percentage of the population, aged 25 to 34, that had acquired higher education was 40 percent in the US versus only 18 percent in France, 25 percent in the UK and Germany, 16 percent in Spain, and 12 percent in Italy. For the population aged 45 to 54, the level in the US was 41 percent, 35 percent in Spain, 33 percent in France, 30 percent in the UK, 22 percent in Germany, and 12 percent in Italy.[55] Another way of looking at these differences is through the money spent on higher education. The US spends 3 percent of GDP on higher education, of which 1.4 percent is public and

TABLE 1.17   Labor Force Skills, Total Economy, 1999

	Higher	Intermediate	Low
US	27.7	18.6	53.7
France	16.4	51.2	32.4
Germany	15.0	65.0	20.0
UK	15.4	27.7	56.9

Source: Britain's Productivity Performance: update and extensions, O'Mahony and De Boer, Processed, NIESR, 2002.

the rest private. The EU spends 1.4 percent of GDP, of which 1.1 percent is public and only 0.4 percent private—less than half that of the US. In the year 2000, enrollment in higher education, as a share of the population aged 20 to 29, was 37 percent in the US versus 24.8 percent in the EU.[56]

Recent research shows that education explains a large part of the US growth rate.[57] While general education allows workers to work in high-tech companies that adopt new technologies, a less costly skill-specific education allows them to work only in low-tech firms that use established production methods. The EU's higher firing and regulation costs cause companies to accept inferior productivity, lowering wages and reducing the incentives to acquire general education; as a result, expected growth rates decline. Recent empirical work suggests that one extra year of education (roughly equivalent to a 10 percent increase in human capital) has raised the long-term output per capita by an average of 4 to 7 percent across OECD countries.[58] Therefore, the EU must create more flexibility in educational choices in upper secondary and higher education and focus more on general education.

2. *According to EUROSTAT, in 2004 total R&D expenditures averaged 3.0 percent of GDP in the US and continue to grow every year, while the EU average remains stagnant at around 2 percent.* The gap is even higher in R&D expenditures by private businesses: The US average is 2 percent and growing, and the EU average is 1.2 percent and falling. In both cases intra-EU variability is very high since the difference between the three highest (Finland, Sweden, and Germany)

and the three lowest (Spain, Greece, and Portugal) is striking and widening. Naturally, part of the difference in R&D spending may just reflect the different sector weights within each economy; some sectors such as chemicals and pharmaceuticals are much more R&D intensive. Nevertheless, when comparing the same sectors in both economies, most of the time US research intensity is higher both in low and high R&D sectors. The only way to enhance private R&D expenditures is for markets to offer sufficient returns and diffusion and for governments to offer adequate incentives, such as strong property rights.

Another important R&D measure is patent activity. According to the OECD (2002), the US has 4.5 patent applications per 10,000 inhabitants each year and that number is growing, while the EU average is only 2 percent and falling. Only Germany has a higher patent rate than the US. There is clear evidence that both R&D spending and patent activity are positively correlated with productivity growth in manufacturing, and that both have social returns that exceed the private returns from spillover effects that accrue to other firms by way of new and improved products, processes, services, and know-how.

3. *The third factor is information and communication technologies (ICT) investment.* The US enjoyed a remarkable economic performance in the second half of the 1990s not only because of stronger employment creation but also because of productivity acceleration. This example has led some researchers and policymakers to ask whether the EU could eventually benefit from the same experience with the *new economy.*

Research in the new economy has basically focused on ICT investment. This general-purpose technology has increased optimism about entering a new industrial revolution that could transform the economic landscape of developed countries. Recent empirical studies have revealed that ICT investment has sizably impacted productivity, accounting for up to three-quarters of the estimated 1 percent rise in US productivity in the second half of the 1990s.[59]

The evidence of ICT's impact in the EU is decidedly smaller. The European Commission calculates that ICT contributed more to

US growth in the first half of the 1990s. This gap of half a decade is consistent with the ICT spending gap.[60]

Nevertheless, while these estimates are encouraging, the evidence does not support ICT's main virtue, namely, productivity gain as it is applied throughout the economy. What is evident is that technological progress has accelerated productivity in IT production. Moore's Law, which quantifies technological progress in the IT sector, demonstrates the economic significance of this progress. On the one hand, the number of transistors per every Intel microprocessor has gone up from 4,000 in 1971 to over 10 million in 2000. On the other hand, prices of processing power have declined noticeably over time, from 6,500 euros in 1994 to fewer than 1,500 euros in 2001, giving rise to incentives for increasing IT capital in the production process. A review of ICT's contribution to the EU economy[61] shows capital deepening resulting from declining prices of ICT capital goods, but does not indicate significant effects of technological progress outside the ICT sector.[62] The contribution gap between the US and EU results mainly from the larger costs of capital adjustment and from the EU's wage rigidity. Another important factor is the EU's smaller share of ICT production, since ICT's main effect on aggregate TFP growth is derived from growth in the sector itself.[63]

Overall, the experience with ICT so far suggests that the emergence and use of new technologies may accelerate EU productivity growth. Over the medium term, the increase in US productivity gives rise to potential catch-up growth, probably repeating the work of forces prevalent in the 1950s and 1960s. The crucial question is whether the conditions exist in the EU's economy to support the application of new technologies.

Table 1.18 shows ICT expenditures as a percentage of GDP. Between 1992 and 2000, when comparing both the annual growth of ICT investment and the level of ICT investment as a percentage of GDP, the United States not only had a higher level than the European Union but also a higher annual rate of growth. Only the United Kingdom and Sweden had higher levels than the United States but a lower rate of growth. Greece and Portugal (because of heavy invest-

TABLE 1.18   International Comparison of ICT Expenditures and Production

	Share of ICT in business sector employment, 1998	Share of ICT in business sector value added, 1998	ICT expenditure as % of GDP, 1998	ICT expenditure as % of GDP, 1992–1999
Belgium	4.3	5.8	5.7	5.6
Denmark	5.1	—	6.7	6.6
Germany	3.1	6.1	5.1	5.3
Greece	—	—	5.1	3.8
Spain	—	—	4.0	3.9
France	4.0	5.3	5.9	5.9
Ireland	4.6	—	6.4	5.9
Italy	3.5	5.8	4.5	4.2
Netherlands	3.8	5.1	6.9	6.7
Austria	4.9	6.8	4.7	4.8
Portugal	2.7	5.6	5.1	4.5
Finland	5.6	8.3	5.7	5.6
Sweden	6.3	9.3	9.5	8.2
United Kingdom	4.8	8.4	9.0	8.1
EU (*)	4.0	6.4	6.0	5.6
Japan	3.4	5.8	6.2	6.0
US	3.9	8.7	8.7	8.1
Switzerland	6.0	—	7.3	7.3
Australia	2.6	4.1	8.5	8.1
Canada	4.6	6.5	8.1	7.6

(*) Weighted average GDP (1990), WIFO calculations
Source: OECD, 2001A, WITSA, 2000, WIFO calculations

ment in telecommunications infrastructures) and Ireland and Finland (because of a deliberate policy to catch up) had higher annual rates of growth, but they began at much lower levels than the United States.[64]

Table 1.19 compares business ICT investment in the EU and the US as a percentage of GDP. The US not only achieved a higher level both in 1992 and in 1999, but had also increased the gap by 1.33 percentage points in 1999. This result is even more impressive if we take into account the share of ICT investment as a percentage of total fixed business investment—between 1992 and 1998, the gap has increased

TABLE 1.19   Business Investment in ICT as a Percentage of GDP

	ICT investment/GDP			Total fixed investment/GDP		
	1992	1999	Difference 1999–1992	1992	1999	Difference 1999–1992
Belgium/Luxembourg	2.12	2.59	0.47	21.29	20.99	−0.30
Denmark	2.04	2.72	0.68	18.14	20.97	2.83
Germany	1.74	2.17	0.43	24.04	21.29	−2.76
Greece	0.75	1.80	1.05	21.32	23.00	1.69
Spain	1.52	1.58	0.06	23.09	23.69	0.60
France	1.70	2.05	0.35	20.93	18.86	−2.07
Ireland	1.82	2.32	0.50	16.59	24.13	7.53
Italy	1.49	1.77	0.28	20.47	18.43	−2.04
Netherlands	2.23	3.09	0.86	21.32	21.47	0.15
Austria	1.61	1.89	0.28	23.50	23.65	0.15
Portugal	0.96	1.81	0.85	25.01	27.48	2.46
Finland	1.61	2.48	0.87	19.61	19.28	−0.32
Sweden	2.49	3.64	1.15	18.26	16.47	−1.79
United Kingdom	2.43	3.76	1.33	16.53	17.97	1.44
EU	1.81	2.42	0.61	20.72	21.26	0.54
US	2.60	4.54	1.94	17.01	20.33	3.32

Source: Daveri, 2001

by 2.78 percent even though the level of total fixed business investment is almost 1 percent higher in the EU. It is important to note that EU business investment has been growing much faster in communications and decreasing in hardware and software.

According to the most recent research,[65] ICT investment's contribution to growth was larger in the US between 1991 and 1999, and even larger between 1996 and 1999. In the first half of the 1990s, the differences were small, 0.53 percent annually in the US versus 0.43 percent. But in the second half of the 1990s, the average annual contribution to growth in the US was almost three times higher—1.45 percent versus 0.57—therefore, the US achieved 0.94 percent versus 0.48.[66]

Two extremely interesting studies[67] have measured ICT's impact on productivity performance by examining 49 industries in 16 OECD countries (2002) and by doing an "ICT growth accounting exercise" for the European Union member countries (2003). The first study shows that between 1990 and 1995, the EU had a larger average productivity growth rate than the US—2.0 percent versus 1.2 percent—and that between 1995 and 2000 the opposite was true—average productivity growth in the US was 2.4 percent versus 1.3 percent. In the ICT sector, increases in productivity growth were high, especially in manufacturing with 11.6 percent in 1995 and 14.2 percent 2000 in the EU versus 14.5 percent and 20.3 percent in the US because of its larger share in output. By contrast, the EU's growth in ICT manufacturing was higher by 0.5 and 2.7 percent in both periods, despite its smaller share in output. In industries using ICT, the growth rate was 1.3 percent for both in the first period, but much larger in the US in the second—4.4 percent versus 1.2 percent. This growth was concentrated mainly in securities, and retail and wholesale trade, because of the larger share in output and employment in the US and more restrictive expansion opportunities in the EU. This study found that the EU's patterns of ICT diffusion are following the US pattern but at a considerably slower pace.

The second study examined how ICT capital contributed to output and productivity growth between 1980 and 2000. The study found that even though real investment and EU capital-service flows increased as rapidly as in the US, the shares of ICT in total EU investment and capital service flows were one-half to two-thirds of the US level up to the mid-1990s. Since then, ICT capital's relative contribution has improved, but overall EU productivity collapsed, suggesting that other factors, such as regulations and structural impediments in labor and product markets, may be preventing the EU from catching up more rapidly.

Another recent study uses the European Union Industry Labor Productivity Database to see if there are marked industry differences in productivity performance.[68] The results show that there are wide differences in performance across industries, countries, and time periods. Double digit annual average growth rates in labor productivity are common in ICT-producing sectors such as office machinery and electronic components. Strongly negative rates occur frequently in transport or business service industries. About half of EU industries show higher growth, but the locus of these industries has changed through time.

If we compare the early 1990s to the period between 1995 and 2002, the US acceleration is by no means ubiquitous, occurring in about half of the 56 individual industries. However, in the European Union fewer than 20 percent of industries show accelerating growth. Weighting each industry's performance by employment shares shows their contribution to aggregate productivity growth. In the US, the post-1995 acceleration is dominated by a few industries, namely ICT production, wholesale and retail trade, and banking and auxiliary financial services. This confirms other findings that stress the importance of services in explaining the US growth advantage.[69] In the EU, the aggregate deceleration in the same period is spread more widely across industries.

Similar findings show that the US average productivity growth was much higher from 1995 to 1999 than from 1973 to1995.[70] In the former it was around 2.5 percent, while in the latter it was around 1.4 percent, that is, an acceleration of more than 1 percent. According to this research, the main sources of acceleration seem to have been ICT-related capital deepening, which oscillates between 0.38 and 0.50 percent, and total factor productivity, which oscillates between 0.31 and 0.90 percent. Nevertheless, the contribution of ICT-related total factor productivity seems to have been smaller than other sources, though one study,[71] finds that the contribution of labor quality has been small but the cyclical effect seems to have been quite large.[72]

NOTES

1 The European Union Economy, 2003 Review (European Economy 2004)

2 European Competitiveness Report, 2002

3 Because of the increasing role of these factors, policymakers have become more important in creating institutional frameworks that enhance these factors, especially research and technology, innovation, and human knowledge and skills.

4 Solow, 1956; Swan, 1956

5 Denison, 1974

6 Studies have tried to reconcile the Solow-Swan model with empirical international evidence on convergence. Mankiw, Romer, and Weil (1992) augmented the aggregate production function with human capital represented by educational attainment. They found out that the Solow model performs well in explaining cross-country differences in income levels when human capital is taken into account, but only when the productivity level and the technical change rate are the same across nations.

7 Romer, 1986; Lucas, 1988; Aghion and Howitt, 1998

8 Lucas, 1988, and Rebelo, 1991

9 Romer, 1986, and Young, 1991

10 Romer, 1990; Grossman and Helpman, 1991; Aghion and Howitt, 1992

11 Bassanini, Scarpetta, and Visco, 2000

12 Denison, 1974

13 OECD 2001D

14 European Competitiveness Report, 2003

15 EUROSTAT, 2002

16 Independent High-level Study Group Report, 2003

17 EU Competitiveness Report, 2003

18 OECD Employment Outlook, 2003

19 Mishel et al. 2003

20 OECD Employment Outlook, 2003

21 In the European Union, these data are weighted by the total employed population by country.

22 Austria and Luxembourg are excluded for lack of data (OECD Employment Outlook, 2003). The Netherlands, with 1,340 hours; Germany, with 1,444; Denmark, with 1,499 and France, with 1,545 hours were the countries with lower effective worked time per year. By contrast, Greece with 1,934 hours was the only country with a higher annual working time than the United States; Spain was the closest to the United States with 1,807. The biggest reduction in

the annual number of hours since 1990 occurred in Ireland with 252, Portugal with 162, Belgium with 118, France with 112, and Germany and the Netherlands with 97 hours.

23 The Economist, 2004

24 Blanchard, 2004

25 Job tenure of less than one year is 27.8 percent in the United States versus 15.8 percent in the European Union; job tenure of more than 10 years is 42 percent in the European Union versus 25.8 percent in the United States.

26 Some European Union countries, such as France and some Nordic countries, have percentages over 25 percent (Algan, Cahuc, and Zyleberberg, 2002).

27 OECD Employment Outlook, 1999

28 Some European Union countries have indices that are five times higher, like Italy, or four times higher, like France.

29 Some countries such as France and Spain have, paradoxically, a lower density than the United States and a much higher coverage.

30 Joumard, 2002

31 The three highest countries in the European Union had rates of 46 percent.

32 The Euro Area refers to the12 countries that have adopted the euro as their single currency.

33 The IMF analysis uses two different instruments. First, it uses the recent empirical studies of Nickell, Ochel, and Quintini (2001) that employ the original data set combining historical series assembled by Nickell and Nunziatta (2001) with the most recent information on labor market institutions made available by the OECD. It then augments this information with simulations performed with the IMF Global Economy Model (GEM), a macroeconomic model incorporating a rigorous characterization of labor and product market imperfections (Pesenti, 2003, and Laxton and Pesenti, 2002). Both approaches convey a unified message.

34 Schnnabel, 2002

35 European Competitiveness Report, 2003

36 Blanchard, 2003

37 European Competitiveness Report, 2003

38 O'Mahony, 2002

39 Blanchard, 2004

40 Daveri, 2004

41 Independent High-level Study Group Report, 2003

42 This has been shown by Gordon (1995), but, at the same time, the trade-off will be subsequently eliminated through a dynamic path of capital adjustment.

43 European Competitiveness Report, 2003

44 The major differences are that EUROSTAT's structural indicators give a higher level of GDP per employed person for the European Union that is compensated for by a lower level of GDP per hour worked. There are also some differences in the purchasing power parities used to convert output in national currency units into a common currency, different methods to calculate hours worked, and different methods to adjust for the informal economy.

45 European Competitiveness Reports, 2001 and 2003

46 O'Mahony, 2002

47 European Competitiveness Report, 2003

48 The only European countries that had a higher average annual growth rate than the United States were Ireland, with 4.0 percent, Finland, with 3.3 percent, Greece and Sweden with 1.9 percent, and Portugal, with 1.8 percent (European Competitiveness Reports, 2001 and 2003).

49 O'Mahony, 2002

50 Independent High-level Study Group Report, 2003

51 Independent High-level Study Group Report, 2003

52 Independent High-level Study Group Report, 2003

53 de la Fuente and Domenech, 2001; European Commission, 2003

54 O'Mahony and De Boer, 2002

55 OECD, 2003

56 UNESCO, OECD, and European Union Commission, 2002

57 Krueger and Kumar, 2003

58 Basanini and Scarpetta, 2001

59 Oliner and Sichel, 2000; Jorgensen and Stiroh, 2000

60 European Economy, 2001A

61 Roger, 2001

62 McMorrow and Roger, 2001

63 European Economy, 2001A

64 European Economy, 2001A

65 Daveri, 2001; European Commission, 2000

66 European Economy, 2001A

67 Van Ark et al., 2002; Van Ark et al. 2003

68 O'Mahony and Van Ark, 2003

69 O'Mahony and Van Ark, 2003

70 Stiroh, 2000

71 Gordon, 2000

72 Gordon, 2000

ADDITIONAL DRAINS
ON EUROPEAN UNION
PRODUCTIVITY

T O explain why EU productivity began to slow in the 1970s, we need to first look at the factors that created the high productivity of the 1960s and the potential for Europe to catch up to the US.[1] The productivity gap with the US widened considerably between the early 1930s and 1950 not only because of World War II but also because of the semiautarkical policies of the 1930s. Furthermore, postwar reconstruction established a modern and highly productive capital stock. Investment ratios in the postwar era were much higher than before the war and contributed to high productivity and output. Moreover, trade barriers were lowered, and the new international monetary system facilitated international trade. Removing European trade protection increased the market's size, intensified competition, enhanced economies of scale, and stimulated growth.

These favorable factors began to vanish after the oil crisis of the early 1970s. Between 1972 and 1974, oil prices increased by almost 400 percent in dollars or more than 350 percent in today's euros. EU oil imports amounted to one-third of total imports, producing a strong negative external contribution to growth and a sharp deterioration of its trade terms. Moreover, real stock prices fell, and the system of fixed exchange rates proved to be unsustainable.[2]

The 1970s economic deceleration slowed fixed capital formation, which fell by 1.3 percent between 1973 and 1975, stabilizing at a level marginally above 3 percent until 1980 and falling again 2 percent in the mid-1980s. Although the capital increases were higher than trend growth, the latter reached its lowest level in 1981, which casts some doubts on the assumed causality between investment and growth. The investment slowdown was also caused by the subsequent shock to factor prices provoked by the oil price hike. The oil crisis was followed by a very large increase in labor costs, which between 1973 and 1975 increased the adjusted wage share in GDP by 3 percent. This increase was not reversed until 1984 when it returned to preoil crisis levels. This persistent shift generated an important capital-labor substitution.

Furthermore, as the oil crisis rapidly increased inflation, monetary policy was strongly tightened to help contain labor costs. However, though the monetary policy improved labor costs, it also raised real interest rates, further decelerating investments until the mid-1980s. At the end of the 1980s, monetary policy tightening was again followed by an increase in long-term interest rates and a drop in investment. Interest rates remained high until 1992. Finally, throughout the 1970s and 1980s, budgetary policies were relaxed, resulting in a rapid increase of public deficits and debt and maintenance of the high interest rates. Each 5 percent increase in the debt to GDP ratio increased interest rates between 100 and 150 basis points.[3]

These shocks to factor prices induced substitution effects between capital and labor and helped to explain capital fluctuations. However, the important question is whether they also accounted for a decline in GDP and capital growth. Some researchers argue that reduced capital profitability due to high wages and high interest rates led to capital stock that was oversized in comparison with employment.[4] Since labor market rigidities prevented wages from adjusting and high budget deficits kept long-term interest rates high, profitability was restored by slowing down capital formation, yielding a new equilibrium with a lower level of employment, capital, and economic activity. According to this explanation, the ongoing investment weakness in the second half of the 1990s in essence reflected unfavorable conditions of demand rather than adverse supply conditions. However, other researchers estimate a less prominent role played by wage developments.[5] They consider that changes in interest rates and productivity were as important as labor markets, and they identify a very close relationship between EU investment and employment rates.

SECTOR SHIFTS

An alternate hypothesis argues that a period of slow technological progress began in the 1970s. Productivity growth decelerates when the production mix of industrial countries breaks down. Whereas the shift from agriculture toward industry inflated productivity estimates in the 1950s and 1960s, the change from manufacturing to services could have depressed productivity. Nevertheless, since the 1970s the decline in the relative share of industrial employment (without construction) had no strong impact on productivity. If employment had been constant in the sectors, aggregate productivity would have been even lower due to low agricultural productivity. A constant share of employment in industry would have raised productivity growth only marginally.

R&D AND HUMAN CAPITAL

A large number of recent studies have tried to identify the determinants of technological progress using the endogenous growth approach, focusing not only on the vintage effect but also on variables and indicators related to R&D and human capital (such as R&D expenditures, level of education, numbers of engineers and scientists, and levels of patent activity).[6] This research points to a significant and positive relationship between these indicators and productivity growth as well as evidence of both the *catching-up effect* by which countries benefit from R&D produced abroad[7] and positive spillovers between firms and industries.[8] Nevertheless, R&D with strong local roots and technology diffusion is fastest at local levels and slower across borders. The distinction between public and private R&D shows that an efficient division of labor between basic and applied research and research marketing does not crowd out private research but rather is mutually reinforcing and beneficial.[9]

Recent empirical evidence reveals that R&D and education have a strong bearing on explaining cross-country differences in productivity growth, especially in developing countries.[10] Since 1973, four EU member states have experienced human capital's strong contribution to productivity.[11] A recent OECD study confirms that upgrading human capital may have a notable impact on output. Furthermore, one additional year of schooling would increase average GDP per capita by up to 6 percent.[12] Another study shows the importance of education on productivity, wage differentials, and changes in relative labor demand, finding that the $1,550 billion spent every year by OECD countries on public education was money well spent and that, given its private and social returns, education should be increased.[13] Also important to increasing growth is social capital—the features of social organizations such as trust, participation, communication, and networking—because it also tends to improve efficiency by facilitating coordinated actions.

However, technological progress does not automatically follow from higher investment in R&D and human capital; its adoption follows much more complex patterns. Engaging economically in R&D depends on individual incentives such as profit-sharing, patent legislation, tax incentives, access to skills and knowledge, efficiency of public investment in research, entrepreneurship, venture capital availability, and competitive pressures. Therefore, there are important institutional issues that need to be in place to make investment in human capital and research produce efficient economic results. It should be noted that human capital and entrepreneurship are distinct concepts that follow different incentive schemes.

ENTREPRENEURSHIP

Government policies may strongly impact productivity because they set the framework for private economic activity that may either encourage entrepreneurship and innovation or discourage them with bureaucratic attitudes or obstacles to economic activity.[14] The effectiveness of taxation and public spending is also important: taxation has an immediate impact on individual incentives because it may discourage entrepreneurs from taking risks and, excessive public spending and debt may crowd out private spending, especially if spending goes mainly to consumption instead of investment.

Capital markets also play an important role in entrepreneurship. The EU's bank-dominated financial system has long been regarded as supportive of industrial activity. But ICT's emergence has changed this perception, allowing the UK and US capital-market-dominated financial systems to develop a very large advantage in venture capital and private equity activities. Even though future cash flows can only be uncertain, entrepreneurs need strong equity backing for start-ups in the inherently risky business of radical innovation. The size of venture capital markets in the EU and US are very different. In 2000, US venture capital funding reached 0.33 percent of GDP versus only 0.13 percent in the EU, and venture capital investment reached 0.52 percent versus only 0.10 percent, although that huge gap is now slowly shrinking.[15] Figure 2.1 compares EU and US levels of equity market capitalization as a percentage of GDP and the ratio of equity financing to bank borrowing. Although the EU has been catching up since 1980, in 2000 the US equity market capitalization was still more than double (110 percent versus 50 percent), and the ratio of equity financing to bank borrowing was 87 percent versus 65 percent.[16]

FIGURE 2.1   Financial Market Indicators

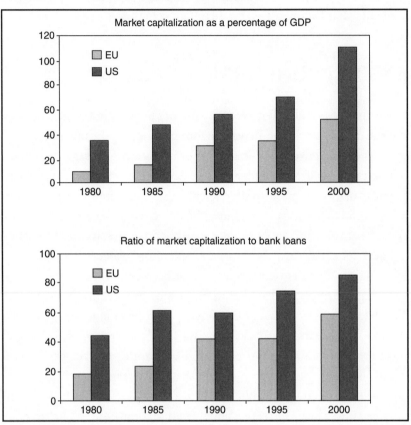

Source: World Bank, World Development Indicators, 2002

TRANSITION EFFECTS

Some recent research argues that aggregate productivity declines when economies are transitioning toward new technology. Therefore, some productivity slowdowns herald a new wave of technological progress and are not the result of structural rigidities or exogenous policy forces.[17] Large-scale technological changes in general purpose technologies, such as the steam engine, electricity, and ICT, make powerful but slow changes to productivity.[18] New ICT developments, for instance, make the existing technology and well-established forms of work organizations obsolete, resulting in older industries suffering a loss of productivity. Older firms do not immediately adjust their factor inputs even though they may be losing market share to new entrants because the change in technology must first be realized and then work practices need to be changed and adjusted. Unless these changes are made, the new technology is not optimally used and the old technology remains in place, generating lower productivity.

Empirical evidence for these arguments has been only very recent because of a lack of relevant statistical sources. Although computers entered economic life in the 1970s, their effect on productivity did not appear until the mid-1990s. It has taken more than 20 years for computers to significantly influence productivity.[19] Stock market prices tend to drop in anticipation of a new technological change, then increase to discount a large profit growth for firms producing these new technologies, and then later decline if the new technology takes more time then expected to spread throughout the economy.[20]

EU IMPROVEMENT IN THE MID-1990s

In the second half of the 1990s, the EU's slowdown in growth seemed to have turned around with average annual real economic growth of 2.6 percent, improving its 1980s performance, but still overshadowed by the US's outstanding economic performance. Output grew mainly through labor accumulation as evidenced by an annual employment growth of 1.3 percent, leaving growth from productivity at only 1.3 percent—much lower than in the previous decade.

Although, in the long run, employment tends to grow in parallel with the working-age population, in recent years this has not been the case in the EU where employment growth since the mid-1990s has outpaced population growth. While the working-age population has grown very slowly, participation and employment have increased considerably because of the large pool of previously unemployed labor. The low participation and employment rates in the first half of the 1990s and their significant increase in the second half are mainly due to cyclical factors, although there has been some help from structural reforms. Over the cycle, participation tends to increase in line with declining unemployment rates. The unemployed and new entrants into the labor market have an incentive when they see a real chance of obtaining a job, which has been the case in the EU for married women, the elderly, and teens. Structural reforms tend to lower the threshold (reservation wage)[21] and reduce the tax wedge; increasing part-time and fixed-term contracts have also played a significant role.[22]

Some small EU labor market reforms have made GDP growth more labor-intensive. Flexible workplace arrangements, such as part-time jobs and fixed-term contracts, have allowed firms to get around job-protection laws and to encourage hiring. Cuts in social security contributions for low-paid workers have allowed some of the jobless back into the workforce. As a consequence, participation and employment rates rose and unemployment fell. Over the second half of the 1990s, EU employment increased at an annual rate of 1.4 percent, even faster than the US rate of 0.8 percent. It is interesting to note that the large increase in the US employment rate from 1992 to 1999 coincided with the highest rates of capital deepening in US history, which shows that there was not a capital-labor substitution. Therefore, employment growth together with a larger capital investment has contributed significantly to US economic growth over the past decades.

A European Commission study[23] looked at how labor inputs contributed to growth using a broader definition of inputs than just the employment rate, that is, working-age people in the total population, labor force participation, total employment as a proportion of labor force, and average hours worked per person employed.[24] In the first half of the 1990s, the estimated contribution of labor inputs to EU GDP growth per capita was negative because of declining employment and shorter work hours. In the second half of the decade, even though average work hours continued to decline, the overall contribution of labor inputs to growth turned positive because employment and participation rates increased enough to compensate for shorter working hours. However, this contribution was only one-third of the US contribution. Estimates for 1998 indicate that lower EU labor accumulation and utilization accounted for two-thirds of the gap with the US, while the remaining third resulted from lower productivity. The EU's labor utilization was lower because of a higher rate of unemployment and shorter working hours. The study concluded that the EU had huge potential in labor utilization and that, if it could match the US employment rate, it would create 18 million new jobs!

Some factors helped increase labor demand. On the one side, continuous wage moderation contributed to making labor utilization in the production process more profitable and inducing some labor-capital substitution. Moreover, the change in demand toward labor-intensive services may have stimulated employment growth and increased the number of regulated industries, contributing to less binding labor market regulation and lower wage growth.

On the other side, technical progress and the strong growth in international trade from globalization increased demand for high-skilled labor at the expense of low-skilled labor. This pattern may have delayed the increase in employment growth until the second half of the 1990s because of the lags involved in increasing skilled labor and the presence of somewhat inflexible wage structures.

Nevertheless, output growth driven exclusively by employment creation is unsustainable over the long run because drop in the working-age population, excluding immigration, puts a natural brake on employment growth. Given the high rate of unemployment, there is still considerable room to increase EU employment, but in the long run productivity will be the key to sustained growth. Lower productivity is often seen as an immediate consequence of rising employment, but in the EU low-skilled labor found employment partly because social security contributions for unskilled labor were reduced.

Figure 2.2 shows that countries with high productivity levels compared to the US tend to have relatively lower labor utilization and vice versa. However, the trend line displayed in the graph is not significant at the 5 percent level; it becomes significant only when we exclude the extremes of Luxembourg, Greece, and Portugal. Without these countries, the trade-off between utilization and productivity is steeper, which implies that high utilization has a less pronounced effect on productivity. Furthermore, with its simultaneous strong growth in employment and productivity, the US demonstrates that both can go hand in hand.[25]

A large part of US performance during the 1990s can clearly be accounted for by the more rapid expansion of labor inputs. US employment grew a full percentage point faster (1.6 percent versus 0.6 percent), of which 40 percent resulted from relative changes in the employment rate over the period. Although part of this difference could result from cyclical factors, the changes in the relative employment rates have a large structural component.

However, employment changes have not proved as important as demographic changes. During the 1990s, the US labor force grew by an average of 1.3 percent versus only 0.6 percent in the EU, which

FIGURE 2.2   Breakdown of the GDP Gap with the US between Labor Utilization and Labor Productivity (1998)

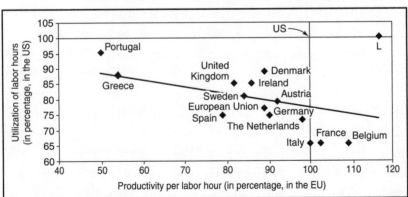

Source: OECD

accounts for over 50 percent of the difference in employment growth and results from the US's higher birth and immigration rates.

In addition, between 1991 and 2000, the number of hours worked in the EU dropped an average of 0.6 percent per year (excluding the UK), while the number of hours worked in the US remained stable. The large increase in the number of holidays and the strong reduction in weekly work hours have both contributed to increasing the working time gap.

DIFFERENT MEASURES OF PRODUCTIVITY GROWTH

Finally, it is extremely important to point out that the US and EU measure ICT investment and pricing methodologies differently, which makes the "new economy" factor less relevant in explaining the differences in productivity growth. First, in the US computer software spending is an investment, but in the EU it is only seen as a current expenditure and so it is excluded from final output.[26] Second, in most EU countries, statistics do not fully account for improvement in the quality and performance of computers; they simply count the number of computers as a measure of output. However, the US uses a *hedonic pricing* methodology that takes into account the prices of computers and other capital equipment and adjusts them accordingly as their power and performance increase over time.[27]

The first factor tends to reduce productivity in the EU and increase it in the US. Therefore, a better way to compare growth in both economies is to use net domestic product (NDP), which deducts capital depreciation so that we avoid accounting for the US's huge increase in capital depreciation resulting from the surge in computer and software investment. Using NDP per hour worked in the last five years, the productivity gap between both economies has been much smaller: from 1996 to 2001, the average annual productivity gap between both economies decreased to only 0.4 percent.

The second factor tends to reduce the size of the ICT sector in the EU and its contribution to economic growth. One estimate[28] concludes that the absence of hedonic pricing in the EU has reduced its average annual growth by more than 0.1 percent during the 1990s.[29] A recent study shows the evidence of large biases in the official price indices of EU capital equipment.[30] When adjusted for quality, productive capital stocks of equipment and software grow 3 percent more annually and quality-adjusted output grows 0.46 percent faster, a 20 percent increase. Therefore, both factors tend to underestimate the impact of IT investment and the use of capital equipment in the EU growth rate, reducing its gap with the US.

Capital investment is also measured differently. US statisticians assume, quite reasonably, that depreciation rates decline over time (equipment loses proportionately more of its value in the first year than in the second and so on) and that depreciation rates vary across different types of capital (a computer depreciates in value faster than a steel press). As proportionately more investment has been made in high-tech capital in the US in the last decade, the US depreciation rate has risen from 6 percent in 1990 to 10 percent today. By contrast, EU statisticians allow only for a steady depreciation rate (around 4 percent) with no variation for different types of equipment. As a result, the EU's depreciation rates are much lower and the accounting value of capital investments tends to be comparatively larger.[31]

NOTES

1 Crafts and Tonilo, 1996; Eichengreen, 1996

2 European Economy, 2001A

3 Tanzi and Lutz, 1993; Ford and Laxton, 1995

4 Blanchard, 1998, and Blanchard and Wolfers, 1999

5 Fitoussi et al., 2000

6 Keeley and Quah, 1998; Cameron, 1998

7 Hanel and Niosi, 1998

8 Hanel and Niosi, 1998

9 Guellec and Van Pottelsberghe, 2001

10 Jones, 1995

11 Hers, 1998

12 Bassanini and Scarpetta, 2001

13 Temple, 2001

14 OECD, 2000

15 de la Dehesa, 2002

16 World Bank, Development Indicators, 2002

17 Greenwood, 1999; Hornstein, 1999

18 David, 1990

19 Oliner and Sichel, 2000; Jorgensen and Stiroh, 2000; Whelan, 2000

20 Jovanovic and Rousseau, 2000

21 The monetary point at which all those seeking employment will accept a job and below which jobs will be rejected.

22 The monetary point at which all those seeking employment will accept jobs and below which jobs will be rejected.

23 European Economy, 2001A

24 European Economy, 2001A

25 Gordon, 1995

26 Lequiller, 2001

27 Daly, 2003

28 Daly, 2003

29 Daly, 2003

30 Sakellaris and Vijselaar, 2003

31 Daly, 2004

THE MEDIUM-
TO LONG-TERM
OUTLOOK

T HE next 10 years do not look much brighter for the EU's growth because the EU's demographic trends are becoming more unfavorable. EUROSTAT labor force projections suggest that during the next decade the EU labor force will grow at an annual rate of 0.1 percent. This estimate may be revised upward if there are substantial flows of labor after the next phase of Central European countries become members, though some restrictions on labor mobility will be imposed for the first seven years of their membership and these countries have even lower fertility rates than the present member countries (1.3 children per woman versus 1.4 children per woman), or from flows from developing countries.

Goldman Sachs analysts expect over the next decade that the EU's working-age population will decline very slowly, because slightly higher immigration rates will partially offset the low fertility rates; the employment rate will continue to improve, especially as more women enter the workforce; average effective hours worked will decline by an annual rate of 0.2 percent—much slower than the 1990s pace when they fell by 0.4 percent per year, and that output per hour worked will remain steady (around 1.8 percent). As a result, in the next decade the EU's overall growth potential could be around 2.2 percent—broadly in line with its performance from 1994 to 2004.[1]

This simple estimate is slightly higher than the OECD's (2 percent—inferred from its output-gap estimations) and the

IMF's (2.1 percent). The European Central Bank's forecast is similar to Goldman Sachs's—around 2.25 percent. However, the same estimates for the United States give an annual growth rate of around 3.0 percent (OECD, 3.1 percent; IMF, 3 percent; and the US Federal Reserve, 3 to 3.5 percent), that is, about 1 percent higher, which will continue to widen the gap.

In the medium term, the EU could grow at the same rate or even faster than the US, because the US needs to reduce its huge deficits. However, since the US has contributed 55 percent of world's growth since 1955, this reduction in growth or a quick and deep drop in the dollar could also negatively impact EU growth. After this necessary adjustment, US growth should eventually outpace that of the EU. In any case, EU growth is expected to be much lower than the 3 percent strategic goal set at the Lisbon summit.[2] Only a higher immigration rate could help the EU grow faster in terms of GDP, but not in terms of GDP per capita. And even a high immigration rate alone would not allow the EU to meet the Lisbon GDP target unless it skyrocketed to an improbable 3 million individuals per year.

THE EUROPEAN COMMISSION'S MEDIUM-TERM OUTLOOK

The European Commission's medium-term outlook is not much different. The latest forecasts estimate EU growth for 2005 and 2006 at 1.6 percent and 2.0 percent, respectively, while US growth is estimated at 3.6 percent and 3.3 percent, respectively, in both years—increasing the present gap.

Since the mid-1990s there have been some important shifts in the underlying growth of the EU and US economies, with a significant gap opening up in terms of GDP, and more importantly, GDP per capita. From 1980 to 1995, EU and US living standards were growing at roughly the same rate, but in the second half of the1990s a significant gap emerged favoring the US.

To understand whether the 1990s were a genuine break in the post-war pattern of convergence with US living standards, the European Union Economy 2003 Review studied the sources of growth in general, paying specific attention to productivity determinants because of their importance in shaping medium- to long-term changes in living standards.

The study develops basic indicators of growth, using not only GDP, but also GDP per capita (which simply adjusts for population changes and represents the widest possible measure of living standards) and GDP per hour worked (which adjusts the GDP per capita for changes in employment and hours worked and constitutes the primary indicator for comparing productivity). Table 3.1 shows how the first two indicators evolved from 1961 to 2000. Between 1981 and 1990, EU GDP growth declined from 3.9 percent to 2.4 percent, and between 1991 and 1995 to 1.6 percent, finally recovering between 1996 and 2000 back up to 2.7 percent. At the same time, the annual

TABLE 3.1   Economic and Demographics Trends, 1961–2000

(annual average % changes for the US and EU-15)

	EU 15	USA
1961–1980		
GDP	3.9	3.7
Population	0.6	1.2
GDP per capita	3.3	2.5
1981–1990		
GDP	2.4	3.2
Population	0.3	1.0
GDP per capita	2.1	2.2
1991–1995		
GDP	1.6	2.4
Population	0.4	1.3
GDP per capita	1.2	1.1
1996–2000		
GDP	2.7	4.1
Population	0.3	1.3
GDP per capita	2.4	2.8

Source: European Commission Services

growth rate of the US also declined but at a less rapid pace—from 3.7 percent to 3.2 percent to 2.4 percent, finally bouncing back to 4.1 percent. Over the 40-year period, US growth has averaged 3.35 percent, while EU growth has averaged only 2.65 percent—0.7 percent less, but doubling in the last period to 1.4 percent.

In terms of GDP per capita, the average annual growth rates have been 2.25 percent for the EU and 2.15 percent for the US, but in the last period the US rate was 0.4 percent higher. This difference results from US's population growth, which has averaged 1.2 percent versus 0.4 percent.

Table 3.2 separates average GDP growth into labor utilization and labor productivity. In terms of labor utilization, the second half of the 1990s witnessed a reversal of labor's strong contribution to US growth—the main feature of US performance since the 1960s. In

TABLE 3.2   **Decomposition of US and EU-15 Average GDP Growth Rates**

	1966–1970	1971–1980	1981–1990	1991–1995	1996–2000	1996–2002
US						
GDP	3.4	3.2	3.1	2.4	4.0	3.2
Labor	1.6	1.6	1.7	1.3	2.4	1.5
(Hours worked)	*(–0.8)*	*(–0.5)*	*(–0.1)*	*(0.2)*	*(0.4)*	*(0.2)*
(Employment)	*(2.4)*	*(2.1)*	*(1.8)*	*(1.1)*	*(2.0)*	*(1.3)*
Labor productivity (hourly)	1.8	1.6	1.4	1.0	1.6	1.7
(TFP)	*(1.2)*	*(1.1)*	*(1.1)*	*(0.8)*	*(1.2)*	*(1.1)*
(Capital deepening)	*(0.6)*	*(0.5)*	*(0.3)*	*(0.2)*	*(0.4)*	*(0.6)*
EU-15						
GDP	5.0	3.2	2.4	1.7	2.6	2.2
Labor	–0.7	–0.6	0.1	–0.7	1.1	0.9
(Hours worked)	*(–0.9)*	*(–0.9)*	*(–0.6)*	*(–0.5)*	*(–0.3)*	*(–0.3)*
(Employment)	*(0.2)*	*(0.3)*	*(0.7)*	*(–0.2)*	*(1.4)*	*(1.2)*
Labor productivity (hourly)	5.6	3.8	2.2	2.4	1.6	1.4
(TPF)	*(3.8)*	*(2.4)*	*(1.5)*	*(1.4)*	*(1.2)*	*(0.9)*
(Capital deepening)	*(1.8)*	*(1.4)*	*(0.7)*	*(1.0)*	*(0.4)*	*(0.5)*

Source: All data are from AMECO/EUROSTAT, except for the hours worked series which are from the Gröningen Growth and Development Centre (GGDC), Gröningen University.

the mid-1990s over 60 percent of US growth came from labor, but by 2002 that number had fallen to only 46 percent. This decline resulted from the US's recent "jobless" growth as well as its high employment rate, which in 2002 was still 8 percent higher than the EU's. On the other hand, in the EU, labor contributes nearly as much to growth as in the US—40 percent. This surge has resulted from wage moderation, structural labor reforms, and a large decline in the capital-labor ratio.

Unfortunately for the EU, this strong recovery has been accompanied by a corresponding negative trend in productivity, which declined from 5.6 percent between 1966 and 1970 to 3.8 percent from 1971 to 1980 to 2.2 percent from 1981 to 1990, rising briefly to 2.4 percent between 1991 and 1995, and then falling again to 1.6 percent between 1996 and 2000 and again to 1.4 percent between 1996 and 2002. The EU now has lower annual growth productivity than the US—0.3 percent. The US is in a relatively unique position internationally because it continues to combine a high level of employment and strong productivity. Since the early 1970s, the US has not only outperformed the EU in employment creation but also in labor productivity.

Therefore, the EU is facing a difficult future since the current recovery in labor utilization is clearly a temporary phenomenon. In a matter of a few years the negative effect of an aging population will really begin to impact the potential growth of a large number of member countries. The EU's future growth will depend on productivity, which at present seems to be engaged in a downward trend.

Because of this inverse relationship between labor utilization and labor productivity, the European Commission study further breaks down both growth components to decipher their underlying determinants in terms of hours worked and employment (Figure 3.1). In the EU, labor's overall contribution is driven by employment rather than by an increase in hours worked. Although the decrease in the number of hours worked is less than in previous decades, the average time spent at work continues to fall. The situation in the US is very different—average hours worked began to rise in the late

FIGURE 3.1   Growth Trend and Its Labor and Labor Productivity Components (1966–2002)

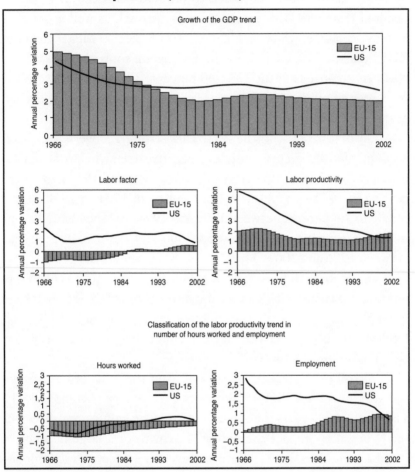

Source: European Commission Services and the Gröningen Growth and Development Centre

1980s and began to decline only in 2000. At the same time, US employment creation is currently on a downward trend driven by the jobless growth pattern of the last few years. This puts the EU in the historically unusual position of having an employment rate that compares favorably with that of the US.

Capital deepening is another crucial factor for productivity and income growth. For over three decades, the EU's capital-labor ratio was significantly higher, but, as Figure 3.2 shows, in the second half of the 1990s a gap emerged that favors the US. While we can question whether the US trend is sustainable given the bubblelike features, what is more puzzling is the poor EU performance exhibited in falling rates of investment despite rising profitability and the declining cost of capital. This could be explained only by a collapse in the equity markets.

Nevertheless, other more worrying factors may also be at play, such as investment location considerations. International choices for investors have increased, and there is a growing flow of investment toward regions that promise favorable ratios between capital produc-

FIGURE 3.2 **Classification of the Labor Productivity Trend and the Intensification of Capital and Total Factor Productivity**

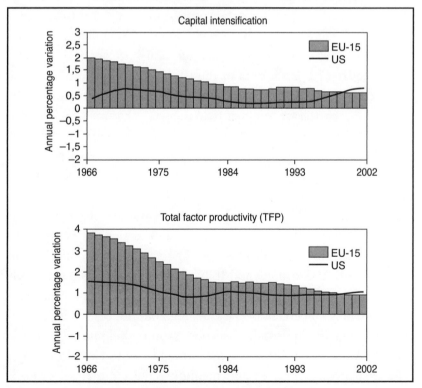

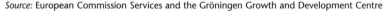

Source: European Commission Services and the Gröningen Growth and Development Centre

tivity and cost. The US is a case in point. Falling US IT investment prices and high rates of innovation (as expressed by accelerating productivity and TFP growth rates) created an extraordinary investment climate that adversely affected EU domestic investment growth. Demographic trends in the EU are going to affect investment negatively. With an increasing dependency ratio, domestic investment as a share of GDP is likely to decline or remain constant as interest rates fall, because a declining population requires less net investment in order to keep the capital-labor ratio constant. In addition, a declining domestic labor force reduces the return prospects for domestic investment as well as the risk associated with overinvestment. In a world of free capital mobility, this effect is likely to be stronger since companies can avoid pressure on domestic returns by investing abroad. Although it seems paradoxical, the falling trend in the investment rate is likely to be accompanied by a decline in interest rates, because borrowing costs will fall with lower returns from capital investments (due to expected decreases in labor supply and domestic demand) rather than act as an stimulus to undertake additional investment.

Finally, TFP is the area of the EU's relative performance that is cause for the most concern. For the first time in a generation, the US's TFP growth rate is higher than the EU's (Figure 3.2). This significant turning point results from a sharp downturn in the EU's growth and a rapid upturn in the US's growth. Given the importance of TFP for long-term growth, this reversal calls the EU's future prosperity into question.

Since the early 1990s, the member countries of the EU have performed very differently, and we can look at this performance by breaking the countries into groups. There is a first group of countries, including Germany and Italy, that stands out as persistently poor performers relative to the EU average. That group represents approximately 40 percent of the EU's total output, constituting a significant drag on the total. A second group—Belgium, Denmark, France, Austria, and the UK—performed close to the EU average. The final group of small and medium-sized countries—Greece, Spain, Ireland, the Netherlands, Portugal, Finland, and Sweden—

managed to grow at a significantly faster pace than the average, especially over the second half of the 1990s. In the period from 1996 to
2002, this last group grew at an average rate of 3.5 percent, compared with 3.25 percent for the US and 2.25 percent for the EU as
a whole. Greece, Spain, Ireland, and Portugal were in effect catching up, because their standards of living in the early 1990s were significantly below the EU average. Ireland has been the best performer
by far. Excluding this final group, the most striking productivity
came from Belgium, Austria, Finland, and Sweden, though Belgium
and Austria could not combine high rates of productivity and labor
utilization, while Finland and Sweden were able to maintain both
rates at a high level.

Finally, the study attempts to look beneath the economywide
trends to assess the broad structural changes that have occurred at
the industry level since 1980. The study examines whether the diver-
gences in productivity growth between the EU and US emanate from
either structural employment shifts from low- to high-productivity
industries or whether they simply reflect higher-productivity growth
rates in specific industries. In addition, the study investigates whether
there are only simple differences from specific industries in the manufacturing or services sectors or if there are more pervasive productivity differentials that result from productivity gains associated with
innovation and ITC adoption.

In order to answer these questions, the study uses two new
industry data sets that are highly disaggregated, internationally comparable, covering the period from 1979 to 2001.[3] The Industry
Labor Productivity Database is used for a *shift and share* analysis,
while the Industry Growth Accounting Database permits a growth
accounting analysis at the industry level.

Shift and Share Analysis

The *shift and share* analysis calculates aggregate productivity as a
weighted average of the underlying industries' productivity. The
weights are determined by each industry's share in overall employ-

ment. Consequently, changes in EU and US productivity rates are determined not only by the productivity growth rate of each individual industry but also by the changes in the industry's employment levels. Therefore, aggregate changes in productivity are separated into three effects from which aggregate productivity changes result:

- An *intra-industry* effect equal to the sum of productivity growth in the individual industries in the absence of structural changes (e.g., changes in the employment shares of specific industries).
- A *structural change* effect equal to the contribution to overall productivity growth resulting from shifting employment resources from low- to high-productivity industries (which shows healthy economic restructuring).
- An *interaction* effect—a residual term—that captures the dynamic component of structural change.

The sum of these last two effects is sometimes used to measure overall reallocation of resources.

In other words, this breakdown gives us three possible explanations for why labor productivity growth rates differ in the EU and US: (1) the differences in average productivity growth rates of individual industries, (2) the differences in the reallocation of employment resources between industries, and (3) the differences in the initial starting conditions, in terms of productivity, that encapsulate any potential catching up.

This shift and share analysis concludes that: (1) the intra-industry growth effect dominates the outcome, accounting for between 89 and 95 percent of the EU's aggregate productivity growth and from 100 to 120 percent of the US's, and (2) that the shift effect in the EU has been positive over the last two decades, compared with a consistent negative pattern for the US. Thus, the EU is still gaining from the employment shift from the low-productivity industries like agriculture to higher-productivity industries like manufacturing and services. For the US, however, this process appears to be finished, and the negative contributions suggest that workers are, on average, moving into lower-productivity service industries. Over the whole period, the EU has been able to use changes in the industry composition of employment as a mechanism for closing the productivity gap with the US. However, the contribution from this catching-up process has been declining over time, more than halving between the 1980s and 1990s—falling from a contribution of 0.5 percent to less than 0.25 percent. This same trend is continuing in the US's increasingly services-dominated economy where employment shifts from manufacturing to service industries are often associated with declines in productivity growth. Over the whole period, the average trend in manufacturing productivity growth in both the US and EU has always been higher than in services, so the only way the EU can reduce its productivity gap is to generate productivity gains at the intra-industry level as the US has done for the last three decades.

The shift and share analysis for the US suggests a surge in pure productivity gains from within industries themselves that more than compensates for the negative effect from reallocating employment resources between industries. The extent of the surge suggests that a new technological regime is emerging that permeates a wide range of industries and positively influences their productivity. This new regime could, at least in part, be driven by the efficiencies being reaped from the use of ICT products and services as well as wider changes associated with the creation and diffusion of ICT-specific knowledge. Figure 2.2 in Chapter 2 shows that while the EU trends in productivity—both in manufacturing and services—have steadily declined since the mid-1980s and seem to have stopped in the last few years, trends in the US have been growing in both sectors, increasing the productivity gap.

Industry-Level Growth Accounting

For this reason, the European Commission study digs a little deeper to see what role ICT has played in the US by separating 56 industrial and services sectors into ICT manufacturing and services with intensive ICT use. Although manufacturing has always produced higher productivity rates than services, the recent surge in US services' productivity suggests that services could shortly challenge manufacturing.

Figure 3.3 looks at the trends in productivity per hour in ICT manufacturing and private services with intensive ICT use. In US ICT manufacturing there is a surge in productivity per hour that reaches close to 25 percent. By contrast, the EU has shown a smaller

FIGURE 3.3   Productivity per Labor Hour Trend in the ICT Production Industries and in Private Sector Businesses that Use ICT Intensively (annual percentage variation)

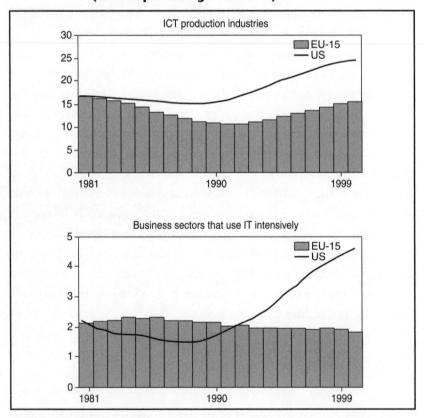

Note: The scales of the two graphs are different.
Source: European Commission Services and the Gröningen Growth and Development Centre

growth, reaching rates close to 15 percent, again increasing the productivity gap. In private services, the gap is even larger because the US rates are close to 4.5 percent. While in the EU productivity per hour has been falling since the mid-1980s and stagnant from the mid-1990s, achieving growth rates of less than 2 percent.

Over the second half of the 1990s, ICT investments and production of ICT goods and services accounted for about 60 percent of US productivity growth, compared with 40 percent in the EU. This translates into an ICT contribution of about 1 percent to productivity growth in the US and 0.66 percent in the EU.

Finally, the study focuses on potential policies to improve the EU's underperformance, encourage TFP and capital accumulation to boost future productivity growth, and achieve the Lisbon target of making the EU the most competitive knowledge-based economy in the world by 2010.

The study concludes that because of the significant negative effects from the regulatory framework on investment, policymakers should consider emphasizing regulatory changes in their reform agendas. The IMF has published a study that concludes that deregulating the EU economy to US levels could increase long-term output by nearly 7 percent and productivity by 3 percent.[4] The Fraser Institute's index of regulation (2003) shows that regulation in the EU is substantially more restrictive than that of the US. While the Lisbon targets aim to eliminate these differences by 2010, even if that were the case—which is very doubtful—it would not lead to sufficient productivity gains over the next seven years to close the 10 percent efficiency gap. Given deregulation's limited dynamic efficiency gains, it should be accompanied by measures to increase knowledge production.

In addition, the Lisbon conference goals seek to boost TFP growth, but this requires increased investment in the knowledge economy in terms of greater spending on higher education, software, and R&D. With respect to R&D, the focus should not be on boosting public spending directly, but on creating conditions—through tax cuts and other instruments—that promote an endogenous increase in market-based research spending. Figure 3.4 compares EU and US

FIGURE 3.4   Investments in the Knowledge Economy: EU versus the US in 1998 (as a percent of GDP)

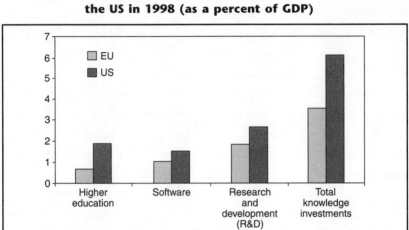

Source: OECD 2000

investment in the knowledge economy in terms of GDP. The biggest gap is in higher education, where the EU spends less than half as much money on software and R&D. The EU's total investment in the knowledge economy is 3.5 percent of GDP versus 6 percent in the US.

The study concludes that introducing such a large package of supply side reforms over the coming years would significantly boost EU growth rates, approximately 0.25 to 0.75 percent. However, even if the US policies remain constant, the EU will need a much longer period to overtake the US.

THE EUROPEAN UNION'S LONG-TERM CHALLENGES

Although it acknowledges that often extrapolating from data is not necessarily accurate, the European Competitiveness Report (2003) develops some interesting extrapolations to show the EU's long-term challenges. The study tries to answer three questions by looking at

EU and US growth in terms of GDP, GDP per capita, productivity per worker, employment, and productivity per hour.

Question 1

On the assumption that GDP per capita in the EU will grow at the same pace as it did from 1996–2002, how much time will the EU need to double its standards of living (measured in terms of per capita GDP)? Table 3.3 shows the study's projections.

TABLE 3.3   Extrapolations for Doubling Standards of Living

Base Period	European Union	United States
1996–2002	35 years	36 years
2001–2002	68 years	210 years
1996–2000	30 years	27 years
2002	98 years	51 years

Question 2

How much additional growth will the EU need in order to catch up with the US in 20 years? In 50 years? To catch up in 20 years, the study suggests that the EU will need an additional 1.6 percent in GDP per capita, 1.2 percent in productivity per worker, and 0.34 percent in productivity per hour worked. To catch up in 50 years, the EU will need an additional 0.65 percent in GDP per capita, 0.48 percent in productivity per worker, and 0.14 percent productivity per hour worked.

Question 3

Judging from the past, how large will the gap be in 10 years and 20 years?

Standard of Living (GDP per capita)
- In 2002, the gap in standards of living between the US and the EU was 28 percent.

- If the 2002 rate is taken as a base, in 10 years the gap will be 32 percent and in 20 years 36 percent.
- If the base period is 2001 to 2002, the gap will be 22 percent in 10 years and 17 percent in 20 years.
- If the base period is 1996 to 2000, the gap will be 29 percent in 10 years and 30 percent in 20 years.
- Finally, if the base period is 1996 to 2002, the gap will be 27 percent in both 10 and 20 years.

Productivity per Worker
- In 2002 the gap between the US and the EU was 23 percent.
- If we use 2002 as a base, the gap will rise to 37 percent in 10 years and 50 percent in 20 years.
- If the base period is 2001 to 2002, the gap will be 30 percent in 10 years and 38 percent in 20 years.
- If the base period is 1996 to 2000, the gap will reach 30 percent in 10 years and 37 percent in 20 years.
- If the base period is 1996 to 2002, the gap will rise to 30 percent in 10 years and 38 percent in 20 years.

Productivity per Hour Worked
- In 2002, the gap in productivity per hour worked was 8.5 percent.
- Using the 2002 rate, in 10 years the gap will rise to 26 percent and in 20 years to 41 percent.
- Using the base period 2001 to 2002, the gap will rise to 13 percent in 10 years and 19 percent in 20 years.
- Using 1996 to 2000, the gap will rise to 11 percent in 10 years and to 16 percent in 20 years.
- Finally, using 1996 to 2002, the gap will rise to 12 percent in 10 years and 17 percent in 20 years.

The obvious conclusion is that for the EU to become the "most competitive economy in the world," a superior performance, not supported by current trends, will be required. Although the productivity gap is narrower today than the standards of living gap, if current productivity trends do not change substantially, the productivity differences will increase further. Meeting the US standard of living would require improving participation and/or employment rates throughout the EU, which will be extremely difficult because its population is aging faster (see Chapter 4).

THE OECD "SOURCES OF GROWTH" STUDY

The OECD has studied sources of growth in OECD countries and assessed the GDP per capita gap and its medium-term developments, proposing a series of structural policies to enhance the EU's future growth. [5]

The study breaks down the GDP per capita growth gap into three major components:

- The ratio of working-age persons (15–64 years) to the total population
- The ratio of employed persons to the working-age population (the employment rate)
- Productivity

Though the total effect is still neutral, demographic trends have started to play a negative role in the evolution of GDP per capita in some member countries. Lower productivity in the EU accounted for 30 percent of the gap with the US, while lower rates of employment and fewer of hours worked accounted for 70 percent. Since hours worked fell quite rapidly, productivity was higher on an hourly basis than on a head-count basis. Declines in hours worked reflected both shorter work weeks and a substantial increase in part-time work.

Thus, relatively lower employment rates combined with the lower number of hours worked per person employed account for most of the difference in EU GDP per capita. To the extent that it seems natural for people to demand more leisure as their income rises, increasing labor use in terms of both employment and number of hours worked does not necessarily imply an improvement. It is likely, however, that the large discrepancies observed in the EU and US employment rates have more to do with the pervasive influence of structural policies on incentives both to hire and to work than differences in preferences for leisure.

Since the mid-1990s, the decline in EU hours worked was more than offset by the positive impact of rising participation and employment rates. While aging rates make it impossible for this trend to continue, there is still room for some member countries' employment and participation rates to offset the demographics. In fact, despite the considerable progress in the last decade in countries such as the UK, the Netherlands, and Ireland, structural unemployment still remains relatively high, leaving significant room for improvement. Also, long-term unemployment remains quite high and did not decline during the 1990s.

Furthermore, high unemployment in several EU countries is compounded by low participation rates, resulting in even larger cross-country differences in overall employment rates, especially in terms of young, older, and female workers.

Following research done in the OECD Jobs Strategy (1999), this OECD study suggests a series of structural measures to improve participation and employment rates, which can be grouped into two broad categories: (1) tax and benefit system reforms, including unemployment support and tax wedges, and (2) labor and market regulation, covering employment protection legislation, rules regarding minimum wages and other working conditions, and administrative burdens on start-up firms and other competition barriers.

Tax and Benefit Reforms

Policymakers are frequently confronted with a trade-off between meeting social objectives and minimizing disincentives to work. For instance, unemployment benefits provide needed support for workers and households after job losses. However, high replacement rates can raise the unemployment rate by lowering the gap between income from work and the income received from benefits. This is particularly the case if high replacement rates are accompanied by a lengthy entitlement period. An extended benefit period can lengthen the average unemployment spell, leading to a loss of human capital and reinforcing insider-outsider mechanisms that potentially reduce overall wage sensitivity to labor market conditions.

In several member countries, the combination of high replacement rates and duration of benefits is quite high.[6] Moreover, despite the empirical evidence that these rates impact unemployment, reform in this area has been difficult and very uneven. Replacement rates have been increasing in the last seven years in the Netherlands, Portugal, Austria, and Germany, while they have decreased in Denmark, Spain, France, Sweden, and the UK, ultimately increasing the gap within member countries. Despite the fact that this issue is especially relevant for those long-term unemployed whose earnings potential is often less than that of the average production worker, net replacement rates for the long-term unemployed are extremely high: over 100 percent in Sweden and Denmark, over 80 percent in Finland, the UK, Portugal, the Netherlands, and Belgium, which are above 80 percent. France and Spain are similar to the US—below 60 percent; the EU average is 75 percent.

While most countries have taken steps to improve this trade-off, the durations of benefits have generally been maintained to avoid adverse social consequences—eligibility and work availability requirements have been tightened by raising the minimum amount of employment time required to qualify and reducing the scope for those who repeatedly reject job offers without penalty. Furthermore, benefit eligibility for certain groups has been made conditional on enrolling in schooling, vocational training, voluntary work, or subsidized jobs. In return, governments are providing more intensive job-search assistance, including personalized job counseling and follow-ups to improve job matching. The majority of countries is actively supporting the unemployed in order to reduce the long-term dependence on benefits, although their expenditures in active labor market policies vary substantially both in terms of GDP and as a percentage of total expenditures on active or passive measures. These active labor market policies need to be well designed and well targeted in order to be effective, otherwise their cost can rise very quickly without achieving their goals.[7]

The trade-off can be particularly difficult for workers with low earnings potential. Significantly reducing unemployment benefits can push many into poverty, which countries try to avoid by providing in-work benefits or payroll tax rebates combined with a minimum wage. To limit these fiscal costs, the benefits are typically based on the worker's earnings, but a rapid withdrawal as earned income increases generates high marginal tax rates, lowering incentives to increase workers work effort beyond a certain threshold (poverty trap). And raising the threshold for benefit withdrawal and/or lowering its pace pushes the problem of marginal tax rates higher up the earnings scale and can rapidly increase the budgetary costs, which may raise tax rates. In order to improve in-work benefits for low-wage earners, the UK, France, Finland, Belgium, and Ireland top off wages of low-income households with in-work benefits.

In order to lower the cost of low-paid jobs and stimulate labor demand, several countries have reduced the wedge between the wage paid by the employers and the take-home pay of employees by cutting labor taxes—mainly employer and/or employee contributions to social security. After rising steadily from the mid-1970s to the mid-1990s, tax wedges have been reduced in several member countries, including France, Italy, and the Netherlands, where wedges were, and still are, relatively high. In fact, in the late 1990s the reduction in tax wedges was a key factor behind the EU's relatively strong employment performance, especially in countries in which the measures were indeed targeted for lower-paying jobs. However, deteriorating public finances have reduced the opportunity for further cutting tax wedges.

With the particularly high rate of inactivity among workers aged 55 to 65, one area that could be given particular attention is incentives for early retirement. Although in a large number of countries the official retirement age remains 65, the average effective retirement age is several years younger. This effective retirement age has declined over time even while life expectancy has increased significantly. In many countries, this pattern has been encouraged by public pension policies of high replacement rates combined with low returns for extra years spent in work beyond a certain age or number of years of contributions. More importantly, older workers have been given an early route out of the labor market through retirement programs, unemployment-related benefits, and disability schemes, even in countries where participation rates of older workers are high. Since the burden of early retirement on output and public finances is going to intensify over the next decades, the disincentives to continue working at older ages should be radically changed.

Labor Market Regulation

Employment protection legislation (EPL) provides a good example of how labor market institutions affect unemployment by influencing the shock transmission mechanism. Raising the cost of dismissal reduces the number of layoffs and hence the flow into unemployment, but strict firing restrictions make firms more hesitant to hire new employees, making it harder for the unemployed to find jobs.[8]

Moreover, employment protection legislation may reduce the speed of real wage adjustments as well as aggregate wage flexibility. Lower job turnover associated with strict employment protection often increases the average duration of unemployment and the proportion of long-term unemployment, raising its persistence and potentially reducing the impact of unemployment on wage setting. As noted earlier, it is striking that the countries with rising long-term unemployment are also the ones generally facing increases in structural unemployment rates. As shown in Figure 3.5, the two were highly correlated between 1990 and 2001.[9] During the last decade, this has been accompanied by a tendency to ease regulations affecting temporary contracts and an increase in the share of temporary jobs as a component of total employment, which has increased the power of *insiders*, those who are typically employed on permanent contracts).[10]

Many member countries also have a statutory minimum wage, which is often a uniform rate applied nationwide. When the rate is moderate relative to the average wage, its effect on overall employment is limited, but when it's disproportionately high, it affects specific categories of workers (e.g., youths in search of a first job experience) or adversely affects employment in regions with higher unemployment. In general, during the past decade minimum wages have slowly fallen, which may prevent relative wages from reflecting productivity differentials. In some cases, collective bargaining agreements impose binding minimum levels on the wages of less productive workers, which can exceed the statutory minimum wage (e.g., Belgium and the Netherlands). This problem is proportionally more

FIGURE 3.5   Changes in Long-Term and Structural Unemployment between 1990 and 2001 in Percentages

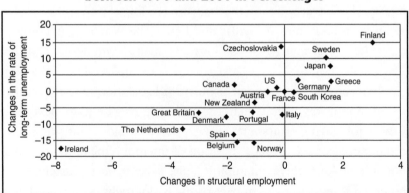

Note: 1991–2001 for Finland and Sweden; 1990–1999 for Ireland and the Netherlands; 1990–2000 for Germany.
Source: OECD, Employment Outlook, June 2002

acute in the countries with larger union membership and where there are more employees covered by collective contracts.

Labor market performance can also be influenced by product market regulations that reduce competition. Regulatory reforms aimed at lowering entry and exit costs, trade barriers, and the stringency of state controls can stimulate output and employment by raising the elasticity of product demand, thereby reducing price markups and lessening labor market segmentation. Over the last two decades, progress in reforming such regulations may have boosted employment rates between 0.5 and 2.5 percent across the EU. While increases in competition put downward pressures on wages in the short run (especially in highly protected sectors where the scope for rent-seeking behavior by workers is largest[11]), in the long run stronger competition tends to boost real wages through its favorable impact on productivity.[12] Reforming labor policies has proven to be difficult because of the associated rents enjoyed by specific groups who are well positioned to resist reform.

Finally, the OECD study looks at how the GDP per capita gap has been affected by skills or human capital and the role played by ICT and multifactor productivity in the gap. Growth in output per employed person is mostly attributable to capital deepening but also to an increase in the average levels of labor force skills, which results more from improving the workforce's education composition than from improving the standard for individual workers. Both the US and EU have invested heavily on education, which has affected the growth of GDP per person employed. Although skill upgrading has been higher in the EU, it was accompanied by lower employment growth. Thus, productivity gains were partly achieved by dismissals or not employing workers with low skills. By contrast, in the US, skill upgrading has played a smaller role in GDP per employed person, and improving labor-market conditions have widened the employment base and allowed low-skilled workers to get a foothold in employment.

ICT affects growth performance through three different channels. The first is an acceleration of productivity in ICT-producing sectors themselves as they increase in size. The ICT sector has accounted for over 13 percent of Finland and Ireland's value-added business sectors and over 10 percent in the US—most EU countries are below 10 percent. In the second half of the 1990s, the US experienced large ICT productivity growth, increasing 364 percent in office, accounting, and computing equipment; 179 percent in radio, television, and communication equipment; and 126 percent in total manufacturing. The second channel is through accumulation of physical capital. The share of ICT equipment and software in total investment rose steadily through the 1990s, accounting for more than 25 percent of the total nonresidential gross fixed capital formation in the US and around 15 percent in the EU. Between 1995 and 1999, ICT capital contributed almost 0.9 percent to growth in the US but was approximately only half that in the EU. The third channel is generated by ICT equipment's positive spillover or network effects in the whole economy, which can be detected by estimates of multifactor productivity growth (MFP). Since MFP growth is the residual of output growth after accounting for quantity and quality of capital and labor, it is very difficult to detect with certainty because of the different accounting methods used in different countries. The fact remains that in most member countries—except the Nordic ones—MFP decelerated in the 1990s, while it accelerated in the US.

The OECD study concludes that the gap in GDP per capita over the past decade results from a combination of *traditional* factors, mainly those related to the efficiency of labor market mechanisms and *new economy* elements related to the size of the ICT-producing sector as well as to how quickly the technology was adopted by other industries. In the medium term, the first factors have a limited margin for improvement in the EU because its population is aging faster, but they can be still enhanced by labor reforms. The second elements can be improved by enriching the EU's policy and institutional environments in order to enhance business conditions for existing firms and new entrepreneurial activities—in other words, strengthening product market and finance reforms.

NOTES

1 Daly, 2005

2 Daly, 2004 and 2005

3 DG Enterprise (European Commission) and GGDC (Groningen Growth and Development Centre) Groeningen

4 Bayoumi et al., 2003

5 OECD, 2003

6 Denmark, the Netherlands, Portugal, Finland, Belgium, France, Austria, Spain, and Germany, all more than double the US rate and nearly double the United Kingdom's rate.

7 Martin, 2000

8 Boeri et al., 2000

9 OECD Employment Outlook, 2002

10 See Dolado et al. (2001) for Spain; Blanchard and Landier (2001) for France, and Nannincini (2001) for Italy.

11 Expending resources in order receive something from another party as the result of a favorable decision in some public policy.

12 Blanchard and Giavazzi, 2001

THE AGING
POPULATION
CHALLENGE

AFTER the next 10 years, the main economic challenge facing both the US and the EU will be the impact of an aging population on public expenditures. The combination of falling fertility rates and a growing life expectancy in most OECD countries will strain public finances. The spending pressure will be higher in the EU because aging trends are faster and social security is more generous, making it much more difficult to comply with the Maastricht Treaty and the Stability and Growth Pact (SGP) budget rules that are necessary to achieve a successful monetary union. However, what is more worrying is that the spending pressure will make it difficult to keep budgets balanced and maintain sustainable debt-to-GDP ratios. The consequences of this could be very severe for the EU's future growth. A graying population means a less active population, less entrepreneurship, less innovation, higher and probably unsustainable public expenditures, all of which will result in lower growth. The five reports discussed in this chapter try to measure the impact of aging on public finances. And while their precise findings may differ, they all reach a similar conclusion: The impact of an aging population is large enough to become the most important economic challenge of the twenty-first century for the OECD countries and especially for the EU.

EUROPEAN UNION COMMISSION REPORT

European Union Demographic Projections

In 1999, the European Commission's Economic Policy Committee established the Working Group on Aging Populations or Aging Working Group (AWG). After two years the group issued its final report, "The Budgetary Challenges Posed by Aging Populations."[1]

The study uses the following demographic assumptions to project the EU's age-related expenditures:

- The average EU fertility rate in 2000 was 1.5 children per fertile woman, ranging from a rate of 1.2 in Spain and Italy and 1.4 in Germany to 1.7 in France and the UK, 1.8 in Denmark, and 1.9 in Ireland.
- By 2050 the average fertility rate is expected to reach 1.7 children, with most of the increase occurring within the next two decades.
- Life expectancy is projected to increase steadily over the same period: from the age of 75 in 2000 for men to 80 in 2050, and for women from the age of 80 in 2000 to 85 in 2050.
- Migration flows will slow from 661,000 in 2000 to 622,000 in 2050, constituting approximately 0.2 percent of the total EU population in 2050.

As a result of these assumptions, the report estimates that the total size of the EU population will continue to grow slowly from 376 million in 2000 to 386 million in 2020 and then fall to 364 million in 2050, a drop of 12 million. Population decreases are expected in countries such as Italy (17 percent), Spain (11 percent), and Germany (8.5 percent), while the population is expected to grow in France (5 percent), the UK (4 percent), Luxembourg (29 percent), and Ireland (26 percent).

According to the study, the EU's working-age population will remain stable at 246 million until 2015, after which it will decline to 203 million by 2050, a drop of 18 percent. The largest declines are projected for Spain (–29 percent) and Italy (–33 percent) with only Ireland increasing (5 percent). As well as declining in size, the labor force will be graying, with workers between 55 and 64 accounting for an increased share of the total workforce. At the same time, the number of elderly persons (65 and over) in the population will rise from 61 million in 2000 to 103 million in 2050, an increase of 70 percent. All member countries will experience increases of over 50 percent.

As a consequence of these outcomes, the EU's old-age dependency ratio—the ratio of people aged 65 to the number of people between ages 15 and 64—will more than double from 24 percent in 2000 to 49 percent in 2050. Striking differences across member countries are evident. Ireland has the lowest ratio at 17 percent compared with ratios of 25 percent and over in Belgium, Greece, Spain, France, Italy, and Sweden. In most member countries the ratio will reach a new plateau by around 2040, reaching 60 percent in Spain and Italy. Finally, the number of people aged 80 and over will almost triple from 14 million in 2000 to 38 million in 2050.

Projected Pension Expenditures

To project pension expenditures, the Committee began with a number of assumptions based on the International Labor Organization's projected participation rates.[2]

- Participation rates for men will grow very slowly from 76.9 percent in 2000 to 77.4 percent in 2050.
- Participation rates for women will approach those of men, rising from 57.7 percent in 2000 to 69.5 percent in 2050.
- * Participation rates for men aged 15 to 54 will fall slightly from 85.1 percent to 84.6 percent, but for men aged 55 to 64 they rise from 52.6 percent to 56 percent.

- Participation rates for women will rise in both age segments—from 67 percent to 77.1 percent for those aged 15 to 54 and from 29.9 percent to 46.7 percent for those aged 55 to 64.[3]

By 2050, unemployment rates are expected to fall to around 8 percent, although some countries like Spain have projected lower rates; rates lower than 8 percent will be very difficult to achieve without major labor reforms.

These demographic projections can be offset by higher participation rates and lower unemployment rates. Thus the key variable is not the old-age dependency ratio but rather the balance between economically active people and the inactive people who must be supported. Therefore, two new ratios must be measured.

- The *potential economic dependency ratio* measures the number of potentially inactive people as a percentage of the labor force, that is, the population aged 15 and over in the labor force, inactive or not, as a percentage of the total number of persons in the labor force.
- The *effective economic dependency ratio* measures the actual number of inactive people as a percentage of total people employed, that is, the number of people aged 15 and over who are not employed, as a percentage of the total number of persons employed.

These ratios are higher than the old-age dependency ratio and rise over the projected period.

The potential economic dependency ratio increases for the EU as a whole from 74 percent in 2000 to 96 percent in 2050, and the effective economic dependency ratio increases from 90 percent in 2000 to 106 percent in 2050. Some countries exceed these percentages.[4] Although most measures of economic dependency include children (ages 0 to 14), children are excluded here from the definition of inactive persons to facilitate comparison with the old-age dependency ratio.[5]

Based on these projections, real GDP growth will fall from an average annual rate of 2.5 percent between 2000 and 2005 to an average of 1.6 percent between 2000 and 2050. Labor productivity growth will stay constant at 1.8 percent.

Table 4.1 shows how these projects will affect pension expenditures in terms of GDP. *Pension measures* refer to all replacement revenues for the older population such as early retirement, disability and survivors pensions, and other transfers to the elderly, such as unemployment benefits to people aged 55 and over and "social pensions." In 2000, spending on public pensions accounted for an average of 10.4 percent of GDP, though with considerable varia-

TABLE 4.1   Public Pension Expenditures Including Most Public Replacement Revenues to People Aged 55 and Over before Taxes

			(% of GDP)				
	2000	2010	2020	2030	2040	2050	Peak change
Belgium	10.0	9.9	11.4	13.3	13.7	13.3	3.7
Denmark (1)	10.5	12.5	13.8	14.5	14.0	13.3	4.1
Germany	11.8	11.2	12.6	15.5	16.6	16.9	5.0
Greece	12.6	12.6	15.4	19.6	23.8	24.8	12.2
Spain	9.4	8.9	9.9	12.6	16.0	17.3	7.9
France	12.1	13.1	15.0	16.0	15.8	—	4.0
Ireland (2)	4.6	5.0	6.7	7.6	8.3	9.0	4.4
Italy	13.8	13.9	14.8	15.7	15.7	14.1	2.1
Luxembourg	7.4	7.5	8.2	9.2	9.5	9.3	2.2
Netherlands (3)	7.9	9.1	11.1	13.1	14.1	13.6	6.2
Austria	14.5	14.9	16.0	18.1	18.3	17.0	4.2
Portugal	9.8	11.8	13.1	13.6	13.8	13.2	4.1
Finland	11.3	11.6	12.9	14.9	16.0	15.9	4.7
Sweden	9.0	9.6	10.7	11.4	11.4	10.7	2.6
UK	5.5	5.1	4.9	5.2	5.0	4.4	–1.1
EU	10.4	10.4	11.5	13.0	13.6	13.9	3.2

Source: AWG

tions among member countries—4.6 percent in Ireland, 5.5 percent in the UK, 13.8 percent in Italy, and 14.5 percent in Austria. In countries where pension entitlements depend on past contributions, pension expenditures are higher, while countries that operate on a more *flat-rate* basis often aim to provide a minimum level of retirement income supplemented with private occupational schemes and/or private savings.

In most member states, these projections show an increase in public pension expenditures between 3 and 5 percent of GDP. The EU average rises from 10.4 percent in 2000 to 13.9 percent in 2050, with Greece (12.2 percent), Spain (7.9 percent), the Netherlands (6.2 percent), Denmark (5 percent), Finland (4.7 percent), Ireland (4.4 percent), and Portugal (4.1) all at the high end. Among these countries there are notable differences because Denmark, Finland, Ireland, and the Netherlands have large funded components of their pension systems, while Greece, Spain, and Portugal rely exclusively on *pay-as-you-go* financing. The UK is the only country to actually project a decrease, which is largely the result of indexing pension benefits to inflation. The increases in Sweden and Italy are small, 2.6 percent and 2.1 percent respectively, resulting from the 1990s *notional defined contribution* pension scheme that mimics funded pensions but remains financed on a pay-as-you-go basis.[6] This scheme limits the impact of aging on expenditures by establishing a close actuarial link between contributions and entitlements and determining the final pension annuity at retirement age by a formula that takes life expectancy into account. Therefore, the impact of increases in life expectancy is shifted from public finances to the individual.

We can explain these expenditure increases by looking at four factors:

- *Population aging or dependency ratio effect*, which measures the change over time in the ratio of people aged 55 and over to the population between ages 15 and 54

- *Employment effect*, which measures the changes in the share of population at working age (15 to 64) that is employed—the inverse of the employment ratio
- *Eligibility effect*, which measures the share of population aged 55 and over that receives a pension
- *Benefit effect*, which measures the changes in the average pension relative to output per worker

The dependency ratio rises substantially in all countries, which places upward pressure on pension expenditures, so it is the main driving force of the increases. The eligibility ratio is the second driving force, increasing expenditures because of the large increase in female participation rates, though this is partly compensated for by the reduction in the number of women receiving survivors' pensions. Increasing the effective retirement age could counteract the increases because it would lower the share of persons receiving pensions. (Benefit and employment ratios tend to offset part of the expenditure increases.)

We should note that these projections could improve or worsen based on the rate of population change, participation, employment, and/or the productivity ratios.

Projected Increases in Public Health and Long-Term Care

The economic implications of increased expenditures on health and long-term care are quite different from pensions because they increase the size of an already relatively large sector of the economy that affects the economy's structure and overall development.

While health care and aging seem to be highly correlated because older people tend to consume more health care than other age groups, this correlation is especially high for the very elderly. Looking at the distribution of health-care expenditures by age for a single year shows that early in life health expenses tend to be high—

up to 5 percent of GDP per capita—mainly because some member countries include the costs associated with birth. After childhood, age-related health-care expenditures per capita tend to increase with age—in all member countries the increase is from 2.5 percent at ages 5 to 9 up to 17 percent at ages 80 to 89. Expenditures tend to fall to 15 percent for those over age 90 because these people are increasingly included in long-term care rather than health care, although it is often difficult to distinguish between both kinds of expenditures. In most member countries, men tend to generate more health-care expenditures with age than do women.

Long-term care expenditures are similar to health-care expenditures, although expenditures in terms of GDP per capita at prime ages tend to be lower and at very old ages tend to be much higher because some member countries supply long-term care in a formal institutional setting. More and more care is being provided at home, which the elderly prefer and which has the added benefit of lower costs. Unlike health-care expenditures, when long-term care is broken down by gender, expenditures for women tend to be higher.

Nevertheless, contrary to the conventional view, the high growth of health-care expenditures in the second half of the twentieth century was not driven by the aging effect but rather by (1) increased public health-care coverage and insurance, (2) increased demand and consumption of health care in line with increased prosperity, and (3) the supply of more expensive technology and medical price inflation. In addition, the effect of aging is limited because these expenditures tend to be concentrated at the end of life, irrespective of when a person dies, which is why they are referred to as *death costs*. Given that mortality rates are higher in older age groups, the concentration of expenditures at the end of life leads to an upward bias in the distribution of health-care expenditures by age. To the extent that future life expectancy will increase and mortality rates at specific ages will decrease, projections based on the single-year age-related expenditures, as above, will overestimate the impact of aging. Thus, aging may not be the key driver of expenditure increases.[7]

The study's projections are limited to the impact of aging on health care and long-term care expenditures up to 2050, because they do not take into account non-age-related factors that will reduce future expenditures. This simple approach has a number of drawbacks. First, the future relationship between age, health care, and long-term care is going to be much more complex. Second, the projections avoid explicitly modeling other important factors such as the diffusion of medical and pharmaceutical technologies, the relative prices for medical inputs, the intensity of care for older ages, and the extent to which long-term care is provided in a formal setting.

While these projections share a common methodology with and are based on the same demographic and macroeconomic assumptions as the ones on pensions, they use two different costs assumptions. The former assumes that expenditures per person on both health and long-term care across all age and sex groups will grow at exactly the same rate as GDP per capita. This assumes that expenditures are neutral in macroeconomic terms—if there is no change in the population's age structure, then the share of the health- and long-term care sectors in GDP will remain the same even if the population size changes. The latter assumes that expenditures per person grow at the same rate as GDP per worker, that is, at the same rate as productivity, which assumes that wages determine costs in both sectors because they are labor-intensive.

Table 4.2 shows the results of these projections up to 2050. The impact of aging on health care and long-term care public expenditures in member countries ranges from between 1.7 and 3.9 percent of GDP. The total EU weighted average rises from 6.6 percent to 8.8 percent if measured by GDP per capita and to 9.3 percent if measured by GDP per worker. The countries with the greatest increases are those that have a strong tradition of providing formal long-term care for the elderly, such as Denmark, the Netherlands, Sweden, and Finland. Therefore, it is long-term care, not health care, that makes up the largest part of the increase. In almost all member countries (except Greece and Spain), GDP per worker projections are higher than GDP per capita because employment growth will be

TABLE 4.2 Total Public Expenditure on Health Care and Long-Term Care

Central demographic variant

Expressed as a share of GDP

	Total health and long-term care			Health care			Long-term care		
	Expenditure as a share of GDP in 2000 (%)	Increase in expenditure in percent of GDP between 2000 and 2050		Expenditure as a share of GDP in 2000 (%)	Increase in expenditure in percent of GDP between 2000 and 2050		Expenditure as a share of GDP in 2000 (%)	Increase in expenditure in percent of GDP between 2000 and 2050	
		Per capita	Per worker		Per capita	Per worker		Per capita	Per worker
Belgium	6.1	2.1	2.4	5.3	1.3	1.5	0.8	0.8	0.8
Denmark	8.0	2.7	3.5	5.1	0.7	1.1	3.0	2.1	2.5
Greece (1)				4.8	1.6	1.7			
Spain (1)				5.0	1.5	1.7			
France	6.9	1.7	2.5	6.2	1.2	1.9	0.7	0.5	0.6
Ireland (2)	6.6		2.5	5.9		2.3	0.7		0.2
Italy	5.5	1.9	2.1	4.9	1.5	1.7	0.6	0.4	0.4
Netherlands	7.2	3.2	3.8	4.7	1.0	1.3	2.5	2.2	2.5
Austria	5.8	2.8	3.1	5.1	1.7	2.0	0.7	1.0	1.1
Portugal (1)				5.4	0.8	1.3			
Finland	6.2	2.8	3.9	4.6	1.2	1.8	1.6	1.7	2.1
Sweden	8.8	3.0	3.3	6.0	1.0	1.2	2.8	2.0	2.1
United Kingdom	6.3	1.8	2.5	4.6	1.0	1.4	1.7	0.8	1.0
EU (weighted average) (3)	6.6	2.2	2.7	5.3	1.3	1.7	1.3	0.9	1.0

(1) Results for public expenditure on long-term care are not yet available for a number of member states.
(2) The results for Ireland are expressed as a share of GNP, not GDP.
(3) Weights are calculated according to the member states for which results are available. Therefore, for health care, it is a weight for EU-14, and for long-term care and total expenditure on health and long-term care, the average is for 10 member states.
Source: AWG

lower than population growth because of the population's changing age composition.

In sum, these simple projections tend to overestimate the direct impact of aging on overall expenditures because they do not take into account other factors that have driven increases in health- and long-term care expenditures and they underestimate the impact of non-demographic factors that drive costs per person or per unit. However, the increase in the fiscal burden implied by the projections is significant and will increase pension expenditures and undermine the sustainability of public finances.

Sustaining Public Finances in the European Union

The previous projections show that by 2050 the aging population could increase pension expenditures across the EU by 3.5 percent and annual health- and long-term care expenditures by 2.7 percent. This translates into a total annual average increase in the EU of 6.2 percent, which will put substantial pressure on member countries to sustain sound public finance positions that comply with the Stability and Growth Pact (SGP) requirements to facilitate growth and employment.

In the absence of an agreed-upon definition of sustainable public finances or assessed sustainable public finances, the working group took a pragmatic approach to projecting sustainability—avoiding excessive deficits, keeping debt levels below 60 percent of GDP, and respecting the SGP's requirement of budgets "close to balance or in surplus." Although the SGP imposes commitments on member country budgets only in the medium term (three to five years) and does not require explicit longer-term targets, sustainability is ensured de facto, provided that budgets respect the "close to balance or in surplus" target.

Based on this simple approach, the working group constructed long-term sustainability indicators using a two-step approach. The first step involves verifying whether existing budgetary policies can ensure continued compliance with EMU budget requirements. The second step involves estimating the budgetary adjustments required to ensure sustainable public finances.

For the first step, a baseline test extrapolates budget balances and debt levels based on baseline age-related expenditure projections, assuming the tax burden and non-age-related expenditures are held constant and a fixed interest-growth differential is maintained. Then the evolution in public debt is estimated, the result of which hinges upon whether the starting budget surplus is sufficiently high so that the decline in the interest burden can absorb the additional age-related expenditures. Given the sensitivity of the results to the underlying assumptions, three stress tests ascertain whether public finances are sustainable under different circumstances: the first sets the initial primary balance at more or less favorable levels compared with the baseline; the second assumes higher or lower growth for age-related expenditures; and the third assumes higher or lower interest-growth differentials.

The second step develops two synthetic indicators for the required adjustment. The first indicator considers the difference between the projected surplus in the baseline projection and the required surplus necessary to ensure a balance budget in all years up to 2050. The second indicator is a *financing gap* or *tax gap*, which measures the difference between the current tax ratio and the constant tax ratio needed to achieve a predetermined budgetary target at a specified date. Both indicators are applied to two stylized countries: an *average-debt country* in which the initial level of public debt is 60 percent of GDP and a *high-debt country* in which initial public debt is set at 100 percent of GDP. In both cases, non-age-related expenditures are assumed to be constant at 23 percent of GDP. Age-related expenditures are assumed to stay constant at 16 percent of GDP until 2010 and thereafter increase by 5 percent by 2030 and then stay constant at 21 percent until 2050. Both countries are assumed to have a balanced budget in 2005. Real interest rates are fixed at 4 percent and inflation at 2 percent. Nominal GDP growth is assumed to be constant at 4 percent over the period. In this setting, the lower-interest burden of the average-debt country results in a lower constant tax burden than in the high-debt country.

The results for the average-debt country show that a budget position below the 3 percent reference level is maintained until 2025. Thereafter, as debt levels increase, deficits increase to unsustainable levels. Government debt stays below 60 percent of GDP until about 2035, but when stress tests are applied, the reference value is unsustainable after 10 to 15 years. Table 4.3 shows the difference between the projected surplus and the one required to achieve a balanced budget in the baseline scenario and with stress tests. The required primary surplus is 3.5 percent of GDP in 2005 and goes down slowly

TABLE 4.3   Indicators of Sustainable Public Finance: Average-Debt Country

	2005	2010	2020	2030	2040	2050
Required primary balance	3.5	3.0	2.0	1.4	0.9	0.6
Difference between required and projected primary surplus						
Baseline	0.1	−0.4	1.1	3.0	2.5	2.2
Worse initial primary surplus	1.1	0.6	2.1	4.0	3.5	3.2
Better initial primary surplus	−0.9	−1.4	0.1	2.0	1.5	1.2
Higher age-related expenditure	0.1	−0.4	1.3	3.5	3.0	2.7
Lower age-related expenditure	0.1	−0.4	0.8	2.5	2.0	1.7

	Financing gap		NPV of	Average
	SGP	Traditional	PB (1)	PB (2)
Baseline scenario	1.4	1.6	22	1.1
Required			45	1.7
Worse initial primary surplus	2.4	2.6	1	−0.9
Better initial primary surplus	0.4	0.6	43	1.1
Higher age-related expenditure	1.7	2.0	17	−0.2
Lower age-related expenditure	1.1	1.2	27	0.4
Higher interest-growth differential	1.5	1.7		
Lower interest-growth differential	1.3	1.5		

(1) NPV of PB = net present value of all primary balances over the period 2000–2050 as a percentage of GDP.
(2) Average PB = simple annual average of primary balances over the period 2000–2050.

to 2 percent in 2020 and to 0.6 percent in 2050. The difference between the required and the projected surplus goes up from 0.1 percent of GDP in 2005 to 2.2 percent in 2050. If the initial surplus is worse than the baseline, the difference goes up from 1.1 percent in 2005 to 3.2 percent in 2050; and if the age-related expenditure is higher than the baseline, the difference goes up from 0.1 percent in 2005 to 2.7 percent in 2050.

The results of the high-debt country's larger initial surplus show that the deficit gradually increases but remains below 1.5 percent of GDP. Public debt levels fall slowly and by 2015 reach 60 percent and stay below 60 percent until 2050. But with the negative stress tests, both deficit and debt levels increase above reference values at the end of the period. The required surplus is 5.8 percent of GDP in 2005 and goes slowly down to 3.3 percent in 2020, to 1.5 percent in 2040, and 1.0 percent in 2050. The difference between the required and the projected primary surplus goes up from 0 percent of GDP in 2005 to 1.5 percent in 2030 and then falls to 0.2 percent in 2050. With a lower initial surplus, the difference goes up from 1 percent of GDP in 2005 to 1.2 percent in 2050. With higher age-related expenditures, the difference goes up from 0 percent of GDP to 2 percent in 2030, and then down to 0.7 percent in 2050.

In both cases, the indicators show that, by having large surpluses, the member countries will be able to meet the costs of the aging population. Nevertheless, history shows how difficult it is to maintain such surpluses over a long period of time. The high-debt country needs to maintain an average primary surplus of 2.8 percent over the whole period, and the average-debt country needs to maintain an average primary surplus of 1.7 percent. Both levels are extremely difficult to meet for that many years. In addition, by looking only at projected changes in primary balances, a paradoxical policy conclusion emerges: high-debt countries are better placed than average-debt countries to meet the budgetary cost of aging because they need to run very high surpluses to cover interest payments and respect the SGP's close-to-balanced or in-surplus rule. Nevertheless, this focus on the changes in surpluses overlooks the fact that high-debt countries will have to sustain a greater degree of *budgetary effort* to keep primary surpluses higher than average for a long period of time.

THE OECD REPORT

Demographic and Expenditure Projections to 2050

The OECD has coordinated a report, "Fiscal Implications of Aging: Projections of Age-Related Spending,"[8] that also uses projections based on the work of national experts, but in this case the experts were not limited by the underlying assumptions on population and macroeconomic parameters agreed to by the participating countries. This study uses the following assumptions:

- Fertility rates go up from 1.54 children per woman in 2000 to 1.66 children per woman in 2050. The EU average fertility rate rises from 1.52 children in 2000 to 1.68 in 2050, Japan from 1.38 to 1.61 in 2050, and the US from 2.05 in 2000 to 1.95 in 2050—all below the required population replacement rate of 2.1.
- Life expectancy for men rises from 74.1 years in 2000 to 79.3 years in 2050, and for women from 80.6 years in 2000 to 84.7 in 2050. The EU average for men is 74.9 in 2000 and 79.9 in 2050 and for women 81.0 in 2000 and 85.2 in 2050. The Japanese figures for men are 77.4 in 2000 and 79.4 in 2050 and for women 84.1 in 2000 and 86.5 in 2050. Finally, in the US, the life expectancy rate for men rises from 73.9 in 2000 to 79.1 in 2050 and for women from 79.6 years in 2000 to 83.5 years in 2050.
- Annual net immigration rates as a percentage of the total population will average 0.22 percent in 2000 and fall to 0.20 percent in 2050. The EU average was 0.16 percent in 2000 and will be 0.19 percent in 2050. The Japanese figures are not available, and the US rates are 0.33 percent in 2000 and 0.25 percent in 2050.

These assumptions show an average fertility rate increase of around 8 percent and a rising life expectancy of about 4.5 years. In the EU, the fertility rate increases by 10 percent, and life expectancy increases by 4.6 years. In the US, the fertility rate declines by 5 percent and life expectancy increases by 5.2 years.[9]

Under these assumptions, the EU baseline projections for old-age dependency ratios increase from 26 percent in 2000 to 52 percent in 2050—the ratio doubles. In the case of Japan, the ratio goes from 23.5 percent in 2000 to 65 percent in 2050—almost triple. For the US, the increase is smaller, going from 22 percent in 2000 to 37 percent in 2050—an increase of only 68 percent. In other words, in 2050 the US dependency ratio will be 15 percent lower than the EU's and 28 percent lower than Japan's.

Under these assumptions, the baseline projections for total old-age-related public expenditures, including pensions, long-term unemployment, disability, early retirement programs, health and long-term care are:

- Total average age-related spending for OECD countries rises from 16.9 percent in 2000 to 22.4 percent in 2050—an increase of 5.5 percent of GDP. In the EU, the average increases from 18 percent in 2000 to 24 percent in 2050—an increase of 6 percent. In the US, the average increases from 11.2 percent in 2000 to 16.7 percent in 2050—an increase of 5.5 percent (but at a much lower level).
- In pensions and early retirement, US expenditures increase from 4.6 percent of GDP in 2000 to 6.7 percent in 2050, while EU expenditures increase from 10.6 percent in 2000 to 13.6 percent.
- US health- and long-term care expenditures rise from 2.6 percent of GDP in 2000 to 7 percent in 2050, while in the EU they increase from 7.4 percent in 2000 to 10.4 percent in 2050.

The OECD report points out the difficulty the EU faces in the next 50 years with an increase of age-related public expenditures of around 6 percent. In 2000, the EU average total budget revenue was around 52 percent of GDP, while in the US it was only around 30 percent of GDP. Thus, the EU has much less room to maneuver, and the adjustment will have to come from greatly reducing surpluses, increasing budget deficits, or both.

The OECD report simulates the fiscal impact of aging on debt levels in a stylized country, where pension spending represents 8 percent of GDP in 2000, the primary surplus is 2.5 percent, and the net debt is 55 percent. Assuming that other government revenues and expenditures remain constant, from 2000 to 2050 the projected increase in age-related spending is 6 percent of GDP, and the change in age-related spending is fully reflected in the overall primary balance. Assuming a 1.9 percent annual real GDP growth and a real interest rate of 4 percent, debt will increase by 100 percent, doubling net debt from 55 percent to 110 percent.

If the stylized country resembles the average EU country, the impact of this rise in age-related expenses could be explosive. At present, the average EU debt-to-GDP ratio is around 70 percent and could surge to 170 percent in 2050 without reforms. In contrast, the present US debt-to-GDP ratio is 50 percent and will increase only to 90 percent without reforms. These figures could be even higher for the EU if we take into account that most of the new potential member countries have little pension coverage for retirees and that their actual average debt-to-GDP ratios are similar to those of current members.

UNITED NATIONS POPULATION DIVISION DEMOGRAPHIC FORECASTS

The latest report of the United Nations Population Division (2003) updates its demographic forecasts to 2050 and shows significant differences with the EU and OECD reports.

Table 4.4 shows long-term demographic projections for the EU and US based on the UN's median world population forecasts. The 2000 average fertility rates are 1.4 children per woman in the EU and 2.0 in the US, the former is lower than the accepted 2.1 population replacement rate, while the latter is much closer. The 12 new EU members from Eastern Europe have an even lower fertility rate—1.2. By 2050, the average fertility rate is expected to increase to 1.7 in the EU as a whole, 1.8 in the 12 new member countries, and to 2.2 in the US. In the EU, life expectancy is currently 78.5 years; it is 68.4 years in the 12 new member countries and 77.5 in the United States. By 2050 it is expected to reach 83.5 in the EU, 82.6 in the 12 new member countries, and 77.8 in the US.

According to these fertility and life expectancy rates, the EU's population of 380 million will fall to 364 million by 2050, while the present US population of 285 million will increase to 397 million,

TABLE 4.4   U.N. Demographic Forecasts

	Year	E.U.	U.S.	NEW EU-12	
Fertility rate	2000	1.4	2.0	1.2	
	2050	1.8	2.2	1.8	
Life expectancy	2000	78.5	77.4	68.4	
	2050	80.5	82.6	77.8	
Median age	2000	39.0	35.6	36.5	
	2050	48.5	41.3	49.6	
Elderly dependency ratio	2000	35%	25%		
Persons aged 60 and over/ persons aged 15–59	2050	70%	35%		
Population aged 60 and over	2000	19.0%	16,1%	18,6%	
	2050	36.9%	35.6%	36.8%	
Net migration rate (per 1,000 population)	2000	1.5	4.2	−0.3	
	2050	1.6	3.0	−0.4	
Population change per year (in thousands)	2000	125	2,800	−1,645	
	2050	−235	1,950	−1,797	
				EU-27	EU-39
Total populations (in millions)	2000	382	283		
	2050	364	397	475	745

Source: U.N. World Population Prospects 2000 and 2004 Revisions

overtaking the EU-15. However, by then, the EU will probably include around 39 members. Today's 25 member states will have been joined by 3 others—Bulgaria and Rumania in 2007 and Croatia in 2009. Between 2012 and 2020, there will be another 5 potential candidates: Turkey, Albania, Bosnia-Herzegovina, Macedonia, and Serbia-Montenegro. In addition, there are another 6 potential candidates, countries that are likely to request membership sooner or later: Iceland, Norway, and Switzerland and possibly Moldova, Ukraine, and Belarus. These new and potential member states will add another 360 million people to the Union so that by 2050 the EU's population could reach 745 million. Even if the EU's membership remains at the committed 27 countries, the 2050 population will still be 475 million—larger than that of the US.

However, according to this report, the average rate of immigration in the last decade has been much higher in the US: 11 million immigrants entered the US versus 6 million in the EU. Extrapolating these rates to 2050, the population of both economies will increase by 55 and 21 million people, respectively. Given that the fertility rate increases in parallel with the immigration rate, since immigrants tend to have more children (especially those immigrants from Latin America who are migrating to the US and who have fertility rates of 2.7 children per woman), the population increase in the US could be much higher. On the flip side, the fertility rates of Central and Eastern European countries are even slightly lower than the current EU's—only 1.3—but in 2050 they are expected to increase to 2.2. Therefore, the likelihood of a big population increase in the fully enlarged EU is much lower than in the US unless the EU sees a massive influx of African immigrants (who are likely to maintain high fertility rates in the next decades). The US has the advantage over the EU in terms of immigration in that it has a long-standing tradition of being a country that welcomes immigration; there are already 40 million Hispanics living in the United States (15 percent of the total population), and immigration from Asian nations is also rapidly increasing.

As a consequence of these assumptions, the UN report forecasts a higher elderly dependency ratio than the EU Commission and OECD reports. Given that the median age of the population is aging faster in the EU and in the 10 most recent members as well as the two projected new members and that the population aged 60 and over is also increasing much faster, the UN forecasts a much higher elderly dependency ratio that is more representative of the EU's early retirement rates. According to the UN, the EU's elderly dependency ratio is currently 35 percent, while the US ratio is only 25 percent. By the year 2050, the EU ratio will double, reaching 70 percent, that is, 70 persons will be supported by every 100 people of working age. In the US the ratio will increase by only 35 percent, half the increase seen in the EU. The EU dependency projection could very well take into account the potential members from Eastern and Central Europe because their fertility and life expectancy will tend to grow over the next 50 years converging with the EU average. However, at present, the UN forecasts that the elderly dependency ratio in Eastern Europe will reach 30 percent in 2050—less than half that of the EU. There is little potential error in these forecasts, given that the population that will be aged between 65 and 100 in 2050 is as quantifiable as that aged between 18 and 35 today.

THE CENTER FOR STRATEGIC AND INTERNATIONAL STUDIES REPORT

The Center for Strategic and International Studies (CSIS) report "Global Retirement Crisis" (2002) projects that aging is going to have a larger impact on public pension expenditures than either the EU and OECD estimate. For both the EU and the OECD report, each member country made its own projections using its own pension model. The EU and OECD then established a common set of demographic and economic assumptions to which all countries adhered. In general, their projections include all publicly financed old-age pensions (both retirement and survivors' benefits), all minimum or social assistance pensions, and all special early retirement pensions. In a few countries, however, there are significant omissions: the Netherlands' early retirement benefits, the UK's civil service pensions, and the US state and local employee pensions, for example. The CSIS report starts with the premise that baseline spending projections should almost always be based on established historical trends. The CSIS uses both official pension expenditure projections from the EU and the OECD as a starting point and then it adjusts them to reflect different assumptions about unemployment, participation, fertility, and life expectancy rates.

First, the official projections assume that unemployment will fall beneath its recent historical average in every developed country except Japan, although the CSIS does not offer any explanation for this despite the fact that unemployment has been chronically high for decades in many EU countries. Most economists agree that the unemployment problem is caused by rigid labor markets, high labor costs, and easy access to generous unemployment, disability, and early retirement benefits. The CSIS also believes that reducing the unemployment rate substantially will be possible only with fundamental reforms. For this reason, the CSIS assumes that unemployment rates will remain stable at their 1990 to 2000 averages. This change in perspective raises projected pension costs significantly in a number of countries, with the largest increase in Spain (2.3 percent of GDP) since it had forecasted a 2050 unemployment rate of only 4 percent, down from the present 11 percent.

Second, the official projections assume that the participation of women in the workforce will rise, sometimes significantly, in every developed country except Norway. The CSIS assumes that the work patterns of women will remain unchanged, except to allow for a possible *cohort effect* based on advances in workforce participation by the previous generation of women workers. In other words, in some countries such as Austria, Belgium, Greece, Ireland, Italy, the Netherlands, Portugal, and Spain, younger women now have higher participation rates than older women. Therefore, the CSIS assumes that women between ages 40 and 54 in these countries will eventually have the same rates as women aged 20 to 39. In other countries, women under age 40 work at lower rates than women over age 40. In this case the CSIS assumes that there will be no cohort effect—a consistent projection will show a declining overall participation rate. In some other countries, the official projections assume an increase in the participation rates of older men because of recent pension reforms. The CSIS allows this assumption except in Austria and Italy, where the projected rise is far greater than can be explained by policy changes. In the former, participation rates for older men are projected to rise 55 percent and in the latter 38 percent; CSIS reduces both to 20 percent.

Third, without much justification, the official projections assume that fertility rates will rise in most developed countries, with the biggest increases in those countries that now have the lowest rates. However, there has been no evidence presented in favor of this shift. In Italy, Austria, Greece, and Spain, fertility rates are declining or flat across every age bracket and have been for decades. The only possible explanation is that fertility rates are now growing in some countries among women in their thirties and early forties, suggesting that they are merely postponing having children rather than reducing the total number of children planned. But the impact of this time shift is very limited, and it is offset by falling fertility rates among younger women. Therefore, the CSIS assumes that fertility rates will remain constant at their 1995 to 2000 averages.

Fourth, the official EU and OECD projections assume that the rate of improvement in life expectancy will slow, despite the fact that most demographers think that it will continue to grow at the present pace, or, more precisely, that mortality will continue to fall at its historical pace. Demographers who expect a slowdown in improved life expectancy argue that it cannot keep rising because medical progress will eventually push everyone to a *natural limit*. But if such a limit existed, mortality improvements for the oldest elderly age brackets would be slowing relative to those for the younger elderly, and variations in life expectancy should be narrowing as more people bunch up against the limit. None of this appears to be happening thus far. For many years, Sweden and Japan had longer life expectancies than the other developed countries, and this difference appears persistent. The

CSIS assumes that age-specific mortality rates in the developed countries will continue to decline at their long-term (1950 to 1994) averages. This assumption will raise life expectancy in every country, ranging from an extra six months in Germany to an extra nine years in Japan. The CSIS report does not change the official assumptions about either net immigration or labor productivity.

Given these adjustments, the CSIS projections increase the EU and OECD's 6 percent prediction of the impact of aging on the economy to 13.1 percent of GDP. In the case of the US, the CSIS increases the 4.4 percent of GDP to 10.1 percent.

INTERNATIONAL MONETARY FUND REPORT

The International Monetary Fund (IMF) has conducted two very interesting analyses of the economic impact of demographic changes, presented in its report (2004B). First, it uses a large 115-country data set, covering the period from 1960 to 2000, to investigate the relationship between demographic variables and GDP per capita, savings, investment, and fiscal balances. Because each variable is considered separately rather than as part of an integrated economic system and because historical correlations may not reflect causality, it uses a second instrument to look at how aging populations will impact on the economy. This second instrument is a multiregion macroeconomic model called INGENUE,[10] which explicitly captures the interactions between variables and across countries within an integrated and consistent framework.

The first analysis yields a number of important observations.

- First, that GDP per capita is positively correlated with changes in the relative size of the working-age population and negatively correlated with changes in the percentage of elderly—that is, the larger the labor force, the greater the positive productive impact and vice versa.[11]

- Second, a higher dependency ratio translates into a lower savings rate and, therefore, lower output growth. According to the life-cycle hypothesis of savings, people try to maintain a smooth pattern of consumption through their lifetime. This means that when current income is low relative to lifetime average income, savings will also be low and vice versa. Young people tend to be net borrowers, older adults tend to be net savers, and elderly people tend not to save or to save less than before.[12]
- Third, the larger the working-age population, the higher the investment rate tends to be because the investment returns tend to be higher.[13]
- Fourth, the higher the working-age population, the more positive the fiscal balances tend to be; and the higher the dependency ratio, the more negative the fiscal balances.[14]
- Fifth, the higher the dependency ratio, the larger the budget deficit and vice versa. Elderly people need increasing public expenditures in pensions and health and long-term care, but a smaller labor force reduces the number of contributors to, and the tax revenue from, social security.[15] Aging populations also affect the financial markets, which may put downward pressure on real equity prices if retirees begin to liquidate their assets.[16]

These conclusions combined with the INGENUE model's projections show that in advanced countries an increase in elderly dependency ratios and a decline in the working-age population could result in slower GDP per capita growth and lower savings and investment. The estimates suggest that these aging trends could reduce real GDP per capita by an average of 0.5 percent by 2050. The EU and Japan will be more negatively affected than the US—Japan's GDP will be reduced by 0.8 percent, the EU's will fall by 0.5 percent, and the US's by less than 0.3 percent. The decline in savings will also negatively affect the fiscal balances of Japan by 2.5 percent of GDP and of the EU by 0.2 percent, while the balances of the US will improve by more than 1.5 percent. Other models, like the MSG3,[17] show the EU's balance also improving because investment will decline faster than savings. The reduction of GDP growth will be larger than that of GDP per capita. Europe, for instance, will see its GDP growth rate reduced by 0.8 percent by 2050.

Besides these estimates, other models predict that the labor supply could drop by as much as 35 percent in Japan, 30 percent in Italy, and 17 percent in Germany.[18] Moreover, according to these economists, solving this serious problem and keeping labor supplies at 2000 levels requires:

- The participation rates among the working age population to increase by an average of 11 percent, but Europe's working-age population will need to increase more than the average: Spain's by 21 percent, Italy's by 19 percent, and Germany's by 14.5 percent. The US's working-age population will need only a 3.5 percent increase. The extreme case is Japan where an increase of 100 percent will not be enough to keep its labor supply constant.
- The required cumulative immigration will need to increase by up to 40 percent of the total population in Spain, up to 37 percent in Italy, and up to 35 percent in Germany, while only up to 22 percent in the US.
- The retirement age will need to be raised by 12 years in Japan, 10 years in Spain and Italy, 9 years in Germany, and only 2.5 years in the US.

Naturally, the solution will mix these three partial measures and will also require an increase in fertility rates, but the main conclusion is that Europe needs to make an extraordinarily huge effort, while the US will only be required to make a moderate one.

Table 4.5 summarizes the differences in public expenditure on pensions and health care as a percentage of GDP between the EU, OECD, and CSIS projections. This synthesis shows that not only are the US expenditure growth rates lower than in the EU,

TABLE 4.5   Summary of Projections of the Impact of Aging on Public Expenditure

(as a percentage of GDP)

	Pensions		Health		Total		Differences EU-US in percentage points
	2000	2050	2000	2050	2000	2050	
EUROPEAN UNION							
EU Report	10.4	13.9	6.6	9.3	17.0	24.2	9.5
OECD Report	10.6	13.6	7.4	10.4	18.0	24.0	9.3
CSIS Report	10.5	17.2	6.9	13.4	17.5	30.6	10.1
UNITED STATES							
OECD Report	4.6	6.7	5.7	98.0	10.3	14.7	
CSIS Report	4.6	7.4	5.7	13.1	10.3	20.5	

between 2.9 and 3.8 percentage points of GDP, but also their total expenditure levels for pensions and health care in 2050 will be much lower, between 9.3 and 10.1 percent of GDP. Thus, the fiscal pressure in the EU is 22 percentage points higher than that in the US (52 percent versus 30 percent), which will require a huge effort to deal with this increase, and the room to expand tax revenue will be very small. Therefore, the EU's challenge is of enormous proportions.

Such a dramatic fiscal situation in the EU could be reduced if:

- Fertility, employment, and productivity rates increase much faster than their present trend.
- Present retirement age increases to 70.
- Immigration rates increase substantially.
- Pay-as-you-go pension systems are changed to a mixed system in which the pay-as-you-go system is maintained for only minimum pension levels while the remainder is based on private, collective, and individually funded systems.

Unfortunately, none of these objectives is easy to achieve. The inflows of immigrants would have to be very large, which is not likely given the restrictive regulations and the increasing rejection of immigrants once a certain threshold level is surpassed. The increase in the retirement age is absolutely necessary to compensate for the increase in the life expectancy, but the trend today has companies lowering the early retirement age to 50. The change from pay as you go to a funded system needs to be financed by issuing new debt to avoid major discrimination among cohorts, but the Stability and Growth Pact imposes very strict rules that reduce debt-to-GDP ratios to less than 60 percent. Increasing employment rates require major labor reform in most member countries and increasing competition by reducing product and factor market regulations. In the absence of these reforms the EU's budgetary and debt situation could become unsustainable.

In the US, the budgetary and debt situations are difficult but could still be manageable. Not only are the age-related public expenditures lower, but the US's room to maneuver in order to increase tax pressure is larger as well as its ability to increase its debt-to-GDP ratio (which is still almost 20 percent lower than the EU's). The US's participation rates are over 10 percent higher, even more in the case of older workers. The participation rate of people aged 60 to 64 is 55 percent versus only 30 percent in the EU, and the participation rate of people aged 65 and older is 18 percent versus only 6 percent in the EU. By 2050, the US old-age dependency ratio is going to be 35 percent, exactly half of the EU's. Moreover, US pension plans possess 59 percent of the total of all global pension assets, while the US's economic weight in the total global economy is only 23 percent. The UK alone has more pension assets than the rest of the EU combined, which makes it the only member country whose public pension system faces no long-term cost challenge. The main weakness of the US is that it spends $4,200 per capita on health care—nearly 50 percent more than the next runner up, Switzerland, and 70 percent more than the EU average. Therefore, the US also needs to greatly reform its health system.[19]

As discussed earlier, this very large projected gap in the future budgetary and debt positions between the US and EU economies could increase the current 1 percent growth gap in favor of the US, making it even more difficult for the EU to catch up in the next 50 years. The EU projections estimate that the pure impact of aging will reduce the potential growth rate from 2 percent to around 1.25 percent in 2040. The cumulative impact of such a decline would be a GDP per capita some 20 percent lower than could otherwise be expected. If the present use of labor potential remains unchanged, potential economic growth will fall to 1.5 percent by 2015. These estimates are even more negative than those of the IMF (2004B).

In confirmation of the seriousness of this impact, a recent report by Standard & Poor's, the credit rating agency, says that if the present aging expenditure trends prevail without major reforms, the cost of aging in pensions and health care will fuel downgrades of credit ratings for France, Germany, the UK, and even the US from their present AAA investment grade to the speculative or junk category. France will achieve a below BBB– grade in 2020, the US in 2027, Germany in 2030, and the UK in 2035, and with these grades will come a large increase in these countries' borrowing costs. Although the US has much healthier demographic trends, its budget deficit will add to the pain when its population's aging rate begins to accelerate in around 2020.[20]

NOTES

1 European Economy, 2001, No. 4

2 International Labor Organization, 1997

3 These participation rates could be smaller since some countries, such as Spain, Ireland, and the United Kingdom, measure participation rates only for those aged 20 to 54.

4 In the first ratio, Belgium increases from 92 percent to 113 percent, Spain from 92 percent to 114 percent, and Italy from 109 percent to 125 percent. In the second ratio, Belgium increases from 114 percent to 128 percent, Spain from

123 percent to 128 percent, and Italy from 134 percent to 142 percent. The countries with lower effective economic dependency ratios are Denmark, with 66 percent in 2050, Sweden, with 76 percent, Ireland, with 77 percent, and Luxembourg, with 32 percent, and countries with ineffective economic dependency ratios are Denmark, with 76 percent, Portugal and Sweden, with 86 percent, and Luxembourg, with 29 percent.

5 When children are included, the potential economic dependency ratio increases from 112 percent in 2000 to 131 percent in 2050, and the effective economic dependency ratio increases from 135 percent to 145 percent. That is, each person employed in 2050 will have to support 1.45 inactive persons.

6 In Sweden a proportion is financed on a funded basis.

7 Jacobzone, 2001

8 OECD, 2001

9 The assumptions for participation rates, unemployment, and labor productivity rates are the same as in the European Union report.

10 INGENUE Team, 2001

11 Bloom, Canning, and Sevilla, 2001; Gomez and Hernandez de Cos, 2003

12 Faruqee, 2002; Loayza, Schmidt-Hebbel, and Servén, 2000

13 Poterba, 2001

14 Feroli, 2003; Chinn and Prassad, 2003

15 Heller, 2003

16 Bosworth, Bryant, and Burtless, 2004

17 Batini, Callen, and McKibbin, 2004

18 Burniaux, Duval, and Jaumotte, 2003

19 The recent book by Nyce and Shieber (2005) achieves similar results.

20 Standard & Poor's, 2005

CHAPTER 5

REDUCING THE FISCAL
IMPACT OF AGING

HOW can the fiscal challenge posed by aging be addressed? The OECD report, using a sylized OECD country, offers some possibilities.[1] In this fictional country, total average age-related spending will increase by approximately 7 percent of GDP (although, as we saw earlier, the increases are significantly higher in some EU countries).

In terms of pension expenditures, the report calculates that to keep the debt-to-GDP ratio constant at 55 percent (currently 70 percent in the EU), by 2050 the fictional country will be required to reduce the average benefits of old-age pensioners and the number of beneficiaries by delaying retirement. The number of beneficiaries should be reduced by close to 8 percent, which would correspond to more than a year's increase in the effective age of retirement, while the required decrease in average benefits would be approximately 17 percent. Pension benefits require a larger decrease because of the feedback effects that fewer pensioners have on higher unemployment and GDP as well as the effect on tax revenues. In reality, however, cutbacks in pension generosity might well induce people to work longer, since later retirement in some countries automatically leads to higher pensions.

Alternatively, the sylized country could choose to further increase its primary surplus now to offset the impact of aging later. The OECD's simulations suggest that the age-related increase in spending alone could be fully offset by an increase in the primary surplus of an additional 1 percent and sustained through the whole period because the higher non-age-related surplus helps counteract age-related fiscal pressures. However, there is a narrow window of opportunity, before dependency ratios begin to rise rapidly, that countries can use to improve their overall fiscal situation and announce reforms. This window will be especially important for those reforms that have to be phased in progressively, because it will give households time to adjust. If these policies are delayed considerably, stronger measures will be required. For example, if they were implemented 10 years later, by 2015, the required reduction of pension beneficiaries would be 9.5 percent, and the reduction in benefits would reach 21.3 percent, or, alternatively, the surplus would need to be higher. If the reforms were carried out by 2025, the reductions would need to increase to 12.3 percent and 29.9 percent, respectively, or the necessary surplus would need to be 1.8 percent of GDP.

We should note that sharp decreases in average pension benefits may mean widening the gap between wage earners and pension beneficiaries, thereby increasing poverty among the elderly. Because the elderly will account for an important share of voters, there will be strong pressure to reverse the reductions, which is why there may be a need to provide alternative sources of retirement income (e.g., mandatory funded private pensions or savings) and to encourage people to work longer in order to qualify for a full public pension. It will also be necessary to encourage higher participation rates of older workers and larger immigration flows, but these policies will be dependent on whether there is employment available. In order to achieve this goal, new labor reforms are needed to reduce unemployment and encourage rapid employment growth.

MEASURES TO IMPROVE PUBLIC PENSION FINANCES

Pensions depend on two basic ratios:

- The rate of pension generosity, which is the outcome of dividing the average pension by the average output per employed person. When the productivity of the employed is higher, then the average pension is higher and vice versa.

• The dependency ratio, which results from dividing the number of employed contributing to the pension system by the number of retired people who benefit from the system. The higher the number of contributors, the higher the number of beneficiaries and vice versa.

If productivity is too low or the number of retirees is too high, the pension system cannot be sustained.

What Can Be Done to Reduce the Dependency Ratio?

The most important step will be to adapt retirement age to life expectancy. In 1960 the average retirement age in OECD countries was 65 and the life expectancy of people reaching 65 years of age was 70. Therefore, the system paid, on average, for five years of full pension. Today, retirement age has fallen to 61 while average life expectancy of the people reaching 65 has increased to 79—increasing the potential pension payout to 18 years! By 2050, average life expectancy may well reach 82 years, increasing the cost to the public even further.

What makes this increase in life expectancy problematic from a public finance perspective is that the legal retirement age (the age at which employees are eligible to receive a pension) has been decreasing in most OECD countries and in the EU. In the OECD, the legal retirement age for men has fallen to 60, and in Japan, Belgium, and France, the average is 64. For women, the legal average retirement age is 63, with some countries giving legal pensions at 57 (Italy) and 58. This trend is completely unsustainable and needs radical change.

The reasons for early retirement are twofold: (1) employers want to reduce the number of older workers with higher salaries and less productivity, and (2) workers, especially those in lower-skilled employment, do not see any incentive to continue working because it will not improve their pension benefits.[2]

One way to solve this dangerous and expensive trend would be for all member countries to agree to increase the legal retirement age to 70. Another easier solution would be to permit the employee to decide on retirement age and to create the incentive for a longer working life by increasing the pension accordingly. In more than half of the OECD countries today, pensions for 55-year-olds do not increase if an additional 10 years are spent in the workforce, while in 1960 they increased by 33 percent over that duration. Only three OECD countries have pension systems that are retirement-age neutral (Iceland, Denmark, and the US) and only two (Germany and the Netherlands) where pensions increase throughout working life. In fact there are disincentives to retire later as well as subsidies like unemployment or temporary disability that discourage people from working longer.

The major problem posed by decreases in the retirement age is that the participation or activity rate of older employees (60 to 64 years) falls dramatically—only 17 percent in France, 18 percent in the Netherlands, 29 percent in Germany, and 31 percent in Italy, which reduces the number of people in the workforce—social security contributors—and increases the number of retirees. The participation rate of young workers is also falling because they come into the workforce later because of increased rates of secondary and higher education. In 1960, the average youth looked actively for a job at age 15 or 16, but today's youths enter the labor market at 21 or 22—six years later. This trend is even more difficult to change because education has enabled the achievement of the more advanced countries, so this delay will continue to grow.

Thus, on one hand, the labor force is shrinking because instead of working from ages 15 to 64 people work from ages 21 to 61—nine years less. On the other hand, the number of retirees is growing because instead of retiring at 65 and dying at 70, they are retiring at 61 and dying at 79—13 years longer. As we have seen, irrespective of the numbers entering and leaving the workforce, fertility rate and life expectancy trends alone may shrink the 2050 EU labor force by 40 percent.

Another way to reduce the dependency ratio is by fostering the fertility rate. France had had reasonable success with an incentive called *les allocations familiales*, which provides incentives, both housing allowances and cash stipends, for families starting with the second child and increasing for each child thereafter. The French government also provides tax exemptions to larger families. However, this solution takes many years to bear fruit, and the current pressures will require member countries to act quickly. While some economists argue that fertility has dropped because more women have entered the workforce, this does not seem to be the case because Denmark and Sweden have maintained reasonable fertility rates with higher employment rates, while Italy and Spain have both low female employment and low fertility rates. In other words, fertility rates do not depend on monetary incentives, but rather on providing working women with adequate childcare at home or nearby as well as proper nursery schools located on the premises where people work.

Another solution would be to admit a greater number of immigrants, which has allowed Canada, Australia, and the US to have lower dependency ratios and more sustainable pensions. However, this solution presents three problems. First, this solution is only temporary because immigrants tend to adopt the same habits and customs as the local population, reducing their higher fertility rates. Second, immigrants who contribute today to sustain the pension system are going to benefit from a pension at retirement as well, so either fertility rates need to rise further or even more immigrants are needed. Third, the number of immigrants needed to balance the EU pension systems is huge.

Until only recently, most EU countries have been net migrants to North and Latin America and Oceania and are not used to receiving large flows of immigrants. And in countries with high unemployment, immigrants are often socially rejected. According to the latest Eurobarometer, 73 percent of EU citizens are unsure about the future of their pensions, but at the same time 60 percent do not think that immigrants can efficiently solve Europe's aging population problem; only 34 percent believe immigrants can help. Moreover, when asked about solving the pension problem, most favor maintaining the retirement age and increasing the social security contributions—few favor working and contributing longer. [3]

Demographers estimate that the EU will need 30 million immigrants a year to balance the negative domestic demographic effects on pensions, but in the last decade EU immigration has averaged 7 million a year. If these 7 million have faced increasing social rejection, what will happen with 30 million? In spite of the European population's strong negative attitude, the fact is that immigration seems the most available and reasonable solution, at least temporarily.

What Can Be Done to Reduce the Pension Generosity Ratio?

The first option is clear: increase productivity per person employed, which will make it possible to finance the generous pensions because the wages of pension contributors will be higher, allowing them to make higher contributions to the system. However, this solution is again only temporary, because those contributors will eventually retire and demand pensions commensurate with their higher contributions.

The second option is to reduce the average pension's generosity. As we have seen, the *replacement rate*, the main measure of pension generosity, is the proportion of the pension in relation to the actual wage received before retiring. The average EU replacement rate is much higher than in the US. In 2000, the average US replacement rate was 20 percent of the wage at retirement, whereas in the EU, the average replacement rate was 60 percent, or triple that of the U.S. Therefore, there is more room to reduce replacement rates. For instance, the highest and lowest gross replacement rates in the US are 75 percent and 20 percent, respectively, but in France they are 119 percent and 43 percent, in Spain 110 percent and 60 percent, in Italy 73 percent and 66 percent, and in Germany 70 percent and 25 percent.

One way of calculating this reduction in generosity is to compute how much the replacement rates need to be reduced to stabilize the pension finances in the year 2030. According to these calculations, the US should reduce pensions by 17 percent, Germany by 19 percent, France by 28 percent, Italy by 9 percent, and Spain by 31 percent. Reducing pensions is problematic because it transfers income from the old to the young and because it breaches a consolidated right of retirees to receive a defined pension. For this reason, governments have looked to other ways of achieving a similar result. For example, France, Germany, Italy, and Spain have increased the years of contributions, while others have moved from a system of defined benefits to one of defined contribution, which is a more radical change. Still others, as we will see, are moving from the today's pay-as-you-go system toward a funded system.

A third option would be to increase the average contribution, but this poses a serious problem because it benefits the old at the expense of the young, introducing intergenerational solidarity issues. Moreover, if young contributors who already pay a high proportion of their disposable income to social security are forced to pay more, they will lose any incentive to work harder and longer, further exacerbating the problem.

In sum, there is no magic solution to a problem so complex; the ultimate solution will likely be some combination of these options. However, one issue is certain: steps must be taken as soon as possible before people over age 60 become the majority of the electorate, making it impossible to pass the necessary laws and regulations!

PAY AS YOU GO VERSUS FUNDED PENSION SYSTEMS

The more radical pension policy alternative is to transition from the present *pay-as-you-go systems* (PAYG) to a fully funded pension system, which has created a heated debate among economists. Martin

Feldstein (1996, 1997), one of the pioneers of PAYG, argues that social security tends to displace savings, both public (by drawing resources from the government budget) and private (by replacing savings for the retirement of forward-looking individuals) with social security taxes or contributions. Therefore, privatizing social security could increase capital accumulation and therefore growth. In some member countries there is a clear correlation between the social security system's generosity and a reduction in the national savings rate. Thus, increasing public pension generosity could displace wealth creation via capital accumulation.

The design of EU pension systems creates disincentives to work beyond certain ages. At the same time, employer-run *defined benefit* systems often have built-in incentives that encourage workers to retire at a relatively early age, due to the increasing costs of pensions as workers extend their working lives. The nonneutrality and disincentives of the EU systems allow companies to ease workers out of the workforce and create an *implicit tax* on work. Workers tend to leave the workforce through any loophole available when the implicit tax on work becomes high.[4] Therefore, unlike the US, both public and private systems result in a very high rate of early retirement and a very low level of economic activity among older employees. This can be seen clearly in the plunge in EU employment rates when workers reach 50 and 60.

We must also consider workers' existing rights in terms of their pension benefits. Within the PAYG system, these rights should be considered as *hidden debt* because they are future liabilities for the social security system. The stock of pension liabilities has a similar nature to explicit government debt and it can amount to, or even exceed, the current resources, that is, the country's GDP. The existence of this debt can go hand in hand with a current social security deficit (as in the EU) or surplus (as in the US until recently).

What options are available to solve these problems? A recent report by Boeri, Brugiavini, and Disney for the European Round Table of Industrialists provides an excellent discussion of this issue and presents three options.[5] The first option is *pure privatization* by creating funded individual accounts. However, in creating the individual accounts, the existing pension system has to honor the existing pension rights or hidden debt, which can be done by raising taxes and/or issuing new government debt. Thus, pure privatization involves some costs that can be spread in different ways across different generations, or it involves using the proceeds from public utility privatization to offset pension liabilities.[6] The second option is *pure prefunding*, which reduces benefits and increases contributions to reduce future liabilities. Any resulting surplus could be invested in either bonds or diversified portfolios. In the US, a social security trust fund has been created with social security surpluses to provide a cushion for future liabilities. The third option is to implement *soft reforms* within the existing PAYG system in order to reduce the dependency ratio, the replacement rate, or both, by delaying the retirement age, encouraging female labor participation, encouraging immigration, or reducing the replacement ratio by reducing benefits and eligibility or changing the indexation rules to inflation or to wages. Of course, these three options can be combined or even sequenced beginning with soft reforms, followed by the prefunding and ending with the privatization.

What are the differences between PAYG and privately funded systems? Both are mechanisms to redistribute resources over time. But while PAYG systems rely on intergenerational redistribution of resources, privately funded systems rely on intertemporal substitution of resources, an element of flexibility that permits sharing the demographic burden over a much longer period. Unless there are portfolio restrictions on investments, funded pensions offer flexibility because international diversification can automatically ease the pressure of an aging population on the social security costs at the time when a PAYG system would suffer the most. If the demographic change is only temporary and does not translate into a permanent shift in the population's age structure, then funded systems can count on a larger horizon than PAYG systems and smooth out the resource crisis. However, the EU is facing a permanent shift in the population structure because of increasing life expectancies, which will negatively affect both PAYG and funded systems.

Whether a funded system is better than a PAYG system ultimately depends on each system's rate of return. If contributions to a PAYG system are seen as "forced savings for retirement," then the relationship between how much employees contribute and how much they get at retirement age can be expressed in terms of the rate of return on those savings. While in a PAYG system, the return depends on workforce and productivity growth, in a funded system workforce and productivity growth *are* the return on investment. One could argue that the annual growth of the real wage bill and the annual growth of the real return of the funded scheme are highly correlated, leaving no substantial difference between the two. However, studies find no evidence of a strong positive correlation, increasing the funded system's attractiveness. But if funding implies that the same result can be achieved through a lower contribution, its advantage is obvious because it implies lower tax rates, fewer distortions in the labor market, less unemployment, and a more competitive economy.

The debate around the two alternative systems has centered on whether a system can provide reasonably priced annuities to replace the public annuities. The PAYG systems are typically *defined benefits* with some form of indexing to preserve the real value of retirement income, while the funded systems would not normally deliver an annuity but a capitalized fund. One issue is protection from risk, although this can be achieved by the funded system provided there are indexed bonds in the capital market. Another issue is that annuities be priced fairly. The reasoning behind unfairly priced annuities is that the annuity market is thin due to an *adverse selection* problem. When annuities are noncompulsory, annuity purchasers tend to be those individuals characterized by greater than average longevity. Because they are a bad risk for the insurance companies, the companies tend to charge *load factors* for all annuity purchasers to compensate for bad risks. However, as the demand for annuities increases, the adverse selection problem will diminish and premiums will eventually fall.

Another highly debated issue is the risk associated with capital markets' rates of return. Higher returns can be achieved by investing private pension funds in equities, but these are typically riskier than bonds, creating a question of how to diversify pension funds by instrument and market. However, the PAYG systems are not risk-free, because they are public and are subject to risks associated with the population's evolution, productivity growth, and political risk. In principle, the higher returns would not be lost if governments invested funds on behalf of the workers. However, there are two problems: the political risk of misusing the fund to finance government deficits and the standard problem of governments not acting in retirees' best interest. Usually, when governments have a social security surplus, they tend to fund other government investments instead of paying down debt or creating a fund for future expected deficits, so they favor certain types of investments instead of maximizing returns for a given risk in the future.

In addition, the costs associated with transitioning from a PAYG system to a funded system need to be financed by raising taxes or issuing new debt, and someone has to pay these extra costs. The way this transition is financed will affect two different generations in different ways. It is not completely true that the existing employees will have to pay twice—once for their own funded retirement and once for the retirement of their parents—because they will have to save for their own retirement and the cost of the PAYG benefit outlays will decrease as new retirees gradually substitute funded benefits for unfunded benefits. However, the transition does raise two economic issues: first, how many generations should share the transition costs—in other words, how quickly should the systems be transitioned—and second, the cost of the reform for the generations that will suffer a net loss is essentially a reduction in consumption lasting a number of years, which may affect GDP growth.

The way the transition is financed affects those who would have to pay differently. If it is financed by taxes on income or wages, only current workers will be affected, so labor supply decisions will be distorted and costs will be spread over very few generations (only the middle ones), leaving very little room left for smoothing consumption. If the transition is financed by taxes on consumption, there will be a higher burden on the elderly because they presumably benefited from a generous PAYG system and they tend to consume more. If it is financed by issuing new debt, taxes will be deferred to younger generations, including newborns, who would benefit most from the new system. Nevertheless, the creation of new EU debt is subject to the constraints included in the Maastricht Treaty and the Stability and Growth Pact, but these limits could be softened if this debt were earmarked toward a strict funding target or if it represented an investment for future generations.

Although not every EU country will want to undertake such a major reform, all members are concerned with pension sustainability. Furthermore, because the issue of limited labor mobility among member countries was high on the Lisbon agenda, measures need to be taken to improve the flexibility of the labor market via social security arrangements. Thus, the EU will need to ensure the portability of pension rights both within a country and across the EU, which will be very difficult under PAYG.

Nevertheless, we should not infer that the existing systems are bad and that those who can opt out should. The PAYG systems are a suitable way of insuring that participants against the uncertainty of life expectancy, ensuring that the income they will receive over their lifetimes as well as permitting people with disabling health conditions to reduce their commitment to work. The PAYG systems are a reasonable expression of social solidarity across generations and between rich and poor within the same generation. Therefore, we don't need to abolish the pension systems to restore their credibility, unless a suitable and affordable private alternative can be provided. In addition, the compulsory nature of the public system should be preserved. Exemptions to the system are going to be dangerous, inducing the best positioned firms or individuals to ride freely on the system, leaving others with less income to suffer the consequences of inadequate coverage and having to find other means of survival after retirement.

It will be very difficult to find a one-size-fits-all solution because the member countries are in very different situations in terms of budget deficits, debt to GDP ratios, and the impact of aging on their PAYG systems. It will be very easy for countries such as Ireland or the Netherlands to move to a fully or substantially funded system because PAYG never really got off the ground, but the transition will be difficult for most EU countries that have very large, and sometimes very generous, PAYG systems.

There is no simple or easy way around the problem of funding the transition costs. Therefore, a gradual and mixed approach seems to be the right way to proceed. This approach will probably require both the involvement of the private sector and instituting some cutbacks for those at or near retirement. To restore its pension system's credibility, each country, according to its initial situation and its future projections, should try to reach the right balance of a public versus private mix.

The conventional view is that the best way to proceed is through a system based on three pillars: The first pillar is the PAYG system, which is best suited for redistributing income from the rich to the poor and guaranteeing the elderly a basic standard of living. This system is already in use in countries that have a flat-rate component to their public schemes. By contrast, where public schemes are earnings-related and pension benefits are not, there will be a substantial redistribution to low wage earners. Finally, in those countries in which large earnings-related benefit schemes are the norm, there is little room for this kind of redistribution, and those countries' reform implementation must take this into account.

The second pillar is based on collective, or occupational, pensions systems that tend to be compulsory, while the third is based on individual or personal pension accounts that are most often voluntary. Occupational pension systems are primarily organized by employers or institutions, individually or collectively, to supplement their employees' retirement income. The individual accounts are maintained primarily by the self-employed and by those who want to augment their PAYG or occupational pensions. Occupational or collective schemes have a number of advantages. They are cost efficient, since there are no costs associated with selling, advising, and administering the funds, and they allow a larger degree of risk sharing not only between employee and employer but also between generations of employees. Those employees who retire when the stock market and asset prices are doing well ought to be able to cross-subsidize those employees who retire during more difficult market situations. Individual accounts tend to be more portable and flexible but also more expensive to manage than collective accounts, so they are better suited to the well-off.

Coverage through occupational private systems ranges from 90 percent of total retirement income in the Netherlands and 50 percent in the UK to less than 10 percent in the rest of the EU. While most pension systems have *defined benefit* arrangements—based on a combination of the final salary and the number of years worked—in the US there has been a substantial shift toward *defined contribution* arrangements, which face fewer risks because benefits depend exclusively on contributions made and returns achieved.

The second and third pillars become essential with the public scheme focusing on its redistribution role. In countries where the public system provides adequate pensions for those who earn two or three times the average, there is not much room for private sector accounts—and vice versa. However, with an aging population and the very high levels of taxation or contributions needed to fund the pension system, there is little or no chance that current pension levels will be met entirely by the government in the future. Even when the government plays the major role in pensions, some pension elements will have to come from the private sector.

Therefore, workers and firms will have to work together to guarantee that each retiree can achieve a given replacement ratio through privately funded systems. This can also help to bring back actuarial fairness into retirement decisions. Workers who are particularly concerned about their retirement can pad their pensions with additional voluntary contributions. Since these goals are better achieved through capital markets, governments should ensure that private pension funds act in the workers' best interest, which will require rules that protect accumulated funds and workers' retirement income by invoking prudent investment decisions while still allowing flexible portfolio choices.

Nevertheless, this issue of partial privatization of social security, recently recommended by the administration of US President George Bush, has reignited the debate over how to address the uncertainty of pension systems in the face of aging populations. Eleven years ago, the World Bank's landmark study "Averting the Old-Age Crisis,"[7] became the reference point for the debate. The bank advocated moving away from the traditional PAYG systems in favor of compulsory funded pensions paid for by workers by saving part of their earnings. Since then, this kind of reform has been carried out in some Latin American countries and some countries in postcommunist transition. Now, after reviewing how these reforms have performed, the World Bank has recently changed its position.[8] In "Old Income Support in the Twenty-First Century," the bank stresses the need to reform pension systems because they do not deliver on their social objectives—contributing instead to significant distortions in the operation of market economies—and because they are financially unsustainable with an aging population.

The main issue for the World Bank is that the number of future pensioners who will benefit from these funded systems is extremely low because many workers will not be covered by the new arrangements. In most developing countries, close to half the workforce is in the informal economy and therefore outside of any publicly managed system. According to the World Bank, a retirement system should cater to people who will be poor throughout their lives and supply a basic pension for all vulnerable elderly. The system should be financed out of general tax revenues either in the form of social assistance, means-tested pensions, or universal payments received from age 70 on, complementing other resources such as family help, housing, and access to health care.

The World Bank's initial position has now added two additional pillars: the tax-financed safety net and the nonfinancial means of support. The experience with the first three pillars made the World Bank much less enthusiastic about mandatory individual retirement accounts. The accounts proved vulnerable to political risk, as in the case of Argentina, which defaulted on its public debt obligations wherein most of the funds had been invested; they have also suffered major volatility problems with equity investments and high management fees, leaving less net income than anticipated.

These problems have also affected developed countries like the UK and the Netherlands, where some managed accounts have not performed according to expectations, leaving the beneficiaries in a difficult situation. A recent report by the United Kingdom Pension Commission warns that at least 75 percent of those with privately managed individual retirement accounts will not have enough savings to provide adequate pensions at retirement age and that yield reductions resulting from providers charges can absorb 20 to 30 percent of individual pension savings.[9] This is one of the reasons why Sweden, for example, has introduced an innovative idea through its *notional accounts*. Notional accounts maintain PAYG financing, but treat worker contributions as if they were paid into individual accounts, which then form the basis of the individual's pension benefits, establishing a tight link between payroll contributions and pension benefits.

MEASURES TO REDUCE HEALTH COSTS

Finally, the EU will need to control health- and long-term care costs. Today, OECD countries' average health- and long-term care public expenditures amount to approximately 10 percent of GDP and are growing by 1 percent annually. In the future, the demand for both these services will rise with the increasing number of older and very old people in the population. At the same time, the shrinking working population, increasing participation rates, and smaller families are likely to limit families' abilities to care for their elderly members. Therefore, it may be necessary to increase health-care efficiency and effectiveness by introducing budgetary caps on the cost of products and services even though these caps could lead to rationing and lower-quality care. Alternately, countries will need to find ways to limit the demand for and the supply of unnecessary health-care services and to improve the match between health-care needs and the supply of services. In the long term, health-care expenditures will be driven not only by aging but also by new technologies and increasingly costly medical services, which suggests that a wider range of policies will be needed to control health-care costs such as disability prevention and in-home elder care.

The efficiency of a country's health-care system should be the most important goal of any health policy. The US health system's public and private costs amount to nearly 14.5 percent of GDP, while in the EU they total around 9.5 percent. US health indicators are worse than the Europeans', making this one of the areas in which US efficiency lags behind that of the EU. The US and the EU finance health-care costs in entirely different ways. In the US, only the elderly and those living below the poverty level are eligible for publicly funded health care, while the majority of Americans and their families are insured voluntarily through their employers. The problem with the US system is that 44 million Americans are not covered by any health insurance. In contrast, most EU countries' governments finance heath care through compulsory contributions from employers and employees, so there is universal coverage. In the EU, publicly financed health care covers approximately 70 percent of the population, while in the US only 41 percent is covered this way. The problem with the EU's system is that high unemployment and a shrinking working population has caused the number of contributors to fall, while the number of beneficiaries continues to grow, making the system increasingly difficult to finance. In both the US and the EU, there is clear evidence that while medical care pays off in healthier and longer lives, costs are soaring, partly due to a high degree of inefficiency and waste. The present systems in the EU and the US allow patients to choose their primary care physician, or specialist, who is then paid for each visit, giving doctors an incentive to maximize visits and encouraging patients to overuse medical services. Medical technology providers have an incentive to maximize prices; surgeons have an incentive to operate; and so on. Moreover, doctors have always been very independent and have always resisted change and government interference with their activities, even more when being pressed to be cost-effective and coordinated in supplying health care.

Because health care is labor intensive, health-care costs are always rising and tend to grow faster than GDP, so higher health-care demand, which is correlated with rising incomes, requires that more people be employed. This is why some economists call health care a *handicraft industry* afflicted by the chronic costs of personal services. Basically, they mean that there are inefficiencies related to coordinating health care and standardizing and integrating the service, because each patient differs as does each doctor and nurse. By contrast, the costs of medical technology tend to go up at the beginning because new technologies are held under patent and because people are willing to pay the higher price of new treatments. But these costs tend to fall in the medium term as quality and availability improve. So with the help of IT, there is the likelihood in the future of an increasing trade-off between more technology and fewer personal services. One foreseeable solution would be to rely increasingly on newer and more sophisticated pharmaceutical and technological products to keep the old healthier and at home while reducing the heavier costs of hospitals and labor-intensive care.

The solutions to reducing health costs are extremely difficult, and, up to now, most of the well meaning and innovative experiments have failed. This is a sector with powerful vested interests that needs structural change so that competitive pressures can push the industry in a more useful direction, enhancing the power of purchasers and increasing competition in the supply of medical services and products. The traditional argument has been that heath care is too important to leave to the forces of the market, but the opposite is also true: it is to important not to be exposed to the market.[10]

The best way to approach such change is constructively, that is, instead of trying to supplant the market, governments, which are the end payers, should strive to promote competition while upholding social values of equity in heath care. For instance, in countries with competing health insurers, governments can direct public money to poorer and ailing people so that they can afford insurance. Another important measure is to acknowledge that even if governments finance most health care, they do not necessarily have to provide it themselves. The current monolithic grip on providing medical services has inhibited experiments that flourish when hospital ownership is more varied. Governments should also review their role as regulators. Historically, regulation has tended to block competition, for example, preventing health-care purchasers from selective contracting with providers. Instead, EU governments should help to foster competition, so that as an end result they pay less. They should set standards and monitor performance, building on some of the initiatives that are proving worthwhile in the US.

The reengineering of health care will also require reforms in the way that medical providers are paid—that is, paying doctors for doing the right thing at the right time. Fee-for-service payments promote productivity but also encourage overuse. Conversely, paying doctors a straight salary in heavily regulated markets may lead to underperformance, because it fails to reward productivity. Successful reform will involve changing the payment structure so that it rewards quality and performance. The overuse issue can be reduced by introducing copayments, which has proved to be a good deterrent. Of course, there is no one-size-fits-all model of health care, and every country's system should reflect its individual history and values, but structural change has to take into account these factors and aim at encouraging medical providers to be more efficient by increasing competition.

NOTES

1 OECD, 2001

2 According to Herbertson and Orszag (2001), early retirement reduces the growth potential of OECD countries by 5 to 7 percent, depending on the country's situation. In the European Union the average is 7 percent.

3 European Commission, 2005

4 Gruber and Wise, 1999

5 Under the direction of Tito Boeri, 2000

6 Chile does this with "recognition bonds."

7 World Bank, 1994

8 World Bank, 2005

9 UK Pension Commission Report, 2004; H. M. Treasury, 2003

10 The Economist, 2004

INCREASING EUROPEAN
UNION EFFICIENCY
AND PRODUCTIVITY

MANY of the EU's economic problems stem from market issues rather than resource shortages and/or excess or deficiency of overall demand. To most economists, the need for structural reforms seems obvious. Such reforms may impose costs on some citizens in the short run but will likely make most citizens better off in the long run. Most economists believe that the opposition of those negatively affected can be overcome through government compensation, which unfortunately rarely happens.

STRUCTURAL REFORM PROBLEMS

The first problem with structural reforms is that the gains to be had from them are never as clear to the public as they are to economists. If, for instance, interest rate ceilings are removed, the prices of loans will reflect risk accurately and loans will be allocated more efficiently. If lenders such as private banks aim to maximize profits, they will simply not lend to projects that require a break-even rate above the ceiling, shutting out risky, though perhaps worthwhile, projects. But if lenders do not care about profits or cannot accurately evaluate risks, they will be inundated with loan applications from high-risk borrowers with financially unviable projects. Because lenders cannot charge an interest rate that exceeds the ceiling, they may use other ways of choosing among applicants willing to pay a higher rate, or a higher bribe. Thus, lenders, often state-owned, will not only succumb to corruption but will make very risky loans. Therefore, when rate ceilings are in place, regardless of whether lenders maximize profits, loans are not optimal, which means that the economy assumes too little or too much risk.[1]

Only a high-minded and highly articulate politician can appreciate these arguments and compress them into persuasive slogans that will sell interest rate liberalization to the public. If this same politician is worried about being reelected, he or she will not introduce the idea. Another problem with selling structural reforms is the short-run costs to some citizens. For example, a reform that makes it easier for companies to make labor reductions enhances a firm's ability to shape its workforce and makes it more willing to hire new workers. In the short run, firms may use the new freedom to lay off many workers, and workers concerned about the job uncertainty that the reform implies may consume less, thereby reducing growth. However, though it may seem paradoxical to the noneconomist, in the long run greater freedom to lay off workers should boost employment and incomes. These same kinds of short-term and long-term trade-offs will result from reducing subsidies or protections on dying industries.

Moreover, the costs and benefits from structural reforms may also accrue to different people. Economists believe that if reform is beneficial overall, those who benefit could, in principle, compensate those who are harmed. If the compensation actually took place, the losers would be more likely to drop their opposition, and everyone would benefit. Unfortunately, such compensation may be hard to implement. How, for instance, should one compensate a steelworker who loves his job and knows that he will never again find work that pays anything remotely near his current salary? And how will compensation arrangements differentiate between good laid-off workers—who will find new jobs—and bad workers without destroying the incentive for the former to remain in the workforce? How can workers be sure that once they give up their job, public opinion will support their benefits into the future when they are powerless? The bottom line is that those who perceive themselves to be potential los-ers, possibly the majority of people given the surrounding uncer-tainty, may oppose reforms, and their cohesiveness makes them a very effective lobby.[2]

The discrepancy between the widely accepted notion of bene-ficial structural reforms and the mixed implementation record in industrial countries highlights the importance of understanding the obstacles to reform. The basic belief is that reforms lack political via-bility, which as the growing literature suggests, arises because the benefits are unevenly distributed across the economy and time.[3] Pol-icymakers who would like to pursue reforms may be confronted with a status quo bias—a situation in which reforms are not supported by a majority or strongly opposed by a key constituency. However, the broad trend toward regulatory reform over the past two decades shows that the status quo bias is not insurmountable even when con-sidering the differences in scope and speed of reforms across coun-tries. Policymakers also face uncertainty about what constitutes optimal government intervention in case of market failure, raising questions about the economy's exposure to shocks as well as people's attitudes toward risk and preferences regarding the sometimes inevitable trade-offs between efficiency and equity.[4]

Despite these major impediments, policymakers do implement reforms. According to the IMF (2004A), reforms take place when:

- There is a period of low or negative growth—such as the one in the UK in the 1980s, the Nordic countries in the 1990s, or more recently in Germany, France, and Italy—which is conducive to reforms because it causes people to see the need for them and weakens opposing interest groups.
- There is room in the budget to compensate for the reforms. It helps to have such flexibility if, for example, interest groups need to be paid off. In the 1980s and 1990s, Dutch labor reforms were aided by sizable budgetary support. While unemployment, sickness, and

disability benefits were cut, taxes and social security contributions were also cut, making the reforms more palatable.

- They feed off other reforms. For example, product market reforms appear to make labor reforms easier, perhaps because when competition pressures are unleashed, organized labor may be forced to worry about the risk to employers if it does not accept greater flexibility.
- They are aided by external pressures. If a country's three main industrial trading partners implement reforms, its own reform efforts typically also increase. It seems that one country's reforms make firms in partner countries less competitive and force them to either change or perish. Thus, external policy competition could be a strong force for improving the business environment rather than, as is often alleged, leading to a race to the bottom.
- A country joins an international economic organization, such as the OECD or IMF, or an area of integration such as the EU. We know that the EU has fostered trade and product market reforms and that the Monetary Union has increased financial reforms in the euro area, while the IMF surveillance system is a global form of international peer pressure.
- Small interest groups have more power in proportional voting systems. In majority-driven systems, a party needs to cater only to a sizable bloc to achieve a majority or the sufficient plurality needed to govern, and it does not have to attract every interest group. This implies that reforms should be easier in majority systems, and indeed they are. We only need to witness the great number of reforms implemented in Anglo-Saxon countries. The most determined reformers in these counties turn out to be those with stronger majorities in parliament.

However, reforms do not always produce benefits. In fact, as argued earlier, labor market reforms seem particularly difficult, not only because they can lead to a short-term dip in growth and employment but also because the costs fall disproportionately on some citizens.

The IMF (2004A) recently enumerated five recommendations for implementing structural reforms:

1. Since every country is unique, reformers in industrial countries have the luxury of timing their reforms (however, this timing may not be available to a developing country or a country in crisis where the distortion costs may be much larger).

2. Reforms should be started during the recovery from an economic downturn when people are focused on the need for reform and recovery promises a faster reward.

3. Budgetary surpluses should be used to buy reforms. Reforms are tough even in the best of times, and the ability to compensate losers helps soften the blow.

4. The first reforms should be those that may realize more immediate benefits. For example, when trade and financial market reforms produce benefits even in the short run, they not only have a demonstration effect but also may increase competitive pressures and make further reform easier.

5. If adequate resources are unavailable, the country should try to secure foreign support either from its surrounding area or from an international organization.

The main obstacle to introducing structural reforms in the EU is that Europe prides itself on a political system that rests solidly on an institutionalized cooperation between governments and social partners. Business associations, unions, and employee and employer representatives have a privileged position in virtually all policy areas and unparalleled access to political leaders. The underlying rationale is that, by consulting with trade unions and employer associations, governments can demonstrate that a cross-section of society backs their policies, which in turn leads to better policymaking and greater justice. Although the social partners' dialogue is an excellent and democratic idea, it has become a stumbling block that makes it more difficult for governments to undertake structural reforms.

In fact, as the IMF (2004) has stressed, the scope and speed of structural reforms has differed widely among industrial countries and sectors. Some countries, such as Australia, Canada, New Zealand, the UK, the US, and some Nordic countries began reforms in the 1980s and 1990s. Others, such as Germany, France, and Italy began partial reform efforts only a few years ago. In addition, despite similar initial conditions, the early reformers' efforts in selected product markets and tax systems typically exceeded those in most continental European countries. As a consequence, despite recent steps by the latter countries, excessive product and labor market regulations continue to impede growth and employment.[5]

The importance of structural reforms is well confirmed by recent IMF empirical analyses (2003) on the relationship of labor and product market institutions and regulations to GDP and unemployment performance. These analyses combined with the IMF Global Economy Model (GEM) show that: (1) if euro area labor markets became as competitive as those of the US, that area's GDP would increase by about 5.5 percent in the long term, and unemployment rates would be reduced by 3.5 percent, and (2) if the euro area product markets were as competitive as those in the US, the total impact would be nearly doubled, with GDP increasing by 10 percent in the long run and unemployment falling by 6.5 percent, bringing unemployment to levels unseen since the 1970s.

NECESSARY STRUCTURAL REFORMS

Welfare State and Labor Reforms

Since the Lisbon Summit, the EU's labor market performance has been disappointing. In 2000, annual employment growth peaked at

2 percent after growing at an average of 0.4 percent since 1960; it then fell almost to 0 in 2004 and is expected to remain weak in 2005. The EU employment rate for people aged 15 to 64 was 63.4 percent in 2000, and it is expected to rise to only 65 percent in 2005. In 2000, the target of achieving an employment rate of 70 percent in 2010 implied that employment had to grow 1 percent annually, but now in 2005 it would need to be 1.5 percent for the remainder of the term, which seems impossible. Thus, to increase the EU employment rate and its labor performance, some structural reforms are needed.

Labor markets differ from all other markets because they deal with humans and so the textbook assumptions behind a competitive economy—complete markets, perfect information, atomistic and homogeneous agents, and perfect competition—rarely apply. Nominal wages result from negotiations between employers and employees, while firms set their prices as markups over labor costs. While in the short run, unemployment is determined by real aggregate demand, in the long run it converges with a level that is compatible with a stable inflation rate.[6] Under this framework, labor market policies influence employment and unemployment by modifying the wage formation mechanism, changing the price elasticity of product demand, and stimulating technological progress.

Another way to look at labor market performance is as the outcome of matching workers and job vacancies.[7] Heterogeneity of workers and jobs, imperfect information about the characteristics of potential employers and employees, and restrictions on labor mobility all generate market frictions, which in turn influence labor market flows. In the steady state, inflows into unemployment are equal to outflows from unemployment, and there is an inverse relationship (the Beveridge Curve) between the number of vacancies and the unemployment rate, that is, the lower the number of vacancies, the higher the unemployment rate.[8] Within this framework, anything that improves the efficiency of matching unemployed people and vacancies and/or increases the exit from unemployment will shift the curve and reduce the steady state of unemployment.

Within both frameworks, labor market institutions—unemployment and welfare-related benefits, wage bargaining, labor market regulation, and labor taxation—affect firms' hiring and firing decisions, individuals' readiness and willingness to take up jobs, and the extent to which unemployment reins in inflationary pressures. However, the impact of labor policies and reforms is often ambiguous, at least in theory. For instance, unemployment benefits are subject to "moral hazard," since job-search efforts cannot be fully observed, thus benefits can reduce the incentive to find a job and raise reservation wages. But in search models with risk-averse workers and imperfect capital markets, the absence of unemployment insurance may lead people to accept jobs too quickly rather than wait for a higher productivity match that would increase their overall welfare.

Current labor market studies have been unable to completely define the effect of labor market institutions on employment performance.[9] First, in trying to correlate the member countries' labor market institutions and their unemployment rate differences, unemployment is positively associated with generous unemployment benefits in terms of replacement rates and duration,[10] a high tax wedge,[11] high minimum wages,[12] high union coverage and density,[13] and low labor sector[14] and geographic mobility.[15] On the other hand, unemployment is negatively associated with active labor market policies[16] and most times, but not always, with a high degree of coordination in wage bargaining.[17] However, empirical evidence shows that labor market institutions were much more unfavorable in the 1960s, when EU unemployment levels were much lower than in the US.[18]

Second, when looking at the interactions of labor market institutions and macroeconomic shocks, it at first seems rather clear that transitory increases in unemployment due to shocks may be prolonged by institutions that restrict labor flows and protract wage adjustments. However, there are cases in which union density or employment protection do not affect the length of these transitory effects, which are instead affected by labor mobility and benefit duration.

Third, when looking at the interactions between different labor market institutions, some studies show that a wide range of institutions may have complementary effects on unemployment, while others show that when they reinforce each other, they may affect performance negatively. For instance, high labor taxes combined with high unemployment benefit replacement rates weaken the financial incentives for employment and increase unemployment. In sum, these studies suggest that labor market institutions can explain a significant share of cross-country differences in unemployment rates and labor market performance but also the need to adapt reforms to the specific labor market institutions in every country. Hence, labor reforms should be country-specific.

Why keep labor markets institutions if they distort performance? There are two points of view: the normative and positive views. The *normative* view—the main argument for employment protection,[19] unemployment insurance,[20] and wage compression[21]—emphasizes the role of institutions in insuring risk-averse workers against income volatility when capital markets fail to protect against unemployment and income risks. This view shows clearly that labor market flexibility is not an end in itself and that some institutions have a clear *raison d'etre*. The *positive* view finds that labor institutions are largely shaped by political interests and interest groups that benefit insiders—unionized workers with permanent labor contracts. According to this view, these institutions lower employment rates and protect insiders at the expense of the unemployed, nonunionized, temporary, young, or female workers, by producing a wedge between labor supply and demand, interfering with the allocation of labor, compressing wage distribution, and restricting mobility.[22]

In practice, both views have some validity and need to be considered. The question is then how to design labor market institutions that secure the needed benefits while avoiding their distortions of labor performance. Designing optimal institutions depends on the financial markets' characteristics and the nature and frequency of labor market demand shocks, both of which determine the need for insurance.[23] Some social protection institutions act as substitutes for each other, as in the trade-off between the stringency of employment protection institutions and the generosity of unemployment insurance.[24] Therefore, institutions cannot be regarded as exogenous, and they need to adapt to increased competition in the product markets and technological development. Institutions that worked well in the past may create large employment losses in a more competitive market.

The recent experience of partial EU labor market reforms offers a number of lessons:

- Macroeconomic stability is a precondition for the labor market to perform well because it helps keep wage growth in line with both price stability and productivity developments.
- Incentives, particularly in unemployment benefits and active labor market policies, have led to improved labor market performance.
- The most successful reforms have combined tightening unemployment benefit eligibility with more intensive measures such as employer subsidies, direct job creation, and improved training for groups at higher risks of inactivity or unemployment. Eligibility conditions and job-search requirements may be even more important than the level of benefits.
- The threat of losing benefits if one or several employment offers are not accepted tends to raise the incentive to find a job.[25]
- Liberalizing temporary contracts without relaxing stringent employment protections for permanent contracts may be a risky strategy, causing excess turnover among temporary workers and strengthening the bargaining position of protected workers.
- Labor reforms need to be comprehensive, especially when the labor market is uncompetitive. Only when labor markets are competitive can the economy react quickly and smoothly to changes in interest rates, thereby facilitating the task of monetary authorities to stabilize inflation.

Most member countries' labor reforms have focused mainly on politically feasible issues such as tax cuts in return for wage moderation, expenditure-based policies, and liberalization of part-time work. One exception has been the important and politically difficult measure of reforming the 35-hour week law in France. But, in most EU countries, politically difficult reforms, such as benefit entitlements, wage bargaining, or employment protections, are still pending. The optimal way to address labor-market reforms is not through partial and relatively easy measures but rather through a comprehensive package that requires major shifts at both the macro and micro level. In other words, shifting the wage setting mechanism by: (1) redefining rules, norms, and the nature of contractual arrangements (perhaps combined with tax reforms), (2) rebalancing measures designed to protect workers from labor-demand shocks (employment protection or unemployment insurance), and (3) reforming the duration and eligibility criteria of unemployment and other benefits while enforcing job-search requirements and implementing measures for those unable to find work. Finally, labor markets need to be inclusive, so policies should reduce the risks of marginalization and long-term unemployment, which are still very high in most EU countries.

The debate on how to reform the EU labor market has been dominated by the perception of a trade-off between efficiency and equity. Blanchard (2004) presents this as a production possibility frontier, with efficiency on one axis and equity on the other. However, several EU countries are located inside such a frontier. Taxes and transfer management entails administrative costs and deadweight losses as well as risks of welfare dependency. Although designing institutions is not a best practice, reform may be done in ways that can improve both efficiency and equity or at least improve one without compromising the other. For example, the equity-efficiency trade-off may be low when transfers go to people with no capacity to change their behavior, when benefits are paid to those conditioned to meet certain behavioral requirements, or when payments change the behavior or opportunities so that income increases in the future.[26]

Unemployment benefit and labor market reforms that withdraw entitlement to benefits for those not actively seeking employment may be perceived as inequitable, but they have been effective, particularly in reducing youth unemployment, so it seems difficult to argue that equity or social cohesion overall have been adversely affected. Employment protection legislation has a clear impact on income distribution, but not necessarily in a way that everybody would agree is equitable, since it protects established employees partly at the expense of groups that are worse off like the unemployed or those on temporary contracts. Moreover, protection often takes the form of administrative and legal costs and delays; thus, a policy that reduces these deadweight costs can increase efficiency and improve income distribution while facilitating redundancy payments. However, there is no clear consensus about labor reforms, and some studies argue against them.[27]

The most successful reforms are those that improve market performance by increasing employment and reducing unemployment in the long term. This is the case of the UK's labor policies, which have improved its performance by tax and benefit reform reinforced by job-search policies. The same can be said for the Netherlands' wage moderation combined with reducing the tax burden on labor and tightening benefit systems and job-search requirements, especially for the younger unemployed. Denmark has reformed unemployment benefits and active labor market policies, shifting the emphasis toward job search rather than automatic benefit entitlement and reducing the unemployment rate among the young. Spain has reduced after-tax entitlements and their duration and has achieved wage moderation.

LEISURE-LOVING EUROPEANS?

The idea that Europeans are "leisure loving" is partly true, but mostly an illusion. While Europeans do work fewer hours than Americans, it is hardly their choice to trade higher productivity for more leisure instead of more income except in high-productivity level countries such as France and Germany.[28] To be unemployed is definitely not a social choice: two-thirds of the gap in hours worked results from the EU's lower employment. The spread of part-time employment in Europe, especially among women, may partly explain the misperception. Although part-time employment rates do not differ much between the US and EU, Europe has more nonworking days or holidays as well as higher taxes on wages.[29]

A survey by Roper Starch Worldwide (2000) asked about social choices on both sides of the Atlantic, and found that 57 percent of Americans said that they would prefer more money to more time off, while only 37 percent prefer more time off. The same survey found that well over 50 percent of Germans, Italians, and British and 67 percent of the French also prefer more income to more leisure time. These results show that Europeans may have reached what they consider the optimal level of leisure time and that they are ready to try to improve their income. However, according to the latest Eurobarometer,[30] when EU citizens are asked about how to improve economic performance, only 13 percent think working hours should be increased![31]

Thus, what seems to be a choice is really more the result of public policies, regulations, and incentives.[32] The low participation rates among older workers result mainly from generous pension systems, while low employment rates among women and younger workers result from institutions that protect insiders by increasing their bargaining power to exclude others. So while women and younger workers might be willing to work for less, they are excluded by weaker incentives and redistributive policies that benefit the elderly.

For this reason, the EU must increase incentives to work and reduce the inefficiencies of welfare state regulations. Among economists there is almost unanimous consensus about reforming the European welfare system. The pay-as-you-go systems absorb too many resources and are unsustainable in the medium to long term. The overall tax on labor reaches distorting levels, creating disincentives to work and reducing demand. In addition, labor regulations create not only unemployment but also allocation distortions that make it more difficult for the EU to benefit from technology. At the same time, despite extensive government intervention and redistribution, some groups are systematically excluded from welfare benefits and valuable job opportunities.

Unfortunately, most Europeans seem not to understand these issues. A 2000 survey of the four largest member countries—with very different welfare systems—(Germany, France, Italy and Spain) reveal some telling results[33]:

- First, despite widespread understanding of their weaknesses, many respondents underestimate the true cost of their pension system, which means that few voters are likely to favor reforms.
- Second, public opinion, and not just a powerful minority, supports the status quo of the welfare state. However, in all countries a large majority also opposes further tax increases, which means, paradoxically, that they oppose reforms that would shrink the current size of the welfare state but favor reforms that would prevent further expansion as the population ages.
- Third, even though a majority opposes changing the overall size of the welfare state, large segments of the population would welcome changes in how benefits are provided or allocated. Most seem willing to opt out of the public pension system and replace it with private pensions, while in Italy the majority wants to shift away from pensions toward unemployment benefits.
- Fourth, conflicts of interest align along three main dimensions: age, income, and insider/outsider status, which suggests that one-dimensional median voter models are too simplistic. In other words, large-scale consensus could be built by strategically packaging and bundling reforms.

Therefore, the survey shows that there are dual labor markets with insiders—those who are employed and protected and do not want more money spent on insurance against unemployment—and outsiders—those who are unemployed, unprotected, or working under unsecured fixed-term or temporary "junk" contracts and want more unemployment benefits. Since this is a major point of disagreement and political conflict, the right package of reforms could attract a large coalition. Clearly, the member countries need to: (1) make insider contracts less permanent and more insecure by reducing firing costs and restrictions, and (2) make outsider contracts more permanent and secure by increasing permanent part-time contracts at the expense of unsecured temporary and fixed-term contracts. In the EU, 17 percent of all employment contracts are part time, ranging from 34 percent in the Netherlands to under 7 percent in Spain and Greece. The latter countries have the lowest employment rates for females and younger workers and the largest number of temporary fixed-term contracts. The spread of permanent part-time contracts has helped the Netherlands and Nordic countries to employ large numbers of young people and women, thus increasing employment rates and contributors to their social security systems, as well as helping the financial sustainability of their pension systems.

The trade-offs between employment protection legislation (EPL) and unemployment benefits (UB) suggest some politically viable reforms. In Italy and Spain, the governments could find it easier to reduce firing restrictions if they were accompanied by extended unemployment coverage. Such a bundle could receive support from both temporary and unemployed workers—those willing to pay for unemployment insurance and those already covered by it. Furthermore, the extended coverage could be self-financed because workers who benefit from it seem to be willing to pay more than required to maintain the insurance. For France and Germany, though, this strategy is less likely to pay off because they already have very generous unemployment benefits. However, they could extend coverage to workers with relatively short contribution records and reduce the maximum duration of benefits for those already covered. These reforms are likely to improve the efficiency of UB systems because long-term unemployment has been linked to long benefit duration. Finally, the survey found that demand for UB declines with age, which suggests that old-age pensions can be regarded as a substitute for unemployment insurance. If this is the case, then opposition to smaller pension benefits could be reduced by expanding UB coverage.

The EU must also address the very heavy tax on labor. The data about the tax wedge—the difference between what workers take home after paying taxes and social security contributions—is extremely high, especially when compared to other OECD countries and the US. The average EU income tax bracket is around 50 percent versus 30 percent in the US.[34] This higher tax wedge is the price the EU pays for a more generous welfare state, but high tax wedges are disincentives to work and have a lot to do with the lower number of hours worked by employees and Europe's earlier retirement age. Economic theory offers ways to tax more efficiently and with less distortion on productive resources. One guiding principle is that it is better to tax consumption than income, because taxing what is spent rather than what is earned does less damage to incentives to save. A heavy tax on wages produces a disincentive to work and an incentive to dedicate more time to leisure. If wages and the interest on savings are both taxed, then any wages saved are taxed twice making the disincentive greater.

Adding to the unemployment benefits problem are the generous minimum wages that were enacted under pressure from protected insiders but that price many people out of the labor market when they might be willing to take a lower-paying job. The generous unemployment benefits and minimum wages reduce the demand for jobs and in turn the employment rate.

The survey also offers some ideas for pension reforms. The majority of the working population in the four countries surveyed does not know, or underestimates, the magnitude of its public pension systems, and almost half incorrectly think that these systems are in balance or even in surplus. Thus, educating the public about the system's costs is important to any politically successful reform. Politicians, union leaders, and opinion makers who minimize both the costs and the future problems faced by social security systems make reforms less likely. Moreover, successful reforms must be simple and transparent so that voters can recognize the true problems and costs.

Despite inadequate quantitative information, more than two-thirds of respondents in France, Germany, and Italy expect a pension crisis, particularly a reduction in pension levels and a significantly higher retirement age. Only workers in Spain were more optimistic. The more pessimistic respondents were willing to opt out of the present pay-as-you-go system, but more optimistic ones were not willing to do so. What is interesting is that those who are less informed are more optimistic, and those more informed are more pessimistic, which is why this issue is less hotly debated in Spain than in Italy or Germany. As we would expect, public pensions are also more popular among older, poorer, less educated, and less informed workers. They are also more popular among individuals with permanent and protected contracts. As with UB, union membership and political position do not seem to affect opinion. The survey finds three relevant divisions: between young and old, rich and poor, and labor market insiders and outsiders. These divisions suggest that opting out proposals could be packaged to appeal to large voting blocs. For example, if poor and older individuals are less willing to opt out, their vote could be attracted by offering them a more favorable deal to opt out.

As we have seen, the EU must undertake pension reform not only because of the system's uncertainty but also to ensure inter-generational solidarity. The EU's older generation suffered through World War II and, in the case of Spain, a civil war, as well as the secondary consequences of the Great Depression. Though the population was decimated, during the golden postwar years it was easy to find jobs and prosper, and as a result this generation is very likely to have acquired decent pensions. However, the current generation is finding it much harder to find jobs because of stronger competition; they eventually find less protected jobs or are unemployed. As a result, they marry later and have fewer children because they are uncertain about future income and because housing is much more expensive. Some face tougher competition for jobs from immigrants, and, what is worse, they are not sure of receiving decent pensions when they retire. It is all really very unfair.

Thus, while shrinking the welfare state may be very difficult politically, it is not impossible because there appears to be room for reforms that redesign its key components—costs and sustainability. By bundling complementary reforms and finding the right voting coalitions, greater labor flexibility can be achieved as well as partial privatization of pension funds. To this end, French and German business associations, firms, and trade unions have agreed to increase the number of working hours without increasing wages in order to remain competitive and avoid outsourcing and off-shoring to third countries.

PRODUCT MARKET REFORMS

There is wide consensus that product market reforms have a significant impact on productivity. Most studies show that reforms that facilitate market entry and raise the level of competition on goods and services result in productivity gains of between 2 percent and 4 percent because of the way in which product markets are open to competition, increase in size and scope, and improve in activity and structure. Regulations may block rather than spur economic activity, stifling initiative rather than encouraging it.[35]

Product market reforms aim to improve the conditions under which business operates. There are four main types of product market reforms:

- Measures to open goods and services markets that were previously sheltered from foreign competition by tariff barriers (trade openness) or legal barriers (liberalization).
- Measures to open markets that were previously sheltered from new competition by stringent regulations on entry (i.e., permits and licenses) or nontariff barriers (i.e., national regulations or deregulation).

- Measures to create a more business-friendly environment, such as reducing the time and costs to set up a new company or creating appropriate levels and systems of taxation.
- Measures to reduce state distortions of markets such as state aid, subsidies, and state-owned firms. (The Single Market Program is the most comprehensive and paradigmatic exercise of product market reform because it removes all barriers to the free movement of goods, services, people, and capital within the EU.)[36]

Product market reforms not only tend to increase productivity,[37] but they also lead to more labor reforms. Once easier reforms are made in trade, product, and financial sectors, reform pressures increase in more contentious areas like labor and taxes. The incentives for mobilizing against reforms are reduced when firms have weaker pricing power in more competitive markets because the rents shared between producers and workers are also reduced. Thus, complementary reform structures need to be efficiently researched.

Product market reforms both directly and indirectly affect productivity. The direct impacts reduce the costs of doing business and remove barriers to penetrating new markets. The indirect effects emanate from liberalizing or improving how markets function, which positively impacts productivity by reallocating scarce resources (allocative efficiency), improving production factors (productive efficiency), and creating incentives to innovate and explore technology (dynamic efficiency). The productivity increases from distributive and productive efficiencies operate in the short to medium term, while those derived from dynamic efficiency operate over the long term.

All product market reforms aim to increase competition, which tends to improve distributive efficiency by putting a downward pressure on prices and markups, reducing the incumbents' market power by increasing the number of competitors, and provoking industry restructuring and a better and more efficient allocation of inputs, labor, and capital. In competition-driven industries when services are restructuring, low-productivity firms exit the market (selection effect), high-productivity firms expand domestically, and some enter the foreign markets (reallocation effect). This leads to an increase in aggregate productivity, even if there is no productivity growth within firms, although in the absence of a strong competition policy it can sometimes produce an excess of concentration and higher mark-ups and prices.

By expanding competition, product market reforms also increase productive efficiency by generating incentives for managers to reduce slack, trim fat, and structure the workplace more efficiently. First, competition tends to increase information about other competitors, creating greater opportunities to compare performance and making it easier for shareholders to monitor managers and reduce slack. Second, in highly competitive markets where price elasticity is higher, cost-reducing productivity improvements are likely to generate large increases in market shares and profits—another incentive for managers to reduce costs. Third, greater competition also increases the probability of bankruptcy, so managers have an incentive to avoid such failure. Fourth, competition may also influence workers' involvement and efforts because they are also likely to capture part of the higher profits.

Finally, product market reforms increase dynamic efficiency because increased competition motivates firms to develop product and process innovations and to quickly upgrade technology. Successful innovations will eventually increase growth and total factor productivity, producing, in the long run, greater profits for innovative firms and higher incomes for their workers.

The single market and active competition policies are the cornerstones of the EU's efforts to improve growth. The single market dates back to 1992, but there are still 134 internal market directives that have not been transformed into national law in all member countries! France has the worst implementation record followed by Greece, Germany, Italy, and the Benelux countries. Moreover, infringements against already implemented directives continue even though the goal was to reduce them by 50 percent. Italy has the most infringement cases, followed by France. Italy alone accounts for 30 percent of all cases, although most infringement cases tend to be solved early through the SOLVIT network. EU progress toward becoming a fully functioning single market has slowed since 2000 because intra-EU trade and direct foreign investment have stagnated. Some 80 percent of intra-EU trade is still in goods, leaving only 20 percent in services. The best measure of the single market is price convergence among countries for standard goods and services. Since 2000, prices for well-known brands have diverged, while others have converged slightly with nonbranded goods, averaging out the convergence.[38]

As proposed by the Lisbon Agenda, fully achieving the single market must be the main priority, because without it the EU will not be able to promote competition, new investment, employment, and growth. The free exit and entry of firms in each market is the only way to ensure a more efficient and prosperous EU, because it will increase competition among firms and reduce incumbent monopoly and oligopoly rents, in turn reducing prices to consumers and investors and proportionately increasing their purchasing power, disposable income, and prosperity. Without a fully functioning and integrated single market, other efforts will be wasted. Thus, every national market regulation should be examined on a case-by-case basis to analyze how it will affect innovation and new firms' entry. Currently, ensuring new entry in single market legislation is not an objective but only the result of an integrated market.

Nevertheless, a functioning single market requires more than implementing regulations. It also requires a physical infrastructure for exchanging people, goods, capital, and ideas. The member countries themselves are responsible for the basic physical infrastructure with the EU Structural Fund contributing to regional or national infrastructures to help resolve "missing links" between national systems. Enlargement makes this effort all the more important since it adds an east-west dimension to the previous north-south effort.

The active competition policy plays an essential role in ensuring that the open market realizes its potential gains. In the past, competition policy has been an effective lever in opening certain markets and checking anticompetitive behavior. In the future, strenuous efforts will be needed to ensure that markets become or remain competitive. When implementing competition policies, particular care should be taken to acknowledge the changing nature of markets in which innovation and new entry take place as well as R&D's role in opening competition.[39]

R&D's role in competition shows how fully today's circumstances differ from those of 1992, and how the structure and nature of the markets have changed. Tools of economic management that proved effective in the past no longer display the same efficiency. The nature of integration itself changes with an economy dominated by services and intangible investments rather than manufactured products and tangible goods. Rights of establishment and therefore direct foreign investment become more important for trade as does knowledge creation through higher education. Thus R&D has become a driver of growth.

Unlike the postwar period when Europe could grow and catch up with the US through factor accumulation and imitation, as European countries move closer to the technology frontier and as new communication and information technologies evolve, innovation has become the main engine of growth. In turn, new organizational forms are required that allow for less vertically integrated firms, greater mobility both intra- and interfirm, more flexible labor markets, further reliance on market finance, and more demand for R&D and higher education.

Accelerating the single market will require either huge improvements or faster implementation. Completing the Single Market for Financial Services is crucial, especially, the Risk Capital Action Plan and Financial Services Action Plans because they increase innovation in the services and utilities sectors. The lack of labor mobility, whether within countries, between EU countries, between the EU and nonmember countries, or between firms, has hindered the economy's capacity to adjust to the new market's changing nature and structure. In Europe, labor mobility is often seen as a negative that creates insecurity rather than as a positive way to seek better earnings and improve status and career. Mobility can be supported through special regulations and changes in the welfare systems, for example, by removing all restrictions on the transferability and compatibility of acquired rights for health, pensions, and unemployment. In addition, all temporary cross-border restrictions put on new member countries should be removed to speed up integration and cohesion. The EU should also have a common immigration policy that encourages legal immigration, especially from third countries in order to counter the effects of the aging population.

The recent OECD Report on Economic Policy Reforms[40] introduces a series of arguments and priorities for reform. Among the methods it suggests to increase labor productivity are:

- Reducing French, German, Spanish, and Italian barriers to entry into network industries such as electricity, telecommunications, railways, and professional services.
- Lowering administrative burdens for start-ups in countries such as Spain, Austria, and Greece.
- Easing the regulations on businesses that arise from price controls or administrative procedures in Belgium, Ireland, and the Netherlands.
- Reducing the extent of public ownership in countries such as Finland, France, Italy, Portugal, and Sweden.

FOSTERING A KNOWLEDGE SOCIETY

As an economy gets closer to the educational frontier, the importance of higher education and R&D becomes greater. One of the major problems that the EU faces going forward is that in comparison to the US it under-invests in R&D and higher education—only 1.9 percent of GDP in R&D and 1.4 percent in higher education.

Research & Development

Only Sweden and Finland invest more in R&D than the US's 3.0 percent. Even more important are the sources of R&D investment—in the US, private R&D investment is twice as high as public and continues to grow, while in the EU it is almost the reverse and declining. Even the amount invested by the US public sector in R&D is higher than that in the EU. Patents provide a good but partial measure of R&D output, and the US is far ahead. Another measure of R&D strength, the number of researchers per 1,000 workers in the labor force, is only 5.5 in the EU versus 8 in the US.

Therefore, the EU should invest much more in R&D in order to quickly reach 3 percent of GDP and obtain the level of knowledge required to reach a higher growth path. Both the EU central organization and the member countries' governments should avoid trying to "pick winners" with an excessive "top-down" approach as well as covert subsidies to private companies, and should use instead a clear, well-planned, and integrated research framework. Deficiencies in private R&D investment can be overcome through tax credits that stimulate R&D at the company level. The problem of insufficient public support should also be addressed at both the EU and member country levels—the government should increase investment in those countries that are below average, and the EU should redirect resources from its budget to finance a pan European research network of the best European researchers.

First, the highly fragmented European research community should be clustered and integrated to gain economies of scale in different areas of specialization as well as the implementation or "development" of this research. Moreover, available resources must only be allocated on the basis of the best research available and with the highest standards to help consolidate and integrate the best research only in major centers of excellence. The main problem today in the EU is "brain drain" to the US. More than 400,000 European researchers are currently living in the US because it offers better salaries, better research incentives to market their output, more time for research activities, better conditions, and a better infrastructure. This brain drain is a huge loss for the EU, and something very urgent and dramatic must be done in order to stem the flow and reattract those who left.

In the face of these issues, it is difficult to understand why half the EU budget is still devoted to subsidizing agriculture, an uncompetitive activity of the past that developing countries do inexpensively and more efficiently than the EU countries can. In addition, the subsidies are regressive because they are financed through value-added tax (VAT) revenue, which is paid mainly by the most modest EU families, because they consume a larger fraction of their disposable income, and is disbursed to a small, aging group of farmers (fewer than 900,000), of which the 40,000 richest get the largest percentage of subsidies. Moreover, in order to keep these few farmers competitive, the EU imposes tariffs on most imported food and agricultural products, making European consumers pay twice the international price and reducing the disposable income of poorer families who spend a higher proportion of their income on food. It is truly a scandal! These resources should be rechanneled to activities that make the European economy more competitive and innovative and that increase regional cohesion. These subsidies are evidence that the EU's resources are not applied to its citizens' real needs and explain why in turn the EU's citizens are not willing to approve increased taxes.

Higher Education

The EU also lags behind the US in higher education. The EU spends 1.4 percent of GDP on higher education, of which 1.1 percent is public and only 0.3 percent private, versus 3 percent in the US of which 1.4 percent is public and 1.6 percent is private. The highest level of education attained by adults (25 to 64) in the EU is: 38 percent below upper secondary, 37.3 percent upper secondary and postsecondary, and 23.8 percent higher education. In the US the breakdown is: 12.3 percent, 50.3 percent, and 37.3 percent, respectively, which makes the US much more integrated into the knowledge society, and thus better adapted to the increasing competition of emerging nations. Moreover, the EU also suffers from a higher education system that is neither sufficiently open to international influences nor sufficiently oriented toward the highest standards of excellence, particularly at the postgraduate level. This means that incentives, performance, evaluation, benchmarking, and competition should play a much greater role in organizing universities and assessing qualifications.

Thus, the areas that need improvement are rather clear. The EU needs more mobility for students and faculty by establishing a total equivalence between undergraduate degrees and curricula across European countries and giving incentives to students and professors to move from one country to another and to the best universities in each area. This effort is also important at the postgraduate level, where promoting excellence and mobility can concentrate education in large graduate centers as in the US. Grants and other subsidies should be allocated to the best postgraduate students. A large pooling of resources could be achieved if the EU created a Pan European Science Foundation, similar to the National Science Foundation, which has proven highly efficient. Based on advice from eminent researchers, this independent foundation would allocate resources to only the best independent research.

The EU also needs to develop an *information society*. The US is far ahead of the EU in all international indexes of information production and use. In the latest IDC index, the US ranks third behind Sweden and Denmark with a score of 950 out of 1,000 points. The EU average is 700 with Germany at 800, France at 750, and Italy at 580. A recent OECD report, "Seizing the Benefits of ICT," shows how important ICT production and use are for growth. First, ICT enhances productivity in firms of all sizes and shapes. Second, it makes firms less vulnerable to business cycle downturns and puts them in a better position to benefit from the upturns. Third, its applications increase continuously, and its prices fall. Finally, in spite of the technology bubble, ICT continues to flourish and make firms that use and produce it more productive by raising their efficiency and productivity, forcing workers to improve their skills, giving more responsibility to workers in flatter management structures, enabling outsourcing so firms can focus on core activities, and encouraging innovation.

One of the puzzles surrounding ICT is that even though it is a generally pervasive technology, some OECD countries like the US, the Nordic countries, and Australia have reported greater productivity gains as a result of it than others like Germany, France, Canada, and Japan. To explain these differences, we need to look at ICT investment. The former countries have invested more in ICT than the latter. They have also fostered environments that are more conducive to new business. Their competitive business environments are also more likely to entice firms to invest in ICT to strengthen performance or survive. However, ICT is not a magic bullet; it needs to be accompanied by complementary policies that:

- Provide overinvesting but avoid misdirecting these technologies
- Foster an open, entrepreneurial, pro innovation, and pro risk environment
- Allow for labor flexibility to help make the necessary changes and adaptations[41]
- Encourage ICT use in small firms by providing legal advice, assessing market opportunities, and building networks
- Build public confidence in ICT by switching to e-government services and reducing uncertainties over payments, contracts, delivery guarantees, and above all security (fighting hackers and viruses)

CULTURAL AND INSTITUTIONAL CHOICES

Robert Gordon (2004) argues that policy reform in Europe has been too narrowly focused on deregulating product and labor markets.

He believes that a broader set of social choices matter for productivity and that some of the productivity differences between the US and EU may be irreversible. He believes that much of the surprising acceleration of US productivity since 1995 originates in the trade sector, particularly retail,[42] and goes far beyond the use of ICT. The US retail sector has been revolutionized by *big box* retailing—large stores offering a wide array of low-priced goods and relatively high use of self-service systems—epitomized by Wal-Mart. Almost all the retail productivity growth in the 1990s resulted from more productive new establishments that displaced less productive ones. The most important factor enabling the big box is a large plot of virgin land, which is more widely available in sprawling US exurban areas than in the tightly regulated European environment of land-use planning and protection of old central city retail zones. Cheap and available land and scarce labor in the US have provided a strong motivation to buy, install, and invent labor-saving machinery as well as to invest in mass production and distribution. Thus, the US explosion in retail productivity is mainly due to basic life-style choices that constitute another form of the "American exception." While the US form of metropolitan organization may promote productivity growth, Europeans are rightly skeptical of their unmeasured costs of low urban density that are promoted by explicit government policies. Europeans think that the US is promoting productivity while simultaneously reducing consumer welfare, including excess energy use, pollution, and time spent in traffic congestion.

Moreover, the superior performance of the US retailing sector in achieving rapid productivity growth may in part be due to a measurement procedure that allows quality improvements in manufacturing to spill over into the retail sector. For example, if a 2005 computer is sold at the same price as a 1995 computer but contains four times the quality measured by a hedonic price regression that includes the computer speed, memory, and additional features, then the 2005 computer represents four times the real output of the manufacturing sector and four times the real sales of the retail sector.

According to Gordon, Europeans find abhorrent the trillions of dollars that the US has spent on extra highways and extra energy to support the population's dispersion into huge metropolitan areas spread over hundreds or thousands of square miles, in many cases with few collective transport options other than cars. Productivity data do not give Europe sufficient credit for the convenience benefits of frequent bus, subway, and trains because private automobile production and use have a higher impact on GDP and productivity statistics than do public expenditures on city and metropolitan transport systems. Many Europeans, by contrast, enjoy shopping at small individually owned shops on lively central city main streets and pedestrian arcades and dislike the large and cheerless malls and big-box retailers common throughout the US; although the malls and big box stores are becoming more prevalent in Europe.

In an earlier work, Gordon explains how GDP comparisons between the US and Europe tend to overstate US living standards.[43] The US has to spend more than Europe on both heating and air conditioning because of its more extreme climates, which boosts GDP but does not enhance society. The US's higher crime rate means that more of its GDP is spent on home and business security. The costs associated with keeping 2 million people in prison—a far larger percentage of the population than in Europe—again boosts GDP but not the common good. Gordon believes that when all these factors are taken into account, Europe's living standards are now less than 10 percent behind the US's. However, the US has two other technology-related advantages: First, English is recognized as the world's second language and is spoken as a first language by a critical mass of the world's educated population; Second, immigrants from India, East Asia, and other countries have provided the skilled labor that has been essential to the rise of Silicon Valley and other technological centers.

According to Edmund Phelps, the cultural productivity and efficiency differences between the US and EU are based on their different economic institutions.[44] Some institutions promote dynamism, while others suppress it. According to Phelps, dynamism, based on Schumpeter's concept of "creative destruction," is composed of entrepreneurship and financiership, which are the keys to innovation and productivity. The US's greater success in encouraging innovation is attributed in part to its capital market-based finance system which places greater emphasis on venture capital and initial public offerings than Europe's bank-based system.

In Phelps's view, the relatively poor economic performance of continental Europe results both from the underdevelopment of capitalist institutions, like venture capital and equity finance, and from the overdevelopment of institutions that are designed to protect incumbent producers and inhibit new entrants. These institutions impose penalties, impediments, prohibitions, and mandates that are generally intended to foil creativity. Among these impediments are licenses and permissions needed to set up a new plant or firm, the need to consult with workers on changes in the mix of products or plants, and employment protection legislation. Because these institutions suppress the changes inherent in "unbridled capitalism," they also lead to the underdevelopment of the stock market, resulting in lower ratios of stock market value to GDP than in the US and other less corporatist economies like the UK, Canada, and Australia. According to Phelps, Europeans view with disdain the money-grubbing Americans with their outsized rewards for CEOs and successful entrepreneurs. Children in the United States begin to work earlier than European children, earning baby-sitting money in their early teens and working in fast-food outlets while in high school. Many are forced to work during college, unlike European youth who attend college on government-paid tuition and stipends. According to Phelps, Europe has developed a culture of dependency that breeds an unduly large share of young people who have little sense of independence and are unwilling to strike out on their own.

NOTES

1 Rajan, 2004

2 Rajan, 2004

3 Drazen, 2000; Drazen and Easterly, 2001; Saint-Paul, 1993; Krueger, 1993; Rodrik, 1996; Tommasi and Velasco, 1996

4 Blanchard and Tirole, 2003

5 Blanchard and Giavazzi, 2003

6 Blanchard, 1986; Layard et al., 1991

7 Mortensen and Pissarides, 1999

8 Nickell et al., 2001

9 Blanchard, 2003; Bertola et al., 2002

10 Belot and Van Ours, 2004

11 Nickell and Layard, 1999; Prescott, 2004

12 Blanchard and Wolfers, 2000; Ghellab, 1998

13 Blanchard and Wolfers, 2000; Nickell et al., 2003

14 Marimon and Zilibotti, 1998

15 Jimeno and Bentolila, 1998

16 Elmeskov et al., 1998; Fitoussi et al., 2000

17 Calmfors, 2001

18 Agell, 2002

19 Bertola, 2004

20 Acemoglu and Shinner, 1999

21 Agell, 2002

22 Lindbeck and Snower, 1988

23 Bertola and Koeniger, 2004

24 Buti et al., 1998; Boeri et al., 2002

25 Jensen, Rosholm, and Svarer, 2003

26 Blank, 2002

27 Cohen et al, 1997; Agell, 1999; Bertola, 2004

28 Blanchard, 2004

29 Prescott, 2004

30 European Commission, 2005

31 The new members show the lowest percentages with an average of 7 percent, while the French were at 25 percent and Germans at 20 percent. Only Spain (9 percent) and Italy (7 percent) resembled the new members' opinions.

32 Boeri and Tabellini, 2004

33 Boeri, Borsch-Supan, and Tabellini, 2000

34 Prescott, 2004

35 European Economy, the European Union Economy: 2003 and 2004 Review; IMF, 2003; OECD, 2005

36 The European Union Economy: 2004 Review

37 Blanchard and Giavazzi, 2003; Boeri, 2004

38 Internal Market Score Board, 2004

39 Independent High Level Group Report, 2004

40 Cotis, 2005

41 Adapting to IT investments takes time to change the organizational structure and accumulate the right skills. Evidence from the United Kingdom, for example, shows that over 50 percent of the companies that had already adopted IT before 1995 were using electronic networks for procurement versus less than 20 percent of the companies that began adopting IT in 2000.

42 Van Ark et al., 2002

43 Gordon, 2002

44 Phelps, 2003

THE LISBON SUMMIT
AND BEYOND

Since the main reasons for the EU's poor growth seem related to the supply side of the economy, the decisions taken at the European Council's Lisbon Summit in March 2000 sent a signal of hope. Realizing the urgent need for reform, the participants set forth major strategic goals—the Lisbon Strategy. These goals (see Table 7.1) attempt to: (1) increase innovation and R&D by liberalizing product markets and improving regulation, (2) increase competition by accelerating progress in the single market, (3) increase the employment rates by opening the labor market and improving the quality of the workforce, and (4) increase the growth rate and reduce the growth gap with the US while maintaining Europe's distinctive social agenda of cohesion and inclusion.

THE LISBON STRATEGY

The Lisbon Strategy is composed of five broad policy priority areas in which the EU, as well and its individual member countries, needs to make progress to ensure both its own economic dynamism and the vigor of the whole European economy. The five areas are summarized below.

TABLE 7.1   Lisbon's Strategic Goals

Innovation	Economic Reform for Single Market	Employment	Modern Social Agenda
• Legal framework for e-commerce in 2000 • Fully liberalized and competitive telecoms market in 2001 • Internet access for all schools in 2001 • Communitywide patent in 2001 • Government procurement and access to basic public services online by 2003 • Better quality of EU regulation	• Faster liberalization of gas, electricity, and transport • EIB to channel €-I bn of venture capital support to SMEs • Reduction in state aid • Small firms charter • Strategy for removal of barriers to services in 2000 • Implementation of Risk Capital Action Plan by 2003 • Implementation of Financial Services Action Plan by 2005	• Increase EU employment rate by 2010 to 70 percent overall and 60 percent for women • Europe-wide database on jobs and training • Benchmark pro vision of lifelong learning • Award for companies that invest in employees • More effective employment guidelines (Luxembourg process)	• Increased per capita investment in human resources • National action plans to combat social exclusion • Halve, by 2010, the number of 18–24-year-olds excluded from the labor market • Report on sustainability of pensions in EU • Set a benchmark for improved child care

Source: HM Treasury 2002

Knowledge-Based Society

Evidence demonstrates that R&D spending generates up to 40 percent of productivity growth and that there are powerful spillover effects into other areas of the economy. In addition, up to 30 percent of the future population will work directly in the production and diffusion of knowledge in manufacturing, services, finance, and creative industries. This goal calls for three areas of policy improvement and action.

1. In the information society:
   - Define a regulatory framework for electronic communications
   - Encourage the spread of ITC
   - Create conditions for e-commerce
   - Support European leadership in mobile communication technologies

2. In research and development:
   - Set up an area of research and innovation
   - Boost R&D spending to 3 percent of GDP
   - Make Europe more attractive to the best scholars and experts to avoid "brain drain"
   - Protect intellectual property in order to promote new technologies

3. In education and human capital:
   - Decrease by half the number of people who leave school early
   - Adapt education and training systems to the knowledge society
   - Foster lifelong learning for all
   - Promote and facilitate mobility

Internal Market

Ten years after launching initiatives allowing the free movement of persons, goods, services, and capital to achieve an EU without frontiers, the internal market exercise has not yet been completed despite its important economic benefits. The EU Commission estimates that the internal market has increased EU GDP growth annually by 0.2 percent, and it has created 2.5 million jobs. This goal calls for:

- Accelerating implementation of the commission's legislation
- Removing obstacles to the free movement of services

- Liberalizing markets and network industries, especially gas and electricity by 2007, postal services by 2006, and rail transport by 2008
- Completing the internal market for financial services by 2005
- Reducing state aid to 1 percent of GDP
- Defining rules for mergers, regime change, and takeover bids
- Updating public procurement rules

Entrepreneurial Climate

Increasing knowledge and achieving a fully open market do not automatically drive innovation, competitiveness, and growth. They require entrepreneurship to design new products and services and to take advantage of market opportunities that create value for customers. Entrepreneurship is also the driving force in creating new firms and small and medium-sized enterprises, which are today's major sources of growth. To foster this climate, the EU must:

- Facilitate access to low-cost financing
- Improve bankruptcy legislation
- Consider the specific needs of small and medium-sized firms
- Improve the industrial framework
- Encourage responsible corporate governance
- Lower the cost of doing business
  - Reduce the time and costs of setting up a company
  - Remove red tape
  - Improve the quality of regulation

Labor Market

The fourth goal is to build an inclusive labor market for stronger social cohesion. In order to achieve this goal the EU needs to:

- Increase the employment rate to 67 percent in 2005 and 70 percent by 2010

- Increase female employment to 57 percent in 2005 and 60 percent by 2010
- Increase older workers' employment rate to 50 percent by 2010
- Progressively increase the effective retirement age by five years
- Define a multiannual program for business adaptability, collective bargaining, wage moderation, improved productivity, lifelong learning, new technologies, and flexible work organizations
- Remove disincentives for female labor force participation
- Facilitate social security in cross-border movement of citizens
- Adopt the temporary agency work directive
- Ensure the sustainability of pension schemes
- Introduce the open method of coordination in the field of social protection
- Eradicate poverty by agreeing on a social inclusion program and addressing specific target group issues

Environmentally Sustainable Future

To achieve an environmentally sustainable future, the EU must:

- Fulfill the Kyoto Protocol target of using renewable energy sources for 12 percent of primary energy needs and 22 percent of gross electricity consumption
- Tackle rising volumes of traffic, congestion, noise, and pollution with full internalization of social and environmental costs
- Develop a community pricing framework for transport infrastructure (euro-vignette)
- Ensure a sustainable use of natural resources and level of waste

IMPLEMENTATION DIFFICULTIES

Unfortunately, the EU is already behind schedule on reaching these goals, even though some improvements have been made in employment creation, telecommunications, energy investment, prices, and access to pensions. Most of the difficulties in implementing the Lisbon Strategy result from politics. First, most of the necessary structural reforms require some short-term costs in order to achieve medium- and long-term benefits. But because there are always national or regional elections scheduled shortly somewhere in the EU, governments with impending elections are unlikely to introduce reforms for fear of losing votes and perhaps the election. Therefore, the expected reforms are postponed, but the problems remain.

Second, the EU governance system and complex decision-making process both slow reform. EU economic policies are managed by a complex patchwork of arrangements: delegation, commitment, coordination, and autonomy of national policies. At the same time, many different instruments are used to execute economic policy, ranging from hard collective rules such as the Stability and Growth Pact to milder instruments of persuasion and procedures for cooperation and dialogue. The picture that emerges is one of confusion that causes tension between goals and means. Currently, there are very important fault lines in the EU's economic governance such as policies that are inappropriately allocated between the EU and member countries in terms of the objective pursued or whether they are correctly allocated, so that they may not reach their objectives because of "spillovers" from failures in other policies. In addition, policies may be correctly allocated, but their design and implementation may be deficient because of an institutional failure or the lack of appropriate instruments. There are also failures that are internal to a policy because the goals, the strategy, or the instruments do not fit appropriately.[1]

In the absence of clear responsibilities and instruments to develop some of the relevant policies directly, the Lisbon Strategy emphasizes coordinating national policies according to the Luxembourg, Cardiff, and Cologne processes.[2] As a result, a new policy instrument, the Open Method of Coordination (OMC), was introduced to set common guidelines for national policies. The OMC develops structural indicators of national performance to compare best practices, encourages countries to adopt national action plans for implementing the guidelines, and introduces a joint monitoring and review of results. Nevertheless, it seems quite doubtful that the OMC alone will be sufficient to implement the Lisbon Strategy and reach its objectives.

For example, the single market methodology has not yielded the expected results for financial services and utilities. The commitment approach to fiscal policy has not yet found an organizing concept for coordinating economic policy. The approach for coordinating and benchmarking employment strategy is promising, but it lacks incentives for member countries to cooperate and change the present policies. The combination approach of centralized action and decentralized initiatives to develop the innovation strategy is not yielding satisfactory results.

Structural indicators such as these are the main tools for assessing progress on the Lisbon Summit's objectives. The spring 2003 *Report of the European Union Commission* presented a simple but very informative exercise, counting the frequency with which each member country was among the best and worst performers on each indicator. The results show that certain countries appeared, again and again, among the top performers, most notably Denmark, Sweden, and Finland. It is important to note that these are precisely the same countries that undertook deep and successful reforms well before the Lisbon Summit. On the other hand, countries such as Germany, France, and Italy are clearly lagging behind. The strong productivity growth of a few member countries demonstrates that there is nothing inherently wrong with the Lisbon policy framework; it is only a question of implementation. Unfortunately, implementation is taking much longer than the optimistic and ambitious leaders at Lisbon believed it would.

The spring 2004 Report of the European Commission shows both positive and insufficient progress. On the positive side, 6 million jobs were created from 1999 to 2002, boosting the employment rate from 62.5 percent to 64.3 percent, which in turn reduced long-term unemployment from 4 to 3 percent. Moreover, several key markets have been completely or partially opened to competition such as telecommunications, rail freight, postal services, electricity, and gas; in 2005 a single European air space will become a reality. The knowledge-based economy is also becoming a reality—Internet adoption has been strong, reaching 93 percent of schools as well as businesses, public administrations, and households. Thanks to the gradual development of the European research area, sustainable development is being taken more fully into account in policymaking, and member countries have adopted 100 Lisbon Strategy regulations, directives, and programs.

On the less positive side, national finances are still not viable in the medium and long term given the challenge of aging populations. In addition, investment is still low and employment and productivity growth are still insufficient. The 64.3 percent employment rate is still low if the EU is to reach the 2010 target of 70 percent and in relation to the US's 72.5 percent. Productivity is still 20 percentage points lower than that in the US. Moreover, the employment rate of the 10 new member countries lowers the EU average by 1.5 percent to 62.8 percent.[3] The productivity growth rate per employed person has been declining since the mid-1990s, fluctuating between 0.5 and 1 percent in contrast with 2 percent in the US. This decline is the result of ICT's decreased contribution and a drop in public and private business investment.[4] Public and private investment in human capital is still inadequate. Although public investment in education is comparable to that in the US—4.9 percent of GDP versus 4.8 percent—private investment is three times higher in Japan and five times higher in the US.

In addition, product market integration in manufacturing and services has been very slow. Restrictions are still high and cross-border trade and investment are very low. Strategic measures to increase competitiveness have not gotten off the ground because of the lack of political will. The adoption rate of internal market directives is falling, and of the 70 directives in this arena adopted under the Lisbon Strategy, only 7 have been implemented by all member countries; the average implementation rate is 58.3 percent.

The Lisbon Summit created very large expectations about the EU's growth, promising to make it the "most competitive economy by 2010" and setting precise numerical targets. At that time, the productivity growth was still satisfactory, and consumers thought that growth rates in excess of 2.5 percent seemed within reach. Consumption expenditures started to show a reasonable rate of growth, but these expectations have turned out to be bitterly disappointing: growth slowed as productivity plummeted. The Lisbon Strategy seems to have already lost its initial credibility.

This bursting of the "Lisbon bubble"[5] and the consequent fall in consumers' and producers' expectations seems to be one of the main reasons why the EU private sector growth was only 1 percent between 2001 and 2002 and was close to .5 percent in 2003. By contrast, consumption in the United States has grown by 3 percent. With productivity growth rates low and the prospects for a quick turnaround dim, consumer expectations are also depressed.

In the Special Eurobarometer on the Lisbon Agenda, when citizens in the EU's 25 member countries are asked: "In your opinion, could the EU become the world's top economic power within the next five years?" only 6 percent reply, "yes, certainly," 32 percent respond, "yes, probably," 37 percent respond, "no, probably not," 17 percent respond, "no, certainly not." The standard deviation of the answers is very high. The citizens of new member countries and Greece tend to be much more optimistic than the citizens of the original EU-15. The Swedes, Germans, Austrians, and Finns are very pessimistic, with negative answers above 65 percent.[6]

In sum, the main problem with the Lisbon Strategy is that its role will inevitably be limited to one of advocacy: promoting the need for reform and highlighting national reform successes and failures. The Lisbon Strategy is little more than a nonexhaustive wish list.

Therefore, to be more pragmatic and efficient, the member countries should try to focus on completing the single market and on continuing their partial labor and product market reforms, while the Commission should focus on improving the employment rate and hourly labor productivity.

THE SAPIR REPORT

In the face of this lack of progress, a renewed positive sign of hope came in 2003 from the excellent Independent High Level Study Group Report, established on the initiative of Romano Prodi, the President of the European Union Commission. Although the resulting Sapir Report represents only the opinion of the Independent Group and "not necessarily" the Commission, it complements the Lisbon Strategy but goes much further, establishing a better base from which to introduce radical change in the EU. In order to make the present "European model" of growth, stability, social cohesion, and inclusion sustainable in the long run, the report presents a new agenda that includes six far-reaching recommendations.

1. **Make the Single Market completion faster and more dynamic to further increase competition.** For product markets, this means substantially reducing entry costs and administrative procedures while enforcing antitrust policies. For capital markets, in addition to quickly completing the single market for financial services, it means promoting those forms of equity-based capital that are particularly suitable for risky ventures. For labor markets, it means increasing the member countries' flexibility and reducing the rigidities that still exist, such as increasing labor mobility within countries, between countries, and from third countries. In order to achieve this goal, the EU must remove the nontransferability or noncompatibility of acquired rights such as basic provisions for health, pensions, unemployment, and work permits that allow free

movement of third-country nationals throughout the EU. It will also require a more open attitude toward immigration.

2. Boost investment in knowledge in order to achieve a higher level of innovation and growth.   Compared to the US, the EU underinvests in higher education and in R&D by exactly half. Member countries need to invest more and smarter. In higher education, as noted earlier, this would mean creating an Independent European Agency for Science and Research similar to the National Science Foundation, making competition for funding an objective process based on scientific criteria and rigorous and transparent peer review. In addition, the number of research centers will need to be increased to cluster the best researchers across universities and topics and to attract the best faculty from around the world. In R&D, tax credits will be needed to increase private investments, and they will need to be larger for small start-up firms.

3. Make the EMU's policy more symmetrical and coordinated over the business cycle.   The European Central Bank's (ECB) monetary policy has succeeded in establishing its anti-inflationary credentials. Nevertheless, its definition of price stability as a year-on-year increase in the harmonized index of consumer prices (HICP) below 2 percent over the medium term has led to the perception that while the 2 percent "upper bound" fights against inflation, the implicitly defined lower bound of 0 percent is too low to fight deflation. Therefore, some economists believe that the ECB cares more about inflation than deflation. As a result, the ECB's monetary policy could eventually become too tight for countries to adjust national price differentials and avoid entering into more or less prolonged deflationary periods. These potential problems could be exacerbated with enlargement. In May 2003, the ECB tried to increase monetary symmetry by sending the message that it will aim at an inflation rate close to, but still below, 2 percent to maintain its anti-inflationary credibility and at the same time dispel deflation fears. This is a step in the right direction that now needs to be perceived as such by the markets.

In terms of fiscal policy, the EU also needs to improve its stabilization framework based on the Stability and Growth Pact and make it more symmetric over the cycle. This recommendation includes three complementary rules to foster symmetric budgetary behavior over the different phases of the business cycle.

i. Enhance budgetary surveillance to detect slippage early.   Budgetary surveillance can be achieved by devoting more resources to monitoring fiscal policies and carrying out high-level missions to member countries. This surveillance can be implemented by creating an independent fiscal auditing board to audit the quality of information on current budgetary situations and short-term prospects as well as the accuracy of governments' evaluations of policy measures.

ii. Provide incentives for good fiscal behavior.   The best way to provide incentives is to establish "rainy-day funds" that can be used in slowdowns and replenished in upturns. To avoid moral hazard, rules should ensure that resources are withdrawn only in the case of protracted slowdowns and require the Council's approval. If the rainy-day funds help maintain sound structural budgetary positions, the 3 percent GDP ceiling should not be overly constraining in normal slowdowns. However, in the event of severe recessions, respecting such a constraint may damage procyclical policies, which could be avoided by redefining the "exceptional conditions" under which a temporary excess over the ceiling is allowed. Instead of defining exceptional as only a 2 percent fall of real GDP, which is overly restrictive, it should be defined as simply an annual drop in real GDP.

iii. Ensure that fiscal rules do not have an inherent procyclical bias.   This third rule combines short-term flexibility with long-term sustainability. The Stability and Growth Pact puts undue weight on budget deficits, largely disregarding longer-term public debt sustainability concerns. Countries with low debt levels should have more flexibility in their budgets because of their previous stability efforts, while countries with high debt levels should maintain budgets close to balance or in surplus. This would give low debt countries with high investment needs more room to maneuver. Therefore, countries with public debt levels below 40 percent of GDP should be allowed to have a deficit of up to 1.5 percent of GDP for the time span covered by their Stability or Convergence Program. At the end of that period, the budgetary requirements should be reassessed, and the implicit liabilities should be estimated. Clearly, countries running deficits of 1.5 percent of GDP may see their nominal budget deficits frequently exceed the 3 percent of GDP threshold during cyclical downturns. The 3 percent limit should be kept for everyone, but the timing for returning to the threshold should be longer for countries with low debt levels.

These three rules will help make monetary and fiscal policy more symmetric; however, it will also be necessary to more effectively coordinate macroeconomic policy. The present institutional setting has three weaknesses: an inappropriate distribution of responsibilities between the Commission and the Council in enforcing fiscal rules, weak "political ownership" of coordination procedures, and the coexistence of euro adopters and nonadopters.

The Council is entrusted with the policy and surveillance functions of the Stability Growth Pact, while the Commission has not been given the legal means to perform its surveillance in an authoritative way. Because the Council has to enforce warnings and recommendations, enforcement could be prejudiced because national authorities apply the rules to themselves. Therefore, the Commission should be entrusted with implementing the Council's decisions, delivering not only early warnings but also determining whether an excessive deficit exists.

In order to increase member countries' ownership of budgetary policy coordination, the national stability and convergence programs must be aligned with the national fiscal policies, leaving the Commission to set the external assumptions for those programs, propose the guidelines for national fiscal policies, and consolidate all the national programs into an aggregate European stability program. At the same time, as noted above, to increase budgetary transparency, an independent national fiscal auditing board should be established to audit the quality of information on budgetary situations and the accuracy of budgetary impact evaluations.

In addition, ECOFIN—a financial think tank made up of an independent group of companies in banking and finance, pensions, investment consulting, and financial planning—is still responsible for all the formal decisions of the euro area. Although non-euro member states do not vote on euro-only issues, it would be better to entrust the Euro Area Council with all the decisions that are specific to euro participants (except when these decisions might be contrary to the EU's general interests), giving them the right to amend and adopt rules rather than waiting for ECOFIN's formal approval. Moreover, at the moment there is no discussion forum for the single monetary authority, as the European Central Bank, and the fiscal authorities of the individual countries sharing monetary sovereignty. The euro group consists of the European Central Bank president face to face with 12 finance ministers and a commissioner, which does not favor dialogue. The reverse is true when the commissioner or the council president attend meetings of the European Central Bank's governing or general council. The best solution would be to hold regular informal meetings between the European Central Bank president, the Council president, and the relevant commissioner.

4. Improve convergence and restructuring policies. With enlargement, reducing income disparities will be a matter of priority and urgency to maintain cohesion. Because of the narrow availability of budget resources, convergence should focus on low-income countries rather than low-income regions, and funds should be allocated on the basis of GDP per capita measured in PPP. During the catching-up process, regional disparities could increase within poorer countries, but these problems could be mitigated by national growth and national transfer schemes. The main objectives of convergence policy should be institution-building to reach a good and stable administration and sustaining high rates of human and physical capital. The main principles underlying the current cohesion policy—multiannual programming of expenditures, national cofinancing, and "additionality"[7] of EU money—should be kept, but the key principle of conditionality should be strengthened. Governments should be free to choose investment projects, but they should declare the expected results so that fund disbursements are contingent upon meeting milestones. The evaluation of these results should follow *output* logic based on quantitative results, rather than *input* logic based on amounts spent.

Restructuring will be another priority because of the potential impact the single market, enlargement, and globalization will have on the necessary industrial changes and upgrades as well as employment in different production sectors. This policy should facilitate allocation and reallocation of all displaced or affected workers regardless of their citizenship or their sector of activity. Restructuring eligibility should be limited, but it should hold the possibility for renewal. It should cover the costs of finding a new job as well as retraining so that people can quickly transition between jobs and improve mobility and employability. The agricultural sector should also be included.

5. Mobilize and refocus the EU budget.   The actual EU budget is a relic of the past and should be radically restructured because its expenditures, revenues, and procedures are all inconsistent with EU integration. Half of its spending supports a sector whose economic significance is very small and declining, while little is spent to provide economic and noneconomic public goods that typically feature large economies of scale. In addition, convergence policy is highly dispersed across member countries and does not support appropriate activities. In terms of revenue, 90 percent is financed via national contributions rather than taxes levied on a Union-wide basis. Finally, the procedures for adopting the European Union Financial Perspectives, the multiannual framework that determines the maximum amount for every expenditure, is currently driven by narrow national calculations of self-interest, bolstered by unanimity voting; its negotiations have followed the line of least resistance.

The EU budget should focus spending on those economic and social areas that can best contribute to European growth and solidarity. This means shifting away from traditional expenditures such as the common agriculture policy (CAP) and toward regrouping the budget into three new funds: economic growth, convergence, and restructuring.

The growth fund should be allocated to projects that would make the largest contribution to EU growth, concentrating on the most relevant growth engines: R&D and innovation, higher education and training, and cross-border infrastructures. The convergence fund should help the catch-up process and be invested in building institutions and physical and human capital. The restructuring fund should facilitate resource allocation as economic integration spreads, compensating affected workers for retraining, reallocating, and setting up new businesses.

To make these new funds fully operational, a very sizable amount of agriculture spending will need to be cut. Because of agriculture's huge absolute and relative size, it is the only expenditure that can be cut to make room for the more necessary new funds. CAP is no longer a reallocation policy trying to promote efficiency and production, but rather a distributive policy benefiting a small group of citizens. The diverse income levels, population density, and climatic conditions across the enlarged EU are indicative of the large heterogeneity of preferences that makes it very difficult to conduct a single agricultural policy from Brussels. Finally, the CAP is not consistent with the Lisbon Strategy because its value-for-money contribution to EU growth and convergence is lower than what is targeted for most other policies. Therefore, there is a solid argument for decentralizing the distributive function of the CAP much like other distributive policies.

On the revenue side of the budget, the huge national contributions—90 percent of the revenue by 2006—feed the tendency of national governments to focus the debate on the net balance or *juste retour* issue, preventing a rational allocation of the budget. Moving forward, the budget should target those sources of revenue that have a clear EU dimension rather than those with a national label. Revenues that directly accrue (partially or totally) to the EU budget should be related to a specific policy so that they are not reapportioned nationally; they should also have a mobile tax base such as the *seignorage*[8] earned from issuing euro banknotes.

In terms of procedures, the EU needs radical change, moving toward: (1) more postexpenditure evaluations to determine if predetermined criteria were met; (2) greater devolution of responsibility for budget execution to relevant local, national, or EU autonomous bodies; and, (3) qualified majority voting for adopting multiyear budgetary guidelines.

6. Effective governance.   There is an urgent need to change the way the EU's governance system works. The assignment of responsibilities between the EU and national levels of governance should be more flexible and more coherently defined. The various roles of the EU institutions—rulemaker, policymaker, regulator, supervisor, and facilitator—should be clarified and properly assigned. In addition, funding, economic law enforcement, and regulatory functions that are currently centralized in the Commission's purview should be transferred to independent European bodies so that they are more flexible and avoid unnecessary overlap. For instance, the responsibility for enforcing competition policy, except state aids, should be assigned to a European competition authority accountable to the Council and Parliament and whose decisions would be subject to formal Commission override.

The enlarged EU should move further toward decentralized market regulations by developing "steered networks" of national and EU bodies that operate within the same legal framework. In addition, the obligations of EU and national regulators should be strictly defined to prevent any attempt to foreclose national markets or depart from commonly agreed-upon principles. The management of the single market should also be improved by strengthening sanctions for failing to apply its directives and by concentrating product and service safety at the EU level. Implementation of the Lisbon Strategy should be accelerated, limiting the open method of coordination to areas where there are no alternatives, such as using the community method more extensively and giving incentives to member countries to direct budget priorities for enhancing growth.

Finally, institutional reform should be more strategic. The European Commission should be leaner, with only 15 commissioners with focused portfolios and a specific commissioner for accelerating the Lisbon Strategy. Its staffing should be improved by hiring high-level professionals. The Council should mainly focus on the growth agenda with the same resolve it used in the macroeconomic arena because a higher degree of cooperation is needed among member countries to lead the way and attract other countries.

Unfortunately, the Sapir report was not welcomed by the European Council because it was too radical and difficult to implement. The Council and Commission lost another opportunity to change the direction of the EU.

THE WIM KOK REPORT

After the Sapir Report's failure, the 2004 European Council invited the Commission to establish another high level group headed by Wim Kok to conduct an independent review. Like the Sapir report, this group's report identifies measures and strategies for achieving the Lisbon targets and objectives.

The report acknowledges that the US economy, building on the emergence of the "new knowledge economy" and its leadership in ICT, has begun to outperform all but the very best European countries. According to the report, if Europe wishes to protect its particular social model and continue to offer its citizens opportunities, jobs, and quality of life, it must act with determination, particularly in the face of both mounting economic challenges from Asia and the slowdown of European population growth. Europe needs to act in concert because the more it can develop its knowledge and market opening initiatives in tandem, the stronger and more competitive each member country's economy will be. Europe needs to innovate on its own behalf because the strength of its knowledge industries and its capacity to diffuse knowledge across the totality of the economy are fundamental to its success as well as to increasing its productivity to compensate for its falling population and pay for its social model. Success in the knowledge economy is the key to allowing Europe to remain both open and socially cohesive.

The report recognizes that the last four years have not been kind to the chances of achieving the Lisbon goals. The overall performance of the European economy has been disappointing. The economic upturn in Europe has been weaker than in the US and Asia, in part because of continuing structural weaknesses and in part because the growth rate of public and private demand has been low. European Union enlargement, while welcome, has made Union-wide achievement of the Lisbon goals even harder. Enlargement makes inequality and cohesion problems more pronounced since the total population of the EU has increased by 20 percent, but these additions have increased GDP by only 5 percent. Nevertheless, even if the goals are now more challenging, the report estimates that there is a continued case for the Lisbon Strategy and its 2010 deadline, because enlargement offers the prospect for new members to achieve rapid growth and productivity as they catch up with the European average, giving new dynamism to the economy.

According to the report, the EU's main economic problems are:

- An average annual growth of output per person that is 0.4 percent lower than that of the US.
- A productivity growth rate per hour worked that averages 1.4 percent and is falling as opposed to the US's 2.2 percent and growing. This relatively poor performance can be attributed equally to a lower investment per employee and to a slowdown in the rate of technological progress.

- A decline in the actual hours worked per person, even though the total number of hours worked has increased as a result of job creation.
- A decline in hourly productivity, while US employment growth has been associated with an increase in hourly productivity.

As a consequence of these negative developments, the EU's average GDP per capita is still 70 percent of the US average—the same as it was in 1970.

The report explains that there is no magic bullet that will deliver the jobs and higher growth that Europe urgently needs. Rather there is a series of interconnected initiatives and structural changes that through their cumulative reinforcement and simultaneous implementation in every member country will release the potential that exists in the European economy. Because member countries begin in different positions, the Lisbon Strategy will need to be reinterpreted with an eye to individual national contexts and challenges.

The Kok report makes a series of recommendations in each of the Lisbon Strategy's five priority areas:

First, to achieve a knowledge society, the report recommends reducing the administrative obstacles so that world-class scientists and researchers and their dependants can move to and within the EU. It recommends establishing an autonomous European research council by the end of 2005 to fund and coordinate long-term research at the European level in order to foster scientific knowledge. To foster the e-Europe 2005 plan and reap the full benefits of ICT, accessibility to broadband needs to be boosted in order to reach at least the 50 percent level by 2010. In addition, an agreement should also be reached to reduce the complexity, time, and costs of protecting intellectual property.

Second, to complete the internal market, the report recommends that the Commission produce a full list of internal market legislation still awaiting implementation in each of the 25 member countries, starting with the worst offenders, and then set final deadlines for implementation. By the end of 2005, the Parliament and Council should agree on legislation to remove the obstacles to free movement of services and ensure that national rules are not used as an excuse to hinder or block providers based in other member countries.

Third, to create the right climate for entrepreneurs, the report recommends that member countries agree on a common definition of administrative burden and set a target for reducing it. To this end, national governments must analyze burdens posed by their national laws, and the Commission and each country must indicate how much and by when they are going to reduce the burden in key sectors. By the end of 2005, member countries must drastically reduce the time, effort, and cost required to set up a business and introduce a one-stop shop for setting up new businesses.

Fourth, to build an inclusive labor market, the report recommends assessing the status of the March 2004 European Employment Taskforce, including progress on employment performance and sustainability of social systems. Member countries should also develop a comprehensive aging strategy by 2006, which will require a radical policy and culture shift away from early retirement, toward: (1) providing the right legal and financial incentives for workers to work longer and for employers to hire and keep older workers; (2) increasing participation in lifelong learning, especially for low-skilled and older workers; and (3) improving working conditions and quality of work.

And fifth, to work toward an environmentally sustainable future, the report recommends that the Commission, Council, and member countries promote the development and diffusion of "eco-innovations," building on existing European leadership in key eco-industry markets. The Commission should report on overall progress of the European Union Environmental Technology Action Plan (ETAP), and member countries should set a roadmap for implementing the ETAP, in particular its research components, technology platforms, risk capital for small and medium-sized companies,

and costs to remove harmful substances. By the end of 2006, national and local authorities should set an action plan for greening public procurement, focusing on renewable energy technology and new vehicle fuels.

Finally, in order to making the Lisbon Strategy work, the report makes the following key recommendations:

- The Lisbon Strategy should be revitalized to send a clear message to EU governments and citizens alike, focusing mainly on growth and employment.
- The Council should also indicate what progress has been made in establishing reform partnerships in order to engage citizens, social partners, stakeholders, and public authorities in the key priorities of growth and employment.
- The Council, heads of state, and governments should commit to delivering the agreed reforms, and national governments should present a national action program before the end of 2005.
- By July 2005, the Council of Ministers should adopt the Broad Economic Policy and Employment Guidelines (BEPGs) for a period of four years.
- The EU budget should be reshaped to reflect the Lisbon priorities, perhaps introducing budgetary incentives for member countries to achieve the Lisbon targets.

The Kok report tries to keep the Lisbon goals and deadlines alive, suggesting the best and most reasonable policy and action initiatives to achieve them. Nevertheless, it has received a mixed reception, because it imposes heavy short-term tasks for member countries to fulfill. Therefore, it will be necessary to wait again until the Spring European Council of 2005 to see if the EU leadership is ready to accept its recommendations, to commit itself to delivering the agreed-upon reforms, and to finally make a major and coordinated effort to revitalize the Lisbon Strategy's 2010 goals, which are essential to catching up with the US.

THE EUROPEAN UNION CONSTITUTIONAL TREATY

The new Constitutional Treaty (CT) could help to speed up the Lisbon goals by making it easier to find a voting majority in the enlarged EU. The CT will need consensus among the largest EU members, which, in principle, should take the leadership role in implementing the reforms. The main problems are that the CT needs to be ratified by all member countries, and, in some of them, a referendum is compulsory. In addition, even if the CT is ratified, it will only come into force in 2009, one year before the deadline set by the Lisbon summit.

As Alesina and Perotti have shown, there are two major problems with the EU's current decision-making process.[9] First, its institutional balance is based on a complex web of institutions with overlapping jurisdictions. Thus, there is a lack of clarity in the allocation of powers between the Commission (the supranational body *par excellence*), the Council (the quintessential intergovernmental body), and the role and structure of the European Council. In traditional federalism, the EU would engage in those policy areas in which economies of scale and externalities are large and heterogeneity of preferences among different member countries are low, but this principle has not been applied coherently. The EU governing bodies are increasingly involved in a variety of areas in which economies of scale and externalities are virtually nonexistent. In addition, there is a lack of transparency and accountability. According to the Eurobarometer, 74 percent of EU citizens see "getting closer to the European citizens by informing them more about the EU" as a priority. Given the multiple roles played by the same body, it is not clear to the citizens how much attention to pay to the different governing bodies. In the end, they accept the European Parliament as the main source of legitimacy and accountability because it alone represents the direct will of the citizens.

The second problem is the strong divide between those who prefer an "intergovernmental" EU and those who opt for a more supranational or federalist EU; the first gives more responsibility to the member countries and the Council, while the second enhances the Commission's power. Basically, this is a confrontation between two views or visions of policymaking and culture: one that favors state control of economic and social issues (*dirigisme*) such as the continental European regulatory approach, with its heavy emphasis on regulation, coordination, intervention, social engineering, and quantitative targets and plans, and the other that favors *laissez-faire* strategies such as the Anglo-Saxon pragmatic and promarket approach.

The CT helps to solve the first problem because it chooses a side by enhancing the Council at the expense of the Commission, clarifying the allocation of powers. The treaty abolishes the EU's rotating presidency in favor of a chairperson who is chosen for two and a half years. The new chairperson will represent the EU in meetings with the President of the United States and the G8.

The CT also helps to improve the EU decision-making process by simplifying the Council's qualified majority voting (QMV) procedure, thus reducing the threshold of votes required to obtain a QMV. Baldwin and Widgren (2004) have computed the "passage probability" of any decision by the Council, which determines the capacity to act in the EU by calculating all the possible combinations of yes and no votes by EU Council members (there are 134 million in the EU with 27 member countries). Using each member's weight in terms of number of votes, the number of members, and populations, they calculate which coalitions can be winning majorities and which can be blocking minorities. With the former Nice treaty, the "passage probability" of any random decision or measure in the 25 member EU was only 2.1 percent, and it could become close to 0 percent with enlargement. The CT increases the probability to 12.9 percent because the threshold of votes, members, and population has been reduced.

Moreover, the CT clarifies the distinction between exclusive and shared responsibilities. There are five areas in which the EU has exclusive responsibility: monetary policy, commercial policy, customs union, conservation of marine biological resources, and certain international agreements. It also declares that, "The Union shall have competence to promote and coordinate the economic and employment policies of the Member States." There are 10 areas in which the EU shares responsibility with the member countries, including such broad and loosely defined areas as economic, social, and territorial cohesion and freedom, and security and justice as well as "supporting, coordination or complementary action by Member States," such as industry, culture, education, and vocational training.

Finally, the CT ends the confusing divide between the European Communities that include the single market with its four freedoms of movement, competition, trade, agriculture and the EU that includes common security, foreign policy, justice, and home affairs. Before the treaty, the European Communities legislation was directly applied to the member countries and had primacy over national legislation, while EU legislation needed unanimity and to be approved by member countries. The EU as a whole now has a separate legal personality, which means that the EU can be represented as a separate legal entity in international forums.

Therefore, the CT should be ratified by all member countries because it helps increase the probability of reaching a QMV in making decisions and directly applying all approved legislation in all member countries. The CT is probably the most important step toward approving and applying the necessary reforms of the Lisbon Strategy and finally improving the EU's economic efficiency.

NOTES

1   Independent Group Report, 2003

2   The Luxembourg process analyzes employment policy; the Cardiff process analyzes structural reforms; the Cologne process involves microeconomic dialogue.

3   The same happens with the employment rate of those aged 55 to 64, which stands at 40.1 percent when the 2010 target is 50 percent; the average of the 10 new members is only 30 percent.

4 The private business investment rate fell from 18.3 percent of GDP in 2000 to 17.2 percent in 2002; public investment is 2.4 percent of GDP versus 3.3 percent in the United States.

5 Gros et al., 2003

6 European Commission, 2005

7 Additionality is the extent to which something happens as a result of an intervention that would not have occurred otherwise.

8 The revenue or profit taken from minting bank notes and coins.

9 Alesina and Perotti, 2004

CAN THE EUROPEAN
UNION PRESERVE
ITS PRESENT
SOCIAL MODEL?

T HE review of official data throughout the seven previous chapters seems to confirm that the US economy is more efficient than that of the EU. The US rate of GDP growth has been consistently higher, and its GDP per capita growth rate has been almost the same during the last 40 years in spite of its significantly faster population growth. Moreover, since 1996 the US GDP growth rate has accelerated 1 percent faster than the EU's growth rate. As a result of this differential, EU GDP per capita remains about 30 percent lower than in the US, and this gap has been growing in the last four years by two extra percentage points.

When looking at the factors behind this large gap, it's rather clear that the main differentiator has been the EU's lower labor utilization, both in terms of employment and working hours. For a while, the EU compensated with higher labor productivity growth resulting from its higher capital deepening growth and total factor productivity. However, since 1995, US productivity has grown at almost twice the EU rate because of its much faster growth in capital deepening and total factor productivity, allowing the US to increase its GDP gap in spite of the EU's increase in employment growth.

Is the divergence of the past eight years temporary or will it be a permanent development? Unfortunately for the EU, there is a clear consensus. All the official data, including those from the European Commission, indicate that this trend will be maintained for many years unless the EU complies with all the institutional and structural reforms laid out in the Lisbon Strategy. And as we have seen, compliance with the Lisbon Strategy is far behind schedule; and the Constitutional Treaty, if ratified, only takes effect in 2009, one year before the Lisbon deadline. In addition, the current challenge of enlargement of the Union may further divert the EU's political efforts.

The real challenge for EU growth is going to come when having incorporated poorer countries into the Union and the continually aging population reduces the EU's room to maneuver. These two events will make it difficult to increase the employment rate and to sustain public finances, putting the present welfare state system—the EU's greatest differentiator with the US—at risk. The United States is not only facing a lower fiscal impact from its aging population, but its starting point is at a much better financial position in spite of its large budget deficit. Thus, we again see that the main instrument for catching up with the US will be enhancing productivity. But there again, EU expenditures or tax incentives to foster research, innovation, and infrastructures will be severely limited because of its increasing pension and health provisions.

This conclusion raises again the issue of the trade-off between efficiency and equality, a debate that has been going on for many years, mainly since the seminal work of Arthur Okun.[1] In Okun's terms, the US economy has proven more efficient than the EU's, but the EU's society is more egalitarian and inclusive.

Data from the Luxembourg Income Study[2] show the differences between the two social models in terms of inequality (Gini coefficient). For instance, in 1999, the Gini coefficient in the US was close to 0.40, while the EU's was only 0.27. The income ratio between the 10 percent richest and the 10 percent poorest individuals in the society was 5.6 times larger in the US and only 3.5 times larger between both uppper and lower deciles in the EU. The percentage of population in relative poverty (percentage of disposable income below the median disposable income) was 17 percent in the US and 9 percent in the EU. The percentage of children in relative poverty was 22.4 percent in the US and 10 percent in the EU, and the percentage of children in absolute poverty (below the US poverty line) was 13.9 percent in the US and 14 percent in the EU, despite the fact that the US poverty line is higher and its income per capita is 30 percent higher.

Nevertheless, in the last few years inequality ratios in both economies have been rising, although increasing much faster in the US, mainly because of profits made during the financial bubble, the widespread use of stock options as pay for top executives, and the recent US income tax reduction for personal and company income.

Economic and social inequality is negative for the economy and society because it is related to a variety of adverse social and economic outcomes and ends up reducing economic growth, especially in democracies.[3] But according to Barro (1996), this is true only in poor countries. The fact is that countries with higher inequality, such as in Latin America, suffer from more violent crime and insecurity, even when controlling for the absolute level of poverty.[4] The main adverse effect of inequality on growth is through the subversion of institutions—the legal, regulatory, and political frameworks—by the most powerful for their own benefit. This subversion is a detriment to the security of property rights and therefore to economic growth, especially in countries with weak legal institutions.[5] However, the United States has been remarkably successful in confronting institutional subversion in ways that many developing and transition countries have not. But we should not forget that there are almost 2 million people in US jails, while there are only 900,000 in prison in the EU despite the fact that its population outnumbers that of the US by 100 million.

For many years there was a clear consensus on both sides of the Atlantic in favor of the EU social model, which achieves a more balanced trade-off between equality and efficiency, making the EU a much more attractive society in which to live. Today, unfortunately, this favorable consensus is clearly diminishing, and there is a growing perception that the EU's social model may be unsustainable because of the aging population and the challenges of globalization.

According to Hassler et al. (2001), the sustainability of welfare states is an issue that may result in multiple self-fulfilling "equilibria" that reinforce themselves. A strong sustainable welfare state with political equilibrium can be achieved if the economy starts with a proredistribution majority in power. Institutions promoted by this majority can survive as they reinforce their own constituency, especially in the face of negative economic shocks. Such was the case in the US and other countries after the Great Depression. Large-scale welfare states as well as universal suffrage were initiated in Europe and reinforced by reconstruction after World War II and the threat of communism in the early 1950s. This equilibrium is maintained despite the fact that the cost of financing the current redistribution increases with future redistribution and as the welfare state becomes more inefficient.

But there's another self-fulfilling equilibrium in dismantling any existing welfare state. The increase in the wages tends to weaken political support for the welfare state because people have stronger private incentives to invest in education, thereby increasing the number of upper income individuals who want lower taxes and at the same time reducing those in favor of redistributive policies. Empirical evidence shows that the largest support for welfare states has coincided with a narrowing wage structure, as in post-war Europe.[6] By contrast, conservative governments that proposed drastically reducing social policies were reelected in the 1980s as wage inequality and private educational investment increased significantly.[7] The same evidence is found in President Bush's 2004 reelection. By contrast, in Continental Europe, political changes have been less dramatic because the increase in wage inequality has been smaller.

The so-called traditional Transatlantic Consensus was based on the argument that increasing globalization and, therefore, greater technical progress and competition, resulted in higher income inequality in the US and higher unemployment in the EU due to a shift in the economy to favor skilled workers. Paul Krugman (1993) was the first to deal with this issue in relation to the phenomenon called then *Eurosclerosis*, showing that the two economies were reacting to the shock of the same market forces but in ways that widened income inequality sharply. While the US let these market forces have their way, maintaining favorable employment levels but allowing poverty to worsen while the rich got richer, the EU leaned against the market forces, cushioning the poor from the impact of declining earnings at the cost of growing unemployment.

André Sapir (2000) summarized this consensus when looking at the challenges of globalization. In the US, markets operate more efficiently and globalization generates more wealth, but they also generate more income inequality through wage differentiation and labor adjustment. Both effects have resulted in a fierce opposition of organized labor to globalization. In Europe, where the welfare state is more generous and product and factor markets are less flexible and efficient, globalization has generated more wealth, but also less income inequality and adjustment. Wage and labor adjustments have come via an increase in the unemployment rate, which has been felt mainly by *outsiders* (the young, women, and immigrants) rather than *insiders* (protected workers). Accordingly, European organized labor voiced much less opposition to globalization.

Thus, the real dilemma is to know whether having more people employed, even if some are the "working poor," as in the US, is better in terms of equality than having more people unemployed, with generous unemployment insurance. If we again look at inequality ratios, the answer to the trade-off is that the EU social model is still preferable, but it needs to be improved with more labor efficiency.

Anthony Atkinson (1999) and others have challenged this Transatlantic Consensus. The challengers believe that it is necessary to move from a simple skilled/unskilled labor force dichotomy to a more realistic earnings capacity continuum because not only have the unskilled lost to median income workers, but the median workers have also lost to those at upper income levels. They argue that the Transatlantic Consensus does not explain the tilt in the upper part of the income distribution spectrum. The main factor behind both models is not the challenge of globalization or the faster rate of technical progress, but a shift in social conventions and social preferences that may reduce governments' redistribution policies. Therefore, the main cause is social rather than trade or technology, meaning that there is room for political leadership to reverse this inequality.

For a long time, the majority of Europeans has preferred a more generous welfare state at the expense of a more progressive tax system and more tax pressure as well as a trade-off between more leisure time versus more income. By contrast, most Americans tend to prefer more efficiency to more equality and more income to more leisure time. Therefore, the increasing inequality gap could again be reduced if redistributive policies in both economies were increased. It is thus a question of developing social policies that can counteract the negative effects of these social preferences.

Nevertheless, taking a very simplistic, schematic, but very real look at the issue, there seems to be a different perception of equality on both sides of the Atlantic. In principle, the United States is a country of immigrants who came looking for opportunities. Its economic institutions are more flexible, and climbing the social ladder appears to be easier. Traditionally, Americans prefer to preserve the option of "equal opportunity," even if it is only partially achieved. Once society believes that a state of equal opportunity has been achieved, those who have not been able to exploit their individual opportunities are met with less compassion. Those who fail, with the exception of the physically or psychologically incapable, are considered "voluntary losers." To illustrate this point, 60 percent of Americans still believe that the poor are lazy.[8]

On the other hand, the EU represents older and more stratified societies with less flexible economies in which social promotion is more difficult. Equal opportunity is more difficult to achieve (54 percent of the European Union citizens believe that luck determines income) because Europeans seem to prefer "equal outcomes." Therefore, redistributive policies are applied after the fact to help those who cannot find jobs or who cannot adapt to globalization and technological change. Still today, 60 percent of Europeans believe that the poor are trapped in poverty, and a majority believes that forces beyond their personal control determine success.

Both of these perceptions seem to fit with reality. In a very large survey of Americans and Europeans, Alesina et al. (2001) found that in the EU the rich and those in the right wing were mostly unaffected by inequality, while the poor and the left had a very strong aversion to inequality. By contrast, in the US none of the four groups (poor, rich, left, and right) was averse to inequality. Contrary to the EU's results, in the US only the wealthy left were averse to inequality. Thus, European aversion to inequality is not in the "genes" and does not originate in different preferences. If the EU reflected a "taste for equality," we would expect to find it at least as strongly in the European rich, assuming that equality is a "luxury good," whose demand increases with income. But a more reasonable interpretation is that opportunities for upward mobility are perceived to be higher in the US. When mobility is perceived to be high, inequality levels may have little influence on individual utility and are a poor indicator of what the future holds.

What's behind these two different perceptions of inequality and welfare? In a recent book, Alesina and Glaesser (2004) suggest two interesting explanations: political institutions and race. US political structures are older, very stable, and governed mostly by conservative forces. By contrast, the EU has suffered a highly turbulent political past of invasions and cruel wars, which promoted political changes and have installed proportional representation in most countries, facilitating the growth of socialist and communist parties and the consequent wider-spread support for welfare. In terms of race, Europe is still highly homogeneous, while the US has always had a high degree of racial diversity. The more racial diversity, the lower the positive perception of the welfare state and the lesser concern with inequality; this is compounded by the fact that most of the poor in the US are people of color. US states with higher racial diversity (such as Alabama, Louisiana, and Mississippi) are less generous with aid to the poor than states primarily populated with Caucasians. According to the polls, people are more likely to support welfare if they live close to welfare recipients of their own race.

Americans have always believed that equal opportunity gave them an edge over old Europe. They are proud of this heritage, and many still believe it, but unfortunately equal opportunity is fading away. In the last two decades, inequality has increased markedly in the US. Since 1979, the real income of households in the lowest 20 percent has grown by only 6.4 percent, while income in households in the top 20 percent grew by 70 percent, and the top 1 percent grew by 184 percent. In 2001, the top 1 percent of households earned 20 percent of all income and held 33.4 percent of all net worth.[9] Moreover, social mobility has declined. A survey of more than 6,000 American families (both black and white) over 32 years has shown that 42 percent of those born into the poorest fifth ended up where they started, another 24 percent moved up slightly, and only 6 percent made it to the top fifth. Therefore, the United States is also becoming a class-based society.

Of course, the trade-off between efficiency and equality is much more complex in real life. Labor market regulations and social policies can serve two distinct purposes: counteracting market failures and redistributing income. For example, if workers cannot access credit, they cannot borrow to sustain consumption if they lose their jobs; in this case, a reasonable unemployment insurance system (to avoid "adverse selection") may allow the risks to be spread throughout the whole population. Social policies may try to redistribute income among different groups in society or to protect rents. While a minimum wage can be justified on efficiency grounds to curb the power of *monopsonistic*[10] employers who can force employment conditions below competitive market levels, in many cases it simply serves to redistribute income from the owners of physical and human capital toward low-skilled labor and prices many unemployed out of the labor market. Other regulations that seek mainly to redistribute income tend to reduce economic efficiency. For instance, labor standards and regulations frequently decrease the labor supply so that mandatory reductions of working time or overly generous unemployment insurance makes the unemployed choosier about jobs; rigid employment security legislation slows the exit rate of workers from obsolete industries and makes expanding firms reluctant to create new jobs. A third kind of social policy achieves neither equality nor efficiency. For instance, in many EU countries, high firing costs, originally intended to protect workers against unfair job loss, help employed insiders by insulating them from the competitive pressure of unemployed outsiders.

There are several different kinds and combinations of social measures in the EU. For example, continental European welfare systems tend to be employment-related, offering generous pensions to former workers and protecting prime-age males who are mainly employed at the expense of the young and women. By contrast, the Anglo-Saxon and Scandinavian welfare models offer benefits mainly on the basis of need. Both models reflect different social preferences, though the Scandinavian model seems more effective. Although they devote an average of one-third of their GDP to transfers (versus one-quarter in France and Germany and only one-seventh in the US), they have much more flexible labor markets than does continental Europe and very low taxes on capital (lower than the rest of the EU and the US). By contrast, they have higher taxes on consumption, mainly on goods and services that are less sensitive to price and that are considered nonessential habits, such as smoking and drinking. These Scandinavian welfare models have proved to be smart and efficient and are still going strong, while the continental European models are ailing.[11] It is interesting to note that in the 1990s, when in the face of financial instability and the requirement to do something radical to preserve their social systems, these Scandinavian countries reacted promptly and reinvented their social systems with strong fiscal and social reforms. The rest of continental Europe's social systems have not yet arrived at such a dramatic situation, so their governments have been very slow to act.

The member states also protect workers differently: some countries have high job security and low unemployment insurance and vice versa. The former have created more jobs than the latter, but they are going to be under greater competitive pressure to change when economic integration deepens. Within the present EU, the situation could be significantly improved if the welfare systems were harmonized, but this will be almost impossible once the new candidates from Eastern Europe are made full members. Harmonization makes sense only for countries with similar standards of development and with similar preferences for efficiency and equality. EU income disparities are already relatively high and will increase even further with enlargement because while the 10 new members will add 100 million new citizens, they will increase GDP by only 5 percent.[12]

Therefore, in order to reduce the persistently high unemployment levels, member states will need to quickly reduce those social policies and labor and tax regulations that negatively affect the social and economic level of efficiency. For instance, the income and payroll taxes that support the welfare states drive a deep wedge between workers' take-home pay and the much higher company costs to employ them, reducing employability in the market. The real problem is that the "European social model" has for many years been used to maintain both high labor market rigidity and a high level of social protection without any electoral pressure for change, suggesting that this choice is a *political equilibrium*. To break this kind of equilibrium will not be easy; change may have to wait for increasing pressures from enlargement, when inflexible and noncompetitive labor markets and the aging population will show that both systems cannot coexist because of increasing competition and larger costs in terms of both member countries' and EU budgetary expenditures.

However, if member countries wait, then the European social model, for so many years the world's example of an optimal welfare system and inclusive society, could end up being phased out by a lack of compatibility with demographics and enlargement trends. Unfortunately for this political equilibrium, there is no time left to spare in reforming labor and social institutions and trying to achieve a new and workable trade-off between efficiency and equality. The Nordic example shows that it is possible to achieve both without major sacrifices, but it requires a larger consensus—among employers, trade unions, governments, and the civil society at large—about the society in which to live and the welfare state's efficiency.

For example, after Sweden's economy collapsed in the early 1990s, the government achieved a wide-ranging consensus and introduced a comprehensive reform of its labor, tax, and welfare systems. As a result, Sweden has achieved great flexibility in its labor market's collective bargaining (but with considerable local autonomy in setting relative wages), extensive active labor market policies, higher shares of part-time and temporary work, a strong reduction in taxes on capital and corporations to increase productivity, a system of redistribution transfers (based on government spending and not on tax rates to compensate for the regressive impact of lower taxes on capital), and a system of individual accounts within a pay-as-you-go system. Today, Sweden has become one of the most efficient countries in the world with an extensive welfare system and a very high quality of life.[13]

There are two different stances on the costs and benefits of the EU's social model versus that of the US: Heckman (2003), a defender of the conventional view, shows that the two economies differ in regulatory welfare incentives. The EU's incentives distort resource allocation and impair efficiency as well as the welfare costs of taxation and regulation—what economists call dead-weight burden—which is 40 percent for each euro raised. Not only does the tax system create disincentives, but collective bargaining and regulation of business entry, banking practices, and employment protection all contribute to a high tax burden. The present EU social systems tend to produce security and even wage gains for protected insiders at the expense of further inequality and job and income losses for outsiders. In other words, far from promoting universal social justice at the price of efficiency, it provides security for some at the expense of exclusion and wage loss for others. Moreover, the costs of preserving the status quo have increased in the new world economy, muting the incentives to invest in ideas, skills, and new technology. According to Heckman, EU unemployment is mainly structural and needs long-term policies, while politicians are unfortunately focused on the short-term performance and being reelected.

By contrast, Blanchard (2004) is still optimistic about maintaining the EU's basic welfare system if product market reforms accelerate. He thinks that the engine of reform is being generated by the steps being taken, through European Commission pressure, in the goods and products markets as well as the utility and financial markets. These reforms are changing the work environment and will eventually reform the labor markets. Protected firms may try to maintain employment protection and regulation, but when product and market reforms decrease their rents, they cannot afford to do so. This is why there is a very high correlation between high product market and high labor market regulations. Thus, the opposite should be true—when product market regulations are strongly reduced, they will eventually force a reform of labor markets.[14] Blanchard believes that there is no need to move toward a full US social model because the Netherlands and Nordic countries have been able to reform their welfare systems without decreasing social insurance, making them more efficient.

Agell (2003) is also optimistic about achieving a more balanced trade-off between efficiency and equality. He notes that during the 1960s and early 1970s the EU achieved much lower unemployment rates than the US with even more rigid labor markets. In addition, the UK, which deregulated its labor markets in the 1980s, did not fare significantly better than the average European economy during the 1990s, which shows that macroeconomic events and their inter-action with institutions also play important roles. Agell recognizes that there is no support for the common view that equality is best served by a tax system with increasing marginal tax rates at the top income brackets because it creates supply disincentives for high-skilled labor and an inefficient labor supply. And rate cuts that increase the labor supply of high-wage individuals provide extra tax revenue that can be distributed to low-wage individuals.

Atkinson (1999B) notes that real-world unemployment benefits should have a limited duration to impose active job search require-ments. Moreover, persons who quit voluntarily, are dismissed because of misconduct, or reject reasonable job offers should be disqualified from receiving benefits. Experimental evidence shows that people are willing to invest in public goods provided they are efficiently man-aged and that freeloaders are punished.

Finally, Agell shows that globalization will not dismantle the labor regulations that support the political equilibrium, because it also increases voters' demand for social insurance when facing higher unemployment risks. Thus, the final political equilibrium may be associated with less but also with more income redistribution because the competing forces of integration and globalization as well as the demand for social protection may roughly balance out.

From this debate it becomes rather clear that reforming market regulations and social and labor policies is a matter of urgency if the EU is to achieve more efficiency, greater employment, and lower costs for its social policies. Without reform, the EU will continue to lag behind the US economically, and the pressures of international competition and the aging population will put its social model and political equilibrium under increasing strain.

The solution has two parts: First, product and service market reforms should be accelerated to increase competition among firms and make them more conscious of the high cost of the labor and social protection that they provide. Second, the welfare state should be reformed to address market failures, pursuing redistribution to those genuinely in need and providing incentives to seek employment for those left out of the labor market. In addition, it should also eliminate or reduce policies and programs that add unnecessary costs and create disincentives to efficiency. The solution is not to replicate the US model with its egalitarian shortcomings, but to make the EU model more efficient and less costly without sacrificing major benefits. The urgency for these reforms is great because they will be extremely difficult to accomplish when the median voter nears retirement age, and by 2020 nearly half the EU's voting population will be 50 or older.

The proposed Constitutional Treaty, by introducing majority rule voting in most decisions and reducing the threshold required to make up a majority, could help to speed up the Lisbon summit's goals by making it easier to find the urgently needed voting majority— provided there is a consensus among the largest EU members who, in principle, should take a leadership role. The problem is that most of these countries are going through a period of very low growth (partly because they have not implemented the necessary reforms), and their governments find it difficult to embark on such a policy process that will, in the short term, reduce their electoral support. Commissioner Fritz Bolkenstein recently commented: "Member States are strong on rhetoric and weak on actions. There is much poetry but precious little motion." Unfortunately, now that the Bolkenstein Directive for a single EU market for services has finally been approved by the Commission, the reaction in the Union and in some countries such as France has been very negative.

Another example of this attitude has been the recent rejection of the most serious and comprehensive analyses of EU weaknesses and corrective policy recommendations (see Chapter 7). Unfortunately, EU governments continue to show that they tend to be oriented toward the short term and that they are reluctant to confront the risks involved in introducing the necessary reforms. Germany has been able to reform its labor market by reducing the unemployment subsidy for long-term unemployed and unemployed people over age 55. In addition, it has reformed its pension system by increasing the pension eligibility age. France has just reformed, for the second time, its 35-hour week law, following the Camdessus' report (2004), by increasing the annual overtime quota and creating another overtime concept called "chosen hours," which allows workers to receive higher salaries by working more hours.

The real issue for the European Union going forward is that, without reforms, the probability of achieving the two main original economic goals—catching up with US efficiency and maintaining a high level of equality through a cohesive and inclusive social model— is going to be extremely low and will decrease with time.

We can only hope that the beginning of the long-expected EU economic recovery, the dynamism of the new member countries from the east, and the adoption of the Constitutional Treaty will give a strong boost to the reform process, allowing the EU to be more efficient and to prepare for its rapidly aging population without losing the best attributes of its hallmark social model.

Finally, it is paradoxical but interesting to confront the different perceptions of the efficiency-equality trade-off by liberal (in the US sense) thinkers and scholars on both sides of the Atlantic. For some US and European scholars living in the US, Europe has a better chance to take over and end US supremacy; they believe that Europe is not doing that badly and has more possibilities to improve and prosper than most economists in Europe believe.[15] They take this view mostly because they do not like the way US inequality is increasing and equal opportunity and social mobility is evaporating; they believe that the great American democratic spirit is tired and languishing, and they believe that the EU is more socially advanced and cohesive and has a greater edge in new ideas. They also believe that Europe has a more advanced culture, and that US efficiency lacks sufficient cohesiveness, which may one day end up disrupting the "American dream." They find as well that Americans seem to be content with their situation, while Europeans are much more self-critical, honestly introspective, and more aware of their reality.

In sum, they think that Europe is a better place to live but not a good place to work and research. This is borne out by US census data: around 400,000 European scientists have moved to the US in the last decades,[16] as well as about 20 percent of European Union Ph.D. recipients, because they receive higher salaries and better tuition and research conditions. These figures alone may cause a drop in EU GDP per capita of around 0.5 percent.[17] They may also explain why before World War II three-quarters of the Nobel Prizes in science went to Europeans, and now that same proportion is awarded to US scientists.

I am also convinced, as are other European economists, that Europe is still a better place to live, but the US is an increasingly more efficient economy and attracts an increasing volume of Europe's best human capital. For this reason, we are very critical and skeptical about Europe's future, because we feel its most attractive social attributes may not be sustainable in the long term. Despite this, Europe should not reject its social model to copy the United States, but rather be aware of its weaknesses and try to correct them through reforms. If we do not change and make our EU policy, society, and economy more efficient and adapt them to the challenges of globalization, enlargement, and the aging of European populations, we may lose, sooner rather than later, our most precious attribute: our highly cohesive society.

NOTES

1 Arthur Okun, 1975

2 Smeeding, 2002

3 Alesina and Rodrik, 1994; Persson and Tabellini, 1994

4 Fajnzylber, Lederman, and Loayza, 2002

5 Glaesser, Scheinkman, and Shleifer, 2002

6 Goldin and Margo, 1992

7 Katz and Murphy, 1992

8 Alesina and Glaesser, 2004

9 *The Economist*, 2005

10 A monopsonistic market has only one buyer in the market, often an input market. (A monopolistic market has only one seller.)

11 Lindert, 2004

12 Bean, Bentolila, Bertola, and Dolado, 1998

13 Thakur et al., 2003

14 Saint-Paul, 2000; Bertola and Boeri, 2003

15 Blanchard, 2004; De Long, 2005; Gordon, 2002 and 2004; Krugman, 2004; Reid, 2004; and Rifkin, 2004

16 Mettler, 2005

17 Saint Paul, 2004

EPILOGUE

T HE recent French and Dutch rejection of the Constitutional Treaty (CT) is a major blow not only to the European Union's constitutional process but also to the reforms envisioned at the Lisbon summit and to the EU's adaptation to globalization. With 11 member countries using referenda to ratify the CT democratically, some countries were expected to say no, mainly Denmark, the Czech Republic, and above all the United Kingdom, but nobody expected two of the EU's founding members to say no. Although the CT's Declaration 30 states that the CT should be abandoned only if more than five member countries reject it, after the French and Dutch vote and the United Kingdom's decision to delay its referendum, the CT for all intents and purposes may be dead.

What can be done to save the CT? First, the decision was wrong to make it a national referendum in some countries while others just ratified it in their national parliaments. If the European Council would have chosen the option of approving the CT in the national parliaments, and later as a European-wide referendum, the results would have been totally different. Second, there is no need to invent a new CT, because the Nice Treaty is in force until 2009. And the long constitutional process involved in agreeing to the CT—convention, intergovernmental conference, and national ratifications—would make renegotiation nearly impossible. And given the October 2006 ratification deadline, it would be extremely difficult to have a second referendum for those who have already rejected the CT.

However, one possibility would be to unanimously agree to extend ratification beyond 2007, that is, after the French presidential elections. After 2007, it would be possible to hold a second referendum in France and the Netherlands. Barring this, the only option left would be to find a consensus in the next European Council to apply all CT elements that do not violate the Nice Treaty. This would table discussions for finding a consensus on "enhanced cooperation" areas and institutional design (which would come into force in 2009 with the newly elected European parliament).

After that, a new intergovernmental conference could try to agree on a new CT for the basic constitutional principles, the Council vote weighting, and the Fundamental Rights Charter. In addition, they would have to agree on a new method of ratification that could be based on: (1) achieving a simultaneous superqualified majority of two-thirds both by the new Euro MPs (elected in 2009) and by the national parliaments, and (2) on a simultaneous European Union-wide referendum, which would require a qualified majority of two-thirds of the European citizens and four-fifths of the member countries.

The CT's rejection poses very serious problems for the future. The majority of French and Dutch citizens who voted against the CT were not really voting against European integration, but rather against their own political leaders and their policies, as well as against enlargement, Turkey's future potential membership, foreign competition, and immigration from developing countries, as well as against structural reforms. At the same time, they are demanding more social protection. In other words, they voted against all the factors and policies included in the Lisbon Strategy, which are absolutely essential for the European Union to prosper in the long term.

As I have explained in the previous chapters, the European leaders decided only five years ago in Lisbon to reform the European Union product and factor markets to make it the most dynamic region in the world. They sought to increase productivity and reform labor markets so that they could enhance growth and compete in an increasingly global economy. In addition, they wanted to reduce expenditures and increase savings so that they could accommodate the large aging population and quickly achieve a single market for goods, services, technology, capital, and labor. Given the very slow pace of reforms, the European Commission tried to revive the Lisbon spirit through the Independent Group Report and the Wim Kok Report, but some governments, pressed by national electoral events, decided not only to do very little in terms of reforms but to distance themselves from the two decisive stumbling blocks, the Stability and Growth Pact and the Single Market Services Directive.

Through the CT referenda and regional elections, we have been able to hear the citizens directly, and they seem not only to reject the Lisbon Strategy but also Gerhard Schroeder and Silvio Berlusconi and Jacques Chirac or Jean-Pierre Raffarin. Moreover, the European citizens do not seem to want more immigrants from the Maghreb or other Islamic countries; they do not even want more immigration from Eastern and Central Europe. They do not want to accept competition in textiles from Asia or new member countries. They do not want to reduce agricultural subsidies from the European Union budget. But they do want more protection against foreign competition and globalization, and they want a more "Social Europe."

They do not seem to recognize that the vulnerable financial situation of Social Europe is not only the result of welfare states being too generous, increasingly inefficient, and creating impediments and reducing incentives to employment, investment, and growth, but also fiscal policies that have been too lax for too long. Now, when Social Europe is needed more than ever to compensate those workers at a competitive disadvantage, it is less able to help them.

In addition, their attitude is arriving at the worst possible moment—in the midst of adapting to new information and communication technologies and increasing global competition for exports goods and services as well as capital and labor. With today's global competition, those firms that cannot adapt to the competitive trends are going to suffer heavy losses, and those countries that do not invest in education, training, R&D, and innovation will not be able to compete with new entrants in the world markets.

The EU cannot afford to retreat from world competition and globalization because its larger export and investment markets are going to be in the developing countries rather than an aging Europe. To stabilize its shrinking labor force it needs large inflows of foreign immigrants, and to compete globally, it needs to outsource part of its labor-intensive production process to developing countries.

Finally, if French, German, Italian, and Dutch citizens think that they are going to reverse the present situation by ousting their reform leaders, they are mistaken. Any newly elected leaders will be forced to try to improve the competitive situation. Ironically, the citizens have voted no to the most democratically drafted treaty of all. In order to fill the growing "European democratic deficit," the new CT began with a convention of elected members from national and European parliaments—a great improvement from previous inter-governmental conferences that created the previous treaties behind closed doors. They have voted no to a CT that reduces the weight and size of the Commission, abolishes the inefficient rotating Council presidency, and gives more weight to population votes than to the national votes. They have rejected a CT that gives more power to the European Parliament and extends its joint "codecision" with the Council. Finally, they have paradoxically rejected a CT that, for the first time in the history of integration, includes a chart of fundamental rights for all European citizens.

There is of course a contending point of view, which sees the present deadlock as *déjà vu*, because the European integration process has traditionally taken one step forward and two steps back. These people consider the ratification failure as a great opportunity for the future because the EU has always advanced more rapidly after major crises. Proponents of this view believe, first, that French and Dutch citizens have not said no to European integration but to issues of internal politics and competition and that they are dissatisfied more with the lack of or a very timid pace of reforms. Moreover, many have voted no because would have preferred a more ambitious CT with a higher degree of political integration. Second, they believe that the ratifying process should go ahead because nine countries and 49 percent of the European Union population have already ratified the CT, so it remains to be seen if 20 countries can ratify it before the end of 2006; if not, the ratification period could be extended beyond 2007, in which case the CT could go forward. Third, some believe that sooner rather than later, Jacques Chirac maybe be replaced by a younger and more liberal Nicolas Sarkozy, as Gerhard Schroeder has been replaced by a more market-oriented Angela Merkel, and that Silvio Berlusconi will give way to the more serious reformer Romano Prodi, thus improving EU leadership and decision making. According to this view, the present deadlock could be better for European integration.

I, personally, am more pessimistic about the EU's future now than when I began drafting this book because decision making is going to be much more difficult under the Nice Treaty. It seems clear that EU citizens do not seem ready to face more competition and further reforms and that they want more protection, thus, delaying the consolidation of the single market—the backbone of integration—and the reforms that will allow the EU to compete globally.

I hope I am mistaken, but I see today very little hope for a change in attitude in the medium term and an even more aggressive push for more protection. Historical experience with reforms shows that only those countries close to economic collapse—such as Ireland, Finland, and Sweden more than a decade ago—can introduce important reforms. Today, these countries are much better positioned to face the challenges of globalization and an aging population. Clear proof of their improvement is their World Economic Forum ranking, where they are among the top eight most competitive countries in the world. Their experience seems to prove that only when facing economic collapse were their populations ready to change the status quo and accept short- to medium-term sacrifices to collect future benefits, or, what is one in the same, to accept deep structural reforms. Let us hope that this will eventually happen without the need to go closer to a collapse.

BIBLIOGRAPHY

Acemoglu, K. D. (1999), "Efficient unemployment insurance," *Journal of Political Economy* 107.

Acemoglu K.D., and Shimer R. (2000), "Productivity gains from unemployment insurance," *European Economic Review* 44.

Agell, J. (1999), "On the benefits from rigid labor markets: Norms, market failures and social insurance," *Economic Journal* 109 (February).

Agell, J. (2002), "On the determinants of labor market institutions: Rent seeking versus social insurance," *German Economic Review* 3, no. 2.

Agell, J. (2003), "Efficiency and equality in the labor market," *CES-Ifo Forum* 4, no. 2.

Aghion, P., and Howitt, P. (1992), "A model of growth through creative destruction," *Econometrica* 60.

Aghion, P., and Howitt P. (1998), *Endogenous Growth Theory.* Cambridge, MA: The MIT Press.

Aghion, P., Harris, C., Howitt, P., and Vickers, J. (2001), "Competition, imitation and growth with step by step innovation," *Review of Economic Studies* 68.

Aghion, P., Bloom, N., Blundell, R., Griffith, R., and Howitt, P. (2002), "Competition and innovation: An inverted U relationship," IFS working paper, no. W02/04.

Ahn, N., Garcia, J.R., and Jimeno, J.F. (2004), "Well-being consequences of unemployment in Europe," *Documento de Trabajo* 11, FEDEA, Madrid.

Ahn, S., and Hemmings, P. (2000), "Policy influences on economic growth in OECD countries: An evaluation of evidence," OECD Economics Department working paper, no 246.

Ahmad, N., Lequiller, F., Marianna, P., Pilat, D., Schreyer, P., and Wolfl, A. (2004), "Comparing labor productivity growth in the OECD area: The role of measurement," paper presented at the Banque de France, CEPII and IFO workshop, Paris.

Algan, Y., Cahuc, P., and Zylerberberg, A. (2002), "Public employment and labor market performance," *Economic Policy* 34 (April).

Alesina, A., and Rodrik, D. (1994), "Distributive policies and economic growth," *Quarterly Journal of Economics* 109.

Alesina, A., Di Tella, R., and MacCulloch, R. (2001), "Inequality and happiness: Are Europeans and Americans different?" CEPR discussion paper, 2877.

Alesina, A., and Glaesser, E. (2004), *Fighting Poverty in the US and in Europe: A World of Difference?* New York: Oxford University Press.

Alesina, A., Glaesser, E., and Sacerdote, B. (2005), "Work and leisure in the US and in Europe: Why so different?" Harvard Institute of Economic Research, discussion paper, no. 2068.

Alesina, A., and Perotti, R. (2004), "The European Union: A politically incorrect view," NBER working paper, 10342.

Atkinson, A. (1999A), "Is rising income inequality inevitable? A critique of Transatlantic Consensus," UNU/Wider 1999 lecture, Helsinki.

Atkinson, A. (1999B), *The Economic Consequences of Rolling Back the Welfare State*, Cambridge, MA: MIT Press.

Auer, P., and Cazes, S. (2000), "The resilience of the long-term employment relationship," *International Labor Review* 139, no. 4.

Bailey, N., and Lawrence, R. (2001), "Do we have a new economy?" Paper presented at the Annual Meeting of the Allied Science Association, New Orleans.

Baldwin, R., and Widgren, M. (2004), "Political decision making in the enlarged EU," CEPR mimeo.

Barro, R.J. (1991), "Economic growth in a cross section of countries," *Quarterly Journal of Economics* 106, no. 2 (May).

Barro, R.J., and Salai Martin, X. (1995), *Economic Growth*. New York: McGraw-Hill.

Barro, R. J. (1996), "Democracy and Growth," *Journal of Economic Growth*, no. 1.

Barro, R.J., and Lee, J.W. (2000), "International data on education attainment, updates and implications," NBER working paper, no 7911.

Bassanini, A., and Scarpetta, S. (2001A), "Does human capital matter for growth in OECD countries? Evidence from pooled mean-group estimates," OECD Economics Department working paper, no 282.

Bassanini, A., and Scarpetta, S. (2001B), "The driving forces of economic growth: Panel data evidence for OECD countries," OECD Economic Studies, no 33.

Bassanini, A., Scarpetta, S., and Visco, I. (2000), "Knowledge, technology and economic growth: Recent evidence from OECD countries," OECD Economics Department working paper, no 259.

Bassanini, A., Scarpetta, S., and Hemmings, P. (2001), "Economic growth: The role of policies and institutions. Panel data evidence from OECD countries," OECD Economics Department working paper, no. 283.

Bassanini, A., and Ernst, E. (2002), "Labor market institutions, product market regulations and innovation: Cross country evidence from OECD countries," OECD Economics Department working paper, no. 283.

Batini, N., Callen, T., and McKibbin, W. (2004), "The global impact of demographic change," IMF working paper, Washington, D.C.

Bayoumi, T., Laxton, D., and Pesenti, P. (2003), "When leaner is not meaner: Measuring the effects and spillovers of greater competition in Europe," IMF working paper.

Bean, C., Bentolila, S., Bertola, G., and Dolado, J.J. (1998), "Social Europe: One for all?" CEPR Report, London.

Belot, M., and Van Ours, J. (2001), "Unemployment and labor market institutions: An empirical analysis," CentER discussion paper, no. 50.

Belot, M., and Van Ours, J. (2000), "Does the recent success of some OECD countries in lowering their unemployment rates lie in a clever design of their labor market reforms?" IZA discussion paper, no. 147.

Bergstrom, F., and Gidehag, R. (2004,) "EU versus USA," TIMBRO Report (June), Stockholm.

Bertola, G., Boeri, T., and Nicoletti, G. (2001), *Welfare and Employment in a United Europe*. Cambridge, MA: MIT Press.

Bertola, G., Blau, F.D., and Kahn, L.M. (2002), "Labor market institutions and demographic employment patterns," CEPR discussion paper, no. 3448.

Bertola, G., and Boeri, T (2003), "Product market integration, institutions and the labor markets," mimeo (September), Bocconi University, Milan.

Bertola, G. (2004A), "Labor market institutions in a changing world," *Moneda y Credito* 218, Madrid.

Bertola, G. (2004B), "A pure theory of job security and labor income risk," *Review of Economic Studies* 71.

Bertola, G., and Koeniger, W. (2004), "Consumption smoothing and the structure of labor and credit markets," 12A discussion paper, 1052, Bonn.

Blanchard, O., and Summers, L. (1986), "Hysteresis and the European unemployment problem," in S. Fischer (ed), *NBER Macroeconomics Annual* 1, Cambridge, MA: MIT Press.

Blanchard, O. (1990), "Suggestions for a new set of fiscal indicators," OECD working paper, no 79.

Blanchard, O. (1998), "Revisiting European unemployment: Unemployment, capital accumulation and factor prices," NBER working paper, no 6566.

Blanchard, O., and Wolfers, J. (1999), "The role of shocks and institutions in the rise of European unemployment: The aggregate evidence," NBER working paper, no. 7282.

Blanchard, O., and Landier, A. (2001), "The perverse effects of partial labor market reform: Fixed duration contracts in France," NBER working paper, series no. 8219.

Blanchard, O., and Giavazzi, F. (2001), "Macroeconomic effects of regulation and deregulation in goods and labor markets," NBER working paper, series no. 8120.

Blanchard, O. (2002), "Designing labor market institutions," MIT, Cambridge, MA.

Blanchard, O., and Landier, A. (2002), "The perverse effect of partial labor market reforms: Fixed-term contracts in France," *Economic Journal* 112 (June).

Blanchard, O., and Giavazzi F. (2003), "Macroeconomic effects of regulation and deregulation of goods and labor markets," *Quarterly Journal of Economics* 118.

Blanchard, O., and Tirole, J. (2003), "Contours of employment protection reform," MIT, mimeo.

Blanchard, O. (2004), "The economic future of Europe," NBER working paper, no. 10310.

Blank, R. (2002), "Can equity and efficiency complement each other?" NBER working paper, no. 8820.

Bloom, D., Canning, D., and Sevilla, J. (2001), "Economic growth and the demographic transition," NBER working paper, no. 8685, Cambridge, MA.

Boeri, T., Nicoletti, G., and Scarpetta, S. (2000), "Regulation and labor market performance," CEPR discussion paper, no. 2420.

Boeri, T., Brugiavini, A., and Disney, R. (2000), "European pensions, an appeal for reform," European Round Table of Industrialists, Brussels.

Boeri, T, Brugiavini, A., and Calmfors, L. (2001), *The Role of Unions in the Twenty-First Century*, Oxford: Oxford University Press.

Boeri, T., Borsch-Supan, A., and Tabellini, G. (2001), "Would you like to shrink the welfare state? The opinions of European citizens," *Economic Policy* 32.

Boeri, T., Conde-Ruiz J. I., and Galasso, V. (2002), "Protecting against labor market risk; Employment protection or unemployment benefits?" CEPR discussion paper, no. 3990.

Boeri, T. (2004), "Labor and product market reforms: Why so many and so difficult?" IMF mimeo.

Bosworth, B., Bryant, R, and Burtless, G. (2004), "The impact of aging on financial markets and the economy: A survey," Brookings Institution working paper, Washington, D.C.

Buiter, W. (1985), "A guide to public sector debt and deficits," *Economic Policy*, no 1.

Burniaux, J.M., Duval, R., and Jaumotte, F. (2003), "Coping with aging: A dynamic approach to quantify the impact of alternative policy options on future labor supply in OECD countries," OECD Economics Department working paper, no. 371, Paris.

Buti, M., Pench, L. R., and Sestito, P. (1998), "European unemployment: Contending theories and institutional complexities," European University Institute of Florence, Robert Schuman Centre Policy Papers, 1998/1.

Calmfors, L. (2001), "Wages and wage-bargaining institutions in EMU—a survey of the issues," Stockholm Institute for International Economic Studies, seminar paper, 690.

Camdessus, M. (2004), "Le sursaut: vers une nouvelle croissance pour la France," La Documentation Française, Paris.

Cameron, G. (1998), "Innovation and growth: A survey of empirical evidence," Nuffield College, Oxford, mimeo.

Chinn, M.D., and Prassad, E. (2003), "Medium-term determinants of current accounts in industrial and developing countries: An empirical exploration," *Journal of International Economics* 59 (January).

Cohen, D., Lefranc, A., and Saint-Paul, G. (1997), "French unemployment: Why France and the US are alike," *Economic Policy* 12 (October).

Coe, D., and Snower, D. (1997), "Policy complementarities: The case for fundamental labor market reform," IMF Staff Papers, vol. 44, no. 1.

Colecchia, A., and Schreyer, P. (2002A), "The contribution of information and communication technologies to economic growth in nine OECD countries," OECD Economic Studies, no 34.

Colecchia, A., and Schreyer, P. (2002B), "ITC investment and economic growth in the 1990s: Is the US a unique case? A comparative study of nine OECD countries," *Review of Economic Dynamics* 5, no. 2.

Cotis, J.P. (2003), "A question of structure: Explaining the divergence of growth in the OECD area," *OECD Observer* (May), Paris.

Cotis, J.P. (2005), "Economic policy reforms: Going for growth," OECD (March), Paris.

Crafts, N., and Toniolo, G. (1996), "Post-war growth: An overview," in N. Crafts and G. Toniolo (eds.), *Economic Growth in Europe Since 1945*, Cambridge: Cambridge University Press.

Dalsgaard, T., Elmeskov, J., and Park, C. J. (2002), "Ongoing changes in the business cycle: Evidence and causes," OECD Economics Department working paper, no. 315.

Daly, K. (2003), "Euroland: Productivity is not the problem," *European Weekly Analyst*, Goldman Sachs, June 27.

Daly, K. (2004), "Euroland's secret success story," Goldman Sachs Global Economics Paper, no. 102 (January).

Daly, K. (2005), "The Lisbon Strategy and the future of European growth," Goldman Sachs Global Economics Paper, no. 121 (January).

Daveri, F., and Tabellini, G. (2000), "Unemployment, growth and taxation in industrial countries," *Economic Policy* 15 (April).

Daveri, F. (2001), "Is growth an information technology story in Europe?" IGIER working paper, 168.

Daveri, F. (2002), "The new economy in Europe, 1992–2001," *Oxford Review of Economic Policy* 345.

Daveri, F. (2004) "Why is there a European productivity problem?" CEPS, Centre for European Policy Studies, Brussels.

David, P.A. (1990), "The dynamo and the computer: An historical perspective on the modern productivity paradox," *American Economic Review Papers and Proceedings* 80, no 2.

De la Dehesa, G. (2002), "Venture capital: The European Union versus the US," The Group of Thirty, Washington, D.C.

De la Fuente, A., and Domenech, R. (2001), "Human capital in growth regressions: How much difference does data quality make?," CEPR discussion paper, 3587.

De Long, B. (2005), "The European model is alive," *El País*, project syndicate.

Denis, C., McMorrow, K., and Roger, W. (2002), "Production function approach to calculating potential growth and output gaps: Estimates for the European Union Member States and the US," DG of Economic and Financial Affairs, Economic Papers, no. 176, Brussels.

Denison, E. (1974), "Accounting for United States Economic Growth, 1929–1969," The Brookings Institution, Washington, D.C.

Deppler, M. (2004,) "Integration: Social preferences with robust growth," Finance and Development, IMF (June), Washington, D.C.

Deroose, S., and Thiel, M. (2001), "Considerations and conjectures on economic growth in the EU," *European Economy*, no. 1, Directorate General for Economic and Financial Affairs, European Commission.

Dolado, J.J., Garcia-Serrano, C., and Jimeno, J.F. (2001), "Drawing lessons from the boom of temporary jobs in Spain," University of Alcalá, mimeo.

Drazen, A. (2000), *Political Economy in Macroeconomics*, Princeton, N.J: Princeton University Press.

Drazen, A., and Easterly, W. (2001), "Do crises induce reform?: Simple empirical tests of conventional wisdom," *Economics and Politics* 13.

Durlauf, S.N., and Quah, D.T (1999), "The new empirics of economic growth," in J. Taylor and M. Woodford (eds.), *Handbook of Macroeconomics*, Amsterdam: North-Holland.

The Economist (2004), "Europe v. America," a report (June 29).

The Economist (2004), "The health of nations: A survey of health-care finance" (July 17).

The Economist (2005), "Special report: meritocracy in America" (January 1).

Eichengreen, B. (1996), "Institutions and economic growth in Europe after World War Two," in N. Crafts and G. Toniolo (eds.), *Economic Growth in Europe Since 1945*, Cambridge: Cambridge University Press.

Elmeskov, J., Martin, J., and Scarpetta, S. (1998), "Key lessons for labor market reforms: Evidence from OECD countries' experiences," *Swedish Economic Policy Review* 5 (Autumn).

European Commission (1985), "Completing the internal market," Technical Report, Brussels.

European Commission (2003), "Delivering Lisbon," Report to the Spring European Council (February).

European Commission (2004), "Delivering Lisbon," Report to the Spring European Council (February).

European Commission (2005), "Special Eurobarometer Lisbon," Brussels, (February).

European Competitiveness Report (2001), European Commission.

European Competitiveness Report (2002), European Commission.

European Competitiveness Report (2003), European Commission.

European Competitiveness Report (2004,) European Commission.

European Economy, no. 1 (2001A).

European Economy (2001), "The budgetary challenges posed by ageing populations," no 4.

European Economy (2001), "The European Union economy: 2000 review" no. 71.

European Economy (2002) "The European Union economy: 2001 review," no. 73.

European Economy (2002), "2002 broad economic policy guidelines," no. 4.

European Economy (2002), "The European Union economy: 2002 review," no. 6.

European Economy (2003), "The European Union economy: 2003 review," no. 6.

European Economy (2004), "The European Union economy: 2004 review," no. 6.

Faruqee, H. (2002) Population aging and its macroeconomic implication: A framework of analysis," IMF working paper 02/16, Washington, D.C.

Fajnzylber, P., Lederman, D., and Lloayza, N. (2002) "Inequality and violent crime," *Journal of Law and Economics* 45.

Feldstein, M. (1996), "The missing piece in policy analysis: Social security reform," *American Economic Review*, Papers and Proceedings.

Feldstein, M. (1997), "Transition to a fully-funded pension system: five economic issues," NBER working paper, no. 6149.

Feldstein, M., ed. (1998), "Privatizing social security," NBER and University of Chicago Press.

Feroli, M. (2003,) "Capital flows among the G-7 nations: A demographic perspective," Finance and Economics Discussion Series, no. 2003/54.

Fitoussi, J.P., Jestaz, D., Phelps, E., and Zoega, G. (2000), "Roots of recent recoveries: Labor reforms or private sector forces," Brookings Papers on Economic Activity, 1, Brookings Institution, Washington D.C.

Ford, R., and Laxton, D. (1995), "World public debt and real interest rates," IMF working paper, no. 95/30.

Ghellab, Y. (1998,) "Minimum wages and youth unemployment," Employment and Training Papers, no. 26, International Labor Office, Geneva.

Glaesser, E., Scheinkman, J., and Shleifer, A. (2002), "The injustice of inequality," NBER working paper, no. 9150.

Goldin, C., and Margo, R. A. (1992), "The great compression: The wage structure in the US at mid-century," *Quarterly Journal of Economics* 107.

Gómez, R., and Hernández de Cos, P. (2003), "Demographic maturity and economic performance: The effect of demographic transition on per capita GDP growth," Bank of Spain working paper, no. 318, Madrid.

Gordon, R.J. (1995), "Is there a trade-off between unemployment and productivity growth?" CEPR discussion paper, no. 1159.

Gordon, R. J. (2000), "Does the new economy measure up to the great inventions of the past?" *Journal of Economic Perspectives* 14, no 4.

Gordon, R.J. (2002), "Two centuries of economic growth: Europe chasing the American frontier," paper prepared for the Economic History Workshop, Northwestern University (October).

Gordon, R. J. (2004), "Why was Europe left at the station when America's productivity locomotive departed?" NBER working paper, no. 10661.

Greenwood, J. (1999), "The third industrial revolution: Technology, productivity and income inequality," Federal Reserve Bank of Cleveland Review.

Gröningen Growth and Development Centre: Faculty of Economics, University of Gröningen (various reports).

Gros, D., Jimeno, J. F., Mayer, T., Thygesen, N., and Ubide, A. (2003), "Adjusting to leaner times," 5th Annual Report of the CEPS Macroeconomic Group, July, CEPS, Brussels.

Gros, D., Mayer, T., and Ubide, A. (2004), "Breaking the reform deadlock," 6th Annual Report of the CEPS Macroeconomic Policy Group, (July), Brussels.

Grossman, G.M., and Helpman, E. (1991), *Innovation and Growth in the Global Economy*, Cambridge, MA: MIT Press.

Gruber, J., and Wise, D. (1999), "Social security and retirement around the world," NBER and the University of Chicago Press.

Guellec, D., and Van Pottelsberghe, B. (2000), "The impact of public R&D expenditure on business R&D," OECD STI working paper, no 4.

Guellec, D., and Van Pottelsberghe, B. (2001), "R&D and productivity growth: Panel data analysis of 16 OECD countries," OECD Economic Studies, no 33.

Hanel, P., and Niosi, J. (1998), "Technology and economic growth: A survey," Statistics Canada research paper.

Hassler, J., Rodriguez Mora, J., Storesletten, K., and Zilibotti, F. (2001), "The survival of the welfare state," CEPR discussion paper, no. 2905.

Heckman, J. J. (2003), "The labor market and the job miracle," *CES-Ifo Forum* 4, no. 2.

Heller, P. (2003), "Who will pay?: Coping with aging societies, climate change and other long-term fiscal challenges," IMF, Washington, D.C.

Herbertsson, T.T., and Orszag, M. (2001), "The costs of early retirement in the OECD," Institute of Economic Studies, University of Iceland (May).

Hers, J. (1998), "Human capital and economic growth: A survey of the literature," CPB Report, no 2.

H.M. Treasury (2002), "Realizing Europe's potential: Economic reform in Europe," (February).

H.M. Treasury (2003), "Meeting the challenge: Economic reform in Europe," (February).

H.M. Treasury (2003B), "Structural indicators of European economic reform: Measuring Europe's progress," (February).

H.M. Treasury (2003), "Long-term public finance report: fiscal sustainability with an ageing population," (December).

Hodrick, R, and Prescott, E. (1997), "Post-war business cycles: An Empirical Investigation," *Journal of Money, Credit and Banking* 29.

Horstein, A. (1999), "Growth accounting with technological revolutions," *Federal Reserve Bank of Richmond Economics Quarterly*, 85 (3).

Horstein, A., and Krusell, P. (2001), "New technology and productivity: A macroeconomic perspective," European Economy, no 1. Directorate-General for Economic and Financial Affairs European Commission.

Hulten, C. (2000), "Total factor productivity: A short biography," NBER working paper, no. 7471.

INGENUE Team (2001), "Ingenue: Une modélisation intergénérationelle et universelle," Banque de France, Paris.

International Labor Organisation (ILO) (1997), "Economically active population," Geneva.

International Monetary Fund (2003), "Unemployment and labor market institutions: Why reform pays off," *World Economic Outlook* (May), Chapter 4, Washington, D.C.

International Monetary Fund (2004A), "Fostering structural reforms in industrial countries," *World Economic Outlook* (May), Chapter 3, Washington, D.C.

International Monetary Fund (2004B), "How the demographic change will affect the global economy," *World Economic Outlook* (September), Washington, D.C.

Independent High-Level Study Group (2003), "An agenda for a growing Europe: Making the European Union economic system deliver," chaired by Andre Sapir on the initiative of the President of the European Commission, July. Its members were Phillippe Aghion, Giuseppe Bertola, Martin Hellwig, Jean Pisani-Ferry, Dariusz Rosati, José Viñals, and Helen Wallace. Its Rapporteurs were Marco Buti, Mario Nava, and Peter M. Smith.

Jackson, R. (2002), "The global retirement crisis," Center for Strategic and International Studies (CSIS), Washington, D.C.

Jacobzone, S., Cambois, E., and Robine, J.M. (2000), "Is health of older persons in OECD countries improving fast enough to compensate for population ageing?" OECD Economic Studies, no 30.

Jacobzone, S. (2001), "Healthy ageing and the challenges of new technologies: Can the OECD social and health care systems provide for the future?" Proceedings of the Tokyo workshop on healthy aging and the biotechnologies, organized by the OECD and the Japanese Ministry of Health.

Jensen, P., Rosholm, M., and Svarer, M. (2003), "The response of youth unemployment to benefits, incentives and sanctions," *European Journal of Political Economy* 19, no. 2.

Jimeno, J.F., and Bentolila, S. (1998), "Regional unemployment persistence (Spain, 1976–1994)," *Labor Economics* 5 (March).

Jimeno, J.F., and Rodriguez-Palenzuela, D. (2003), "Youth unemployment in the OECD: Demographic shifts, labor market institutions and macroeconomic shocks," ENEPRI working paper, no. 19.

Jones, C.I. (1995), "Time-series tests of endogenous growth models," *Quarterly Journal of Economics* 110.

Jorgenson, D.W., and Stiroh, K.J. (2000), "Raising the speed limit: US economic growth in the information age," Brookings Papers on Economic Activity.

Joumard, I. (2002), "Tax systems in European Union countries," OECD Economic Studies, no. 34.

Jovanovic, B., and Rousseau, P.L. (2000), "Technology and the stock market: 1885–1998," mimeo.

Katz, L.F., and Murphy, K.M. (1992), "Changes in relative wages 1963–1987: Supply and demand factors," *Quarterly Journal of Economics* 107.

Keeley, L.C., and Quah, D. (1998), "Technology in growth," Centre for Economic Performance discussion paper, no. 391.

King, R.G., and Rebelo, S.T (1993), "Transitional dynamics and economic growth in the neoclassical model," *American Economic Review* 83.

Kok, W. (2004), "Facing the challenge: The Lisbon strategy for growth and employment," Report from the High-Level Group chaired by Wim Kok, European Communities, Brussels.

Krueger, A. O. (1993), *Political Economy of Policy Reform in Developing Countries*, Cambridge, MA: MIT Press.

Krueger, D., and Kumar, K. (2003), "US-Europe differences in technology-driven growth: Quantifying the role of education," NBER working paper, 1001.

Krugman, P. (1993). "Inequality and the political economy of Eurosclerosis," CEPR discussion paper, 867.

Krugman, P. (2004), *The Great Unraveling: Losing Our Way in the New Century.* New York: W.W. Norton.

Laxton, D., and Pesenti, P. (2002), "Monetary rules for small, open, emerging economies," Carnegie Rochester Conference on Public Policy, Pittsburgh, PA (November).

Layard, R., Nickell, S., and Jackman, R. (1991), *Unemployment: Macroeconomic Performance and the Labor Market,* Oxford: Oxford University Press.

Lequiller, F. (2001), "The new economy and the measurement of GDP growth," INSEE working paper.

Lindbeck, A., and Snower, D. (1988), *The Insider-Outsider Theory of Employment and Unemployment.* Cambridge, MA: Cambridge University Press.

Lindert, P. (2004), *Growing Public: Social Spending and Economic Growth Since the Eighteenth Century.* Cambridge, MA: Cambridge University Press.

Loayza, N., Schmidt-Hebbel, K., and Servén, L. (2000), "Saving in developing countries: An overview," *World Bank Economic Review* 14, no. 3, Washington, D.C.

Lucas, R. (1988), "On the mechanics of economic development," *Journal of Monetary Economics* 22 (July).

Lucas, R. (2000), "Some macroeconomics for the 21st century," *Journal of Economic Perspectives* 14.

Luxembourg Income Study (2002), www.lisproject.org/keyfigures. University of Luxembourg and University of Syracuse (US).

Mankiw, G., Romer, D., and Weil, D. (1992), "Contribution to the empirics of economic growth," *Quarterly Journal of Economics* 107 (May).

Marimon, R., and Zilibotti, F. (1998), "Actual versus virtual employment in Europe: Is Spain different?," *European Economic Review* 42 (January).

Martin, J. (2000), "What works among active labor market policies: Evidence from the OECD countries experiences," OECD Economic Studies, no 280.

McMorrow, K., and Roger, W. (2001), "Potential output: Measurement methods, new economy influences and scenarios for 2001–10: A comparison of the EU-15 and the US," European Commission Economic and Financial Affairs, economic paper, no 150.

Mettler, A. (2005), "Europe is steadily losing its scientific elite," *Financial Times*, London.

Mishel, L., Bernstein, J., and Boushey, H. (2003), *The State of Working America*, Ithaca, NY: Cornell University Press.

Mortensen, D.T., and Pissarides, C.A. (1999), "Unemployment response to skill-biased technology shocks: The role of labor market policy," *The Economic Journal* 109.

Nannincini, T. (2001), "The take-off of temporary help in the Italian labour market," mimeo, European University Institute, Florence.

Nelson, R. (1998), "The agenda of growth theory: A different point of view," *Cambridge Journal of Economics* 22.

Nicoletti, G., Scarpetta, S., and Baylaud, O. (1999), "Summary indicators of product market regulation with an extension to employment protection legislation," OECD Economics Department working paper, no. 226.

Nicoletti, G., and Scarpetta, S. (2003), "Regulation, productivity and growth: OECD evidence," *Economic Policy*, no 36 (April).

Nickell, S., and Layard R. (1999), "Labor market institutions and economic performance," in O. Ashenfelter and D. Card (eds.), *Handbook of Labor Economics*, vol. 3, North-Holland: Elsevier.

Nickell, S., and Nunziata, L. (2000), "Employment patterns in OECD countries," OECD (March).

Nickell, S., and Nunziatta, L. (2001), "Labor market institutions database," London School of Economics, London.

Nickell, S., Nunziatta, L., Ochel, W., and Quintini, G. (2003), "The Beveridge curve, unemployment and wages in the OECD from the 1960s to the 1990s," in P. Aghion et al. (eds.), *Knowledge, Information, and Expectations in Modern Macroeconomics: In Honor of Edmund Phelps*, Princeton, NJ.: Princeton University Press.

Nordhaus, W.D (2001A), "Alternative methods for measuring productivity growth," NBER working paper, no. 8095.

Nordhaus, W.D. (2001B), "Productivity growth and the new economy," NBER working paper, 8096.

Nyce, S.A., and Schieber, S. (2005), *The Economic Implications of Aging Societies*, Cambridge, MA: Cambridge University Press.

Obstfeld, M., and Peri, G. (2000), "Regional non-adjustments and fiscal policy: Lessons for EMU," NBER working paper, 6431, Cambridge, MA.

OECD (1999), "Implementing the OECD jobs strategy: Assessing policy and performance," OECD, Paris.

OECD (2000), "A new economy?: The changing role of innovation and information technology in growth," OECD, Paris.

OECD (2001A), "The OECD productivity manual," OECD, Paris.

OECD (2001B), "Productivity growth in ICT producing and ICT using industries: A source of growth differentials in the OECD?" OECD, Paris.

OECD (2001C), "The impact of ICT technologies on output growth: Issues and preliminary findings," OECD, Paris.

OECD (2001D), *Economic Studies*, no 33, OECD, Paris.

OECD (2001E), "Fiscal implications of ageing: projections of age-related spending," OECD Economic Outlook, no 69, OECD, Paris.

OECD Employment Outlook (2002), OECD, Paris (July).

OECD Employment Outlook (2003), OECD, Paris.

OECD (2003A), "The sources of economic growth in OECD countries," OECD, Paris.

OECD (2003B), "Seizing the benefits of ITC: An international comparison of the impacts of ITC on economic performance," OECD, Paris.

OECD (2004A), "Understanding economic growth," OECD, Paris.

OECD Economic Surveys (2004B), "Euro area," vol. 2004/5, OECD, Paris (September).

OECD (2005), "Economic policy reforms: going for growth," OECD, Paris (March).

Okun, A.M. (1975), "Equality and efficiency: The big trade-off," The Brookings Institution, Washington, DC.

O'Mahony, M. (2002), "Productivity in the EU, 1979–1999," National Institute of Economic and Social Research, published by H.M. Treasury (February).

O'Mahony, M., and De Boer, W. (2002), "Britain's productivity performance: Update and extensions," NIESR, mimeo.

O'Mahony, M., and Van Ark, B. (2003), "EU productivity and competitiveness: An industry perspective," European Commission, Enterprise Publications, Brussels.

Onliner, S., and Sichel, D. (2000), "The resurgence of growth in the late 1990s: Is information technology the story?" Federal Reserve Board Finance and Economics discussion paper, no 20.

Onliner, S., and Sichel D. (2002), "IT and productivity: Where are we now and where are we going?" Federal Reserve Bank of Atlanta Economic Review (3rd quarter).

Persson, T. and Tabellini, G. (1994), "Is inequality harmful for growth?" *The American Economic Review* 84.

Pesenti, P. A. (2003), "The global economy model (GEM): Theoretical framework," IMF working paper, Washington, D.C.

Phelps, E. S. (2003), "Economic underperformance in Continental Europe: A prospering economy runs on the dynamism from its economic institutions," lecture, Royal Institute for International Affairs, London (March 18).

Pilat, D. (1997), "Competition, productivity and efficiency," OECD Economic Studies, no 27.

Pilat, D. (2003), "Digital economy: Going for growth," OECD Observer, Paris (May).

Pissarides, C. (1986), "Unemployment and vacancies in Britain," *Economic Policy*, no. 3.

Poterba, J. (2001), "Demographic structure and asset returns," *Review of Economics and Statistics* 83.

Prescott, E. C. (2004), "Why do Americans work so much more than Europeans?" NBER working paper, 10316 (February).

Rajan, R. (2004), "Why are structural reforms so difficult?," *Finance and Development* (June 2004), IMF.

Rebelo, S. (1991), "Long-run policy analysis and long-run growth," *Journal of Political Economy* 99 (3).

Reid, T.R. (2004), *The United States and Europe*. London: Penguin.

Rifkin, J. (2004), *The European Dream*, New York: Polity.

Rodrik, D. (1996), "Understanding economic policy reform," *Journal of Economic Literature* 34.

Roger, W. (2001), "The contribution of information and communication technologies to growth in Europe and the US: A macroeconomic analysis," European Commission Economic and Financial Affairs economic paper, no. 147.

Romer, P.M. (1986), "Increasing returns and long-run growth," *Journal of Political Economy* 94 (5).

Romer, P.M. (1990), "Endogenous technical change," *Journal of Political Economy* 98.

Roper Starch Worldwide (2000), "Workers prefer more money to more leisure," New York.

Saint-Paul, G. (1993), "On the political economy of labor flexibility," *NBER Macroeconomics Annual* 8.

Saint-Paul, G. (2004), "The brain drain: Some evidence from European expatriates in the US," CEPR discussion papers, 4680.

Sakellaris, P., and Vijselaar, F.W (2003), "Capital quality improvement and the sources of growth in the euro area," mimeo (September).

Sapir, A. (2000), "Who is afraid of globalization? The challenge of domestic adjustment in Europe and America," mimeo.

Scarpetta et al (2000), "Economic growth in the OECD area: Recent trends at the aggregate and sectoral level," OECD Economics Department working papers, no. 248.

Schnabel, G. (2002), "Output trends and Okun's Law," BIS working papers, no. 111, Bank for International Settlements, Basel.

Schneider, F. (2002), "Size and measurement of the informal economy in 110 countries around the world," World Bank working paper, Washington, D.C. (July).

Schreyer, P., and Pilat, D. (2001), "Measuring productivity," OECD Economic Studies, no. 33, Paris.

Schreyer, P. (2001), "Computer price indices and international growth comparisons," OECD, Paris.

Smeeding, T. (2002), "Globalization, inequality and the rich countries of the G-20: Evidence from the Luxembourg Income Study," LIS working paper, no. 320, Luxembourg.

Snower, D. J., and de la Dehesa, G. (eds.) (1997), *Unemployment Policy: Government Options for the Labour Market*. New York: CEPR, and Cambridge: Cambridge University Press.

Solow, R. (1956), "A contribution to the theory of economic growth," *Quarterly Journal of Economics* 70 (February).

Solow, R. (1957), "Technical change and the aggregate production function," *Review of Economics and Statistics* 39.3.

Standard & Poors (2005), "In the long run, we are all debt: Aging societies and sovereign ratings," March.

Stiroh, K. J. (2000), "What drives productivity growth?" *Economic Policy Review* 7 (March), Federal Reserve Bank of New York, New York.

Stiroh, K. J. (2002), "Are ITC spillovers driving the new economy?," *Review of Income and Wealth* 48, no. 1.

Swan, T. (1956), "Economic growth and capital accumulation," *Economic Record* 32.

Tanzi, V., and Lutz, M.S. (1991), "Interest rates and government debt: Some linkages and consequences," Finance and Development, IMF (December)" in A. Harry (ed.) *The Political Economy of Government Debt*. Amsterdam: North Holland.

Temple, J. (1999), "The new growth evidence," *Journal of Economic Literature*, no 37 (March).

Temple, J. (2001), "Growth effects of education and social capital in OECD countries," *OECD Economic Studies*, no 33.

Thakur, S., Keen, M., Horváth, B., and Cerra, V. (2003), "Sweden's welfare state," International Monetary Fund, Washington, D.C.

Thiel, M. (2001), "Finance and economic growth: A review of theory and empirical evidence," European Commission Economic and Financial Affairs paper.

Tommasi, M., and Velasco, A. (1998), "Where are we in the political economy of reform?" *Journal of Policy Reform* 1, no. 2.

United Nations Population Division (2003), "World Population Prospects: The 2002 Revision," New York.

UK Pensions Commission Report (2004), "Pensions, risks and capital markets" (April).

Van Ark, B., Melka, J., Mulder, N., Timmer, M., and Ypma, G. (2002), "ITC investment and growth accounts for the European Union, 1980–2000," Report to the European Commission (September).

Van Ark, B., Inklaar, R., and McGuckin, R. (2003), "Productivity, ITC investment and services industries: Europe and the United States," Groningen Growth and Development Centre, research memorandum GD-60 (December).

Whelan, K. (2000), "Computers, obsolescence and productivity," Federal Reserve Board Finance and Economics discussion paper, no 9.

Young, A. (1991), "Invention and bounded learning by doing," NBER working paper, 3712.

INDEX

ABOUT THE AUTHOR

Guillermo de la Dehesa is chairman of the Center for Economic Policy Research, CEPR, a member of the Group of Thirty, and chairman of the Instituto Empresa. He is also director of Banco Santander and vice-chairman of Goldman Sachs Europe, an independent director of four European firms, and a member of the European advisory board of U.S.–based corporations Eli Lilly and Coca-Cola. De la Dehesa is the author and coauthor of numerous books on economics and the author of over 200 articles and papers.